# Keystone Biology Exam Success

By Lewis Morris

www.insiderswords.com/KeystoneBiology

ISBN-13: 978-1792144813

# Table of Contents

# What is "Insider Language"?

Recent research has confirmed what we have known for decades: The strongest students and leaders in industry have a mastered an Insider Language in their subject and field. This Insider language is made up of the technical terms and vocabulary necessary to communicate effectively in classes or the workplace. For those who master it, learning is easier, faster, and much more enjoyable.

Most students who are surveyed report that the greatest challenge to any course of study is learning the vocabulary. When we examine typical college courses, we discover that there is, on average, 250 Insider Terms a student must learn over the course of a semester. Further, most exams rely heavily on this set of words for assessment purposes. The structure of multiple choice exams lends itself perfectly to the testing of this Insider Language. Students who can differentiate between Insider Language terms can handle challenging exam questions with ease and confidence.

From recent research on learning and vocabulary we have learned:

- Your knowledge of any subject is contained in the content-specific words you know. The more of these terms that you know, the easier it is to understand and recall important information; the easier it will be to communicate your ideas to peers, professors, supervisors, and co-workers. The stronger your content-area vocabulary is, the higher your scores will be on your exams and written assignments.

- Students who develop a strong Insider Language perform better on tests, learn faster, retain more information, and express greater satisfaction in learning.

- Familiarizing yourself with subject-area vocabulary before formal study (pre-learning) is the most effective way to learn this language and reap the most benefit.

- The vocabulary on standardized exams come directly from the stated objectives of the test-makers. This means that the vocabulary found on standardized exams is predictable. Our books focus on this vocabulary.

- Most multiple-choice exams are glorified vocabulary quizzes. Think about the format of a multiple-choice question. The question stem is a definition of a term and the choices (known as distractors) are 4 or 5 similar words. Your task is to differentiate between the meanings of those terms and choose the correct word.

- It takes a person several exposures to a new word to be able to use it with confidence in conversation or in writing. You need to process these words several different ways to make them part of your long-term memory.

**The goals of this book are:**

- To give you an "Insider Language" for your subject.
- Pre-teach the most important words before you set out on a traditional course of review or study.
- Teach you the most important words in your subject area.
- Teach you strategies for learning subject-area words on your own.
- Boost your confidence in your ability to master this language and support you in your study.
- Reduce the stress of studying and provide you with fun activities that work.


**How it works:**

The secret to mastering Insider Language is through repetition and exposure. We have eleven steps for you to follow:

1. Read the word and definition in the glossary out loud. "See it, Say it"
2. Identify the part of speech the word belongs to such as noun, verb, adverb, or adjective. This will help you group the word and identify similar words.
3. Place the word in context by using it in a sentence. Write this sentence down and read it aloud.
4. Use "Chunking" to group the words. Make a diagram or word cloud using these groups.
5. Make connections to the words by creating analogies.
6. Create mnemonics that help you recognize patterns and orders of words by substituting the words for more memorable items or actions.
7. Examine the morphology of the word, that is, identify the root, prefix, and suffix that make up the word. Identify similar and related words.
8. Complete word games and puzzles such as crosswords and word searches.
9. Complete matching questions that require you to differentiate between related words.
10. Complete Multiple-choice questions containing the words.
11. Create a visual metaphor or "memory cartoon" to make a mental picture of the word and related processes.

By completing this word study process, you will be exposed to the terminology in various ways that will activate your memory and create a lasting understanding of this language.

The strategies in this book are designed to make you an independent expert at learning insider language. These strategies include:

- Verbalizing the word by reading it and its definition aloud ("See It, Say It"). This allows you to make visual, auditory, and speech connections with its meaning.

- Identifying the type of word (Noun, verb, adverb, and adjective). Making this distinction helps you understand how to visualize the word. It helps you "chunk" the words into groups, and gives you clues on how to use the word.

- Place the word in context by using it in a sentence. Write this sentence down and read it aloud. This will give you an example of how the word is used.

- "Chunking". By breaking down the word list into groups of closely related words, you will learn them better and be able to remember them faster. Once you have group the terms, you can then make word clouds using a free online service. These word clouds provide visual cues to remembering the words and their meanings.

- Analogies. By creating analogies for essential words, you will be making connections that you can see on paper. These connections can trigger your memory and activate your ability to use the word in your writing as you begin to use them. Many of these analogies also use visual cues. In a sense, you can make a mental picture from the analogy.

- Mnemonics. A device such as a pattern of letters, ideas, or associations that assists in remembering something. A mnemonic is especially useful for remembering the order of a set of words or the order of a process.

- Morphology. The study of word roots, prefixes, and suffixes. By examining the structure of the words, you will gain insight into other words that are closely related, and learn how to best use the word.

- Visual metaphors. This is the most sophisticated and entertaining strategy for learning vocabulary. Create a "memory cartoon" using one or more of the vocabulary terms. This activity triggers the visual part of your memory and makes fast, permanent, imprints of the word on your memory. By combining the terms in your visual metaphor, you can "chunk" the entire set of vocabulary terms into several visual metaphors and benefit from the brain's tendency to group these terms.

The activities in this book are designed to imprint the words and their meanings in your memory in different ways. By completing each activity, you will gain the necessary exposures to the word to make it a permanent part of your vocabulary. Each activity uses a different part of your memory. The result is that you will be comfortable using these words and be able to tell the difference between closely related words. The activities include:

A. Crossword Puzzles and Word Searches- These are proven to increase test scores and improve comprehension. Students frequently report that they are fun and engaging, while requiring them to analyze the structure and meaning of the words.

B. Matching- This activity is effective because it forces you to differentiate between many closely related terms.

C. Multiple Choice- This classic question format lends itself to vocabulary study perfectly. Most exams are in this format because they are simple to make, easy to score, and are a reliable type of assessment. (Perfect for the Vocabulary Master!) One strategy to use with multiple choice questions that enhance their effectiveness is to cover the answer choices while you read the question. After reading the question, see if you can answer it before looking at the choices. Then look at the choices to see if you match one of them.

Conducting a thorough "word study" of your insider language will take time and effort, but the rewards will be well worth it. By following this guide and completing the exercises thoughtfully, you will become a stronger, more effective, and satisfied student. Best of luck on your mastery of this Insider Language!

## Insider Language Strategies

## "See It, Say It!" Reading your Insider Language set aloud

*"It is better to fail in originality than to succeed in imitation."*
–Herman Melville

Reading aloud is the foundation for the development of an Insider Language. It is the single most important thing you can do for vocabulary acquisition. Done correctly, it engages the visual, auditory, and speech centers of the brain and hastens its storage in your long-term memory.

Reading aloud demonstrates the relationship between the printed word and its meaning.

You can read aloud on a higher level than you can initially understand, so reading aloud makes complex ideas more accessible and exposes you to vocabulary and patterns that are not part of your typical speech. Reading aloud helps you understand the complicated text better and makes more challenging text easier to grasp and understand. Reading aloud helps you to develop the "habits of mind" the strongest students use.

Reading aloud will make connections to concepts in the reading that requires you to relate the new vocabulary to things you already know. Go to the glossary at the end of this book and for each word complete the five steps outlined below:

1. Read the word and its definition aloud. Focus on the sound of the word and how it looks on the paper.
2. Read the word aloud again try to say three or four similar words; this will help you build connections to closely related words.
3. Read the word aloud a third time. Try to make a connection to something you have read or heard.
4. Visualize the concept described in the term. Paint a mental picture of the word in use.
5. Try to think of the opposite of the word. Discovering a close antonym will help you place this word in context.

# Create a sentence using the word in its proper context

*"OPPORTUNITIES DON'T HAPPEN. YOU CREATE THEM." –CHRIS GROSSER*

Context means the circumstances that form the setting for an event, statement, or idea, and which it can be fully understood and assessed. Synonyms for context include conditions, factors, situation, background, and setting.

Place the word in context by using it in a sentence. Write this sentence down and read it aloud. By creating sentences, you are practicing using the word correctly. If you strive to make these sentences interesting and creative, they will become more memorable and effective in activating your long-term memory.

## Identify the Parts of Speech
"SUCCESS IS NOT FINAL; FAILURE IS NOT FATAL: IT IS THE COURAGE TO CONTINUE THAT COUNTS." –WINSTON S. CHURCHILL

Read through each term in the glossary and make a note of what part of speech each term is. Studying and identifying parts of speech shows us how the words relate to each other. It also helps you create a visualization of each term. Below are brief descriptions of the parts of speech for you to use as a guide.

VERB: A word denoting action, occurrence, or existence. Examples: walk, hop, whisper, sweat, dribbles, feels, sleeps, drink, smile, are, is, was, has.

NOUN: A word that names a person, place, thing, idea, animal, quality, or action. Nouns are the subject of the sentence. Examples: dog, Tom, Florida, CD, pasta, hate, tiger.

ADJECTIVE: A word that modifies, qualifies, or describes nouns and pronouns. Generally, adjectives appear immediately before the words they modify. Examples: smart girl, gifted teacher, old car, red door.

ADVERB: A word that modifies verbs, adjectives and other adverbs. An "ly" ending almost always changes an adjective to an adverb. Examples: ran swiftly, worked slowly, and drifted aimlessly. Many adverbs do not end in "ly." However, all adverbs identify when, where, how, how far, how much, etc. Examples: run hot, lived hard, moved right, study smart.

## Chunking

**"YOUR POSITIVE ACTION COMBINED WITH POSITIVE THINKING RESULTS IN SUCCESS." SHIV KHERA**

Chunking is when you take a set of words and break it down into groups based on a common relationship. Research has shown that our brains learn by chunking information. By grouping your terms, you will be able to recall large sets of these words easily. To help make your chunking go easily use an online word cloud generator to make a set of word clouds representing your chunks.

1. Study the glossary and decide how you want to chunk the set of words. You can group by part of speech, topic, letter of the alphabet, word length, etc. Try to find an easy way to group each term.
2. Once you have your different groups, visit www.wordclouds.com to create a custom word cloud for each group. Print each one of these clouds and post it in a prominent place to serve as constant visual aids for your learning.

## Analogies

**"CHOOSE THE POSITIVE. YOU HAVE CHOICE, YOU ARE MASTER OF YOUR ATTITUDE, CHOOSE THE POSITIVE, THE CONSTRUCTIVE. OPTIMISM IS A FAITH THAT LEADS TO SUCCESS."– BRUCE LEE**

An analogy is a comparison in which an idea or a thing is compared to another thing that is quite different from it. Analogies aim at explaining an idea by comparing it to something that is familiar. Metaphors and similes are tools used to create analogies.

Analogies are useful for learning vocabulary because they require you to analyze a word (or words), and then transfer that analysis to another word. This transfer reinforces the understanding of all the words.

As you analyze the relationships between the analogies you are creating, you will begin to understand the complex relationships between the seemingly unrelated words.

__A__ is to __B_ as __C_ is to __D_

This can be written using colons in place of the terms "is to" and "as."

A:B::C:D

The two items on the left (items A & B) describe a relationship and are separated by a single colon. The two items on the right (items C & D) are shown on the right and are also separated by a colon. Together, both sides are then separated by two colons in the middle, as shown here: Tall: Short :: Skinny: Fat. The relationship used in this analogy is the antonym.

**How to create an analogy**

Start with the basic formula for an analogy:

____ : ____ :: ____ : ____


Next, we will examine a simple synonym analogy:

<u>automobile</u> : <u>car</u> :: <u>box</u> : <u>crate</u>

The key to figuring out a set of word analogies is determining the relationship between the paired set of words.


**Here is a list of the most common types of Analogies and examples**

| | |
|---|---|
| Synonym | Scream : Yell :: Push : Shove |
| Antonym | Rich : Poor :: Empty : Full |
| Cause is to Effect | Prosperity : Happiness :: Success : Joy |
| A Part is to its Whole | Toe : Foot :: Piece : Set |
| An Object to its Function | Car : Travel :: Read : Learn |
| A Item is to its Category | Tabby : House Cat :: Doberman : Dog |
| Word is a symptom of the other | Pain : Fracture :: Wheezing : Allergy |
| An object and it's description | Glass : Brittle :: Lead : Dense |
| The word is lacking the second word | Amputee : Limb :: Deaf : Hearing |
| The first word Hinders the second word | Shackles : Movement :: Stagger : Walk |
| The first word helps the action of the second | Knife : Bread :: Screwdriver : Screw |
| This word is made up of the second word | Sweater : Wool :: Jeans : Denim |
| A word and it's definition | Cede: Break Away :: Abolish : To get rid of |

Using words from the glossary, make a set of analogies using each one. As a bonus, use more than one glossary term in a single analogy.

_____ : _____ :: _____ : _____

Name the relationship between the words in your analogy:_____

_____ : _____ :: _____ : _____

Name the relationship between the words in your analogy:_____

_____ : _____ :: _____ : _____

Name the relationship between the words in your analogy:_____

# Mnemonics

*"It isn't the mountains ahead to climb that wear you out; it's the pebble in your shoe."* –Muhammad Ali

A mnemonic is a learning technique that helps you retain and remember information. Mnemonics are one of the best learning methods for remembering lists or processes in order. Mnemonics make the material more meaningful by adding associations and creating patterns. Interestingly, mnemonics may work better when they utilize absurd, startling, or shocking examples and references. Mnemonics help organize the information so that you can easily retrieve it later. By giving you associations and cues, mnemonics allow you to form a mental structure ordering a list or process to help you remember it better. This mental structure allows you to create a structure of association between items that may not appear to have any relationship. Mnemonics typically use references that are easy to visualize and thus easier to remember. Through visualization of vivid images and references, the information is much easier to imprint into long-term memory. The power of making mnemonics lies in converting dull, inert and uninspiring information into something vibrant and memorable.

## How to make simple and effective mnemonics
Some of the best mnemonics help us remember simple rules or lists in order.

Step 1. Take a list of terms you are trying to remember in order. For example, we will use the scientific method:

observation, question, hypothesis, methods, results, and conclusion.

Next, we will replace each word on the list with a new word that starts with the same letter. These new words will together form a vivid sentence that is easy to remember:

Objectionable Queens Haunted Macho Rednecks Creatively.

As silly as the above sentence seems, it is easy to remember, and now we can call on this sentence to remind us of the order of the scientific method.

Visit http://www.mnemonicgenerator.com/ and try typing in a list of words. It is fun to see the mnemonics that it makes and shows how easy it is to make great mnemonics to help your studying.

Using vivid words in your mnemonics allows you to see the sentence you are making. Words that are gross, scary, or name interesting animals are helpful. Profanity is also useful because the shock value can trigger memory. The following are lists of vivid words to use in your mnemonics:

**Gross words**

Moist, Gurgle, Phlegm, Fetus, Curd, Smear, Squirt, Chunky, Orifice, Maggots, Viscous, Queasy, Bulbous, Pustule, Putrid, Fester, Secrete, Munch, Vomit, Ooze, Dripping, Roaches, Mucus, Stink, Stank, Stunk, Slurp, Pus, Lick, Salty, Tongue, Fart, Flatulence, Hemorrhoid.

**Interesting Animals**

Aardvark, Baboon, Chicken, Chinchilla, Duck, Dragonfly, Emu, Electric Eel, Frog, Flamingo, Gecko, Hedgehog, Hyena, Iguana, Jackal, Jaguar, Leopard, Lynx, Minnow, Manatee, Mongoose, Neanderthal, Newt, Octopus, Oyster, Pelican, Penguin, Platypus, Quail, Racoon, Rattlesnake, Rhinoceros, Scorpion, Seahorse, Toucan, Turkey, Vulture, Weasel, Woodpecker, Yak, Zebra.

**Superhero Words**

Diabolical, Activate, Boom, Clutch, Dastardly, Dynamic, Dynamite, Shazam, Kaboom, Zip, Zap, Zoom, Zany, Crushing, Smashing, Exploding, Ripping, Tearing.

**Scary Words**

Apparition, Bat, Chill, Demon, Eerie, Fangs, Genie, Hell, Lantern, Macabre, Nightmare, Owl, Ogre, Phantasm, Repulsive, Scarecrow, Tarantula, Undead, Vampire, Wraith, Zombie.

There are several types of mnemonics that can help your memory.

**1. Images**

**Visual mnemonics** are a type of mnemonic that works by associating an image with characters or objects whose name sounds like the item that must be memorized. This is one of the easiest ways to create effective mnemonics. An example would be to use the shape of numbers to help memorize a long list of them. Numbers can be memorized by their shapes, so that: 0 -looks like an egg; 1 -a pencil, or a candle; 2 -a snake; 3 -an ear; 4 -a sailboat; 5 -a key; 6 -a comet; 7 -a knee; 8 -a snowman; 9 -a comma.

Another type of visual mnemonic is the word-length mnemonic in which the number of letters in each word corresponds to a digit. This simple mnemonic gives pi to seven decimal places:

3.141582 becomes "How I wish I could calculate pi."

Of course, you could use this type of mnemonic to create a longer sentence showing the digits of an important number. Some people have used this type of mnemonic to memorize thousands of digits.

Using the hands is also an important tool for creating visual objects. Making the hands into specific shapes can help us remember the pattern of things or the order of a list of things.

## 2. Rhyming

Rhyming mnemonics are quick ways to make things memorable. A classic example is a mnemonic for the number of days in each month:

"30 days hath September, April, June, and November.
All the rest have 31
Except February, my dear son.
It has 28, and that is fine
But in Leap Year it has 29."

Another example of a rhyming mnemonic is a common spelling rule:
"I before e except after c
or when sounding like a
in neighbor and weigh."

Use **rhymer.com** to get large lists of rhyming words.

## 3. Homonym

A homonym is one of a group of words that share the same pronunciation but have different meanings, whether spelled the same or not.

Try saying what you're attempting to remember out loud or very quickly, and see if anything leaps out. If you know other languages, using similar-sounding words from those can be effective.

You could also browse this list of homonyms at http://www.cooper.com/alan/homonym_list.html.

## 4. Onomatopoeia

An Onomatopeia is a word that phonetically imitates, resembles or suggests the source of the sound that it describes. Are there any noises made by the thing you're trying to memorize? Is it often associated with some other sound? Failing that, just make up a noise that seems to fit.

Achoo, ahem, baa, bam, bark, beep, beep beep, belch, bleat, boo, boo hoo, boom, burp, buzz, chirp, click clack, crash, croak, crunch, cuckoo, dash, drip, ding dong, eek, fizz, flit, flutter, gasp, grrr, ha ha, hee hee, hiccup, hiss, hissing, honk, icky, itchy, jiggly, jangle, knock knock, lush, la la la, mash, meow, moan, murmur, neigh, oink, ouch, plop, pow, quack, quick, rapping, rattle, ribbit, roar, rumble, rustle, scratch, sizzle, skittering, snap crackle pop, splash, splish splash, spurt, swish, swoosh, tap, tapping, tick tock, tinkle, tweet, ugh, vroom, wham, whinny, whip, whooping, woof.

## 5. Acronyms

An acronym is a word or name formed as an abbreviation from the initial components of a word, such as NATO, which stands for North Atlantic Treaty Organization. If you're trying to memorize something involving letters, this is often a good bet. A lot of famous mnemonics are acronyms, such as ROYGBIV which stands for the order of colors in the light spectrum (Red, Orange, Yellow, Green, Blue, Indigo, and Violet).
A great acronym generator to try is: www.all-acronyms.com.

A different spin on an acronym is a backronym. A **backronym** is a specially constructed phrase that is supposed to be the source of a word that is an acronym. A backronym is constructed by creating a new phrase to fit an already existing word, name, or acronym.

The word is a combination of *backward* and *acronym*, and has been defined as a "reverse acronym." For example, the United States Department of Justice assigns to their Amber Alert program the meaning "**A**merica's **M**issing: **B**roadcast **E**mergency **R**esponse." The process can go either way to make good mnemonics.

Visit: https://arthurdick.com/projects/backronym/ to try out a simple backronym generator.

## 6. Anagrams

An anagram is a direct word switch or word play, the result of rearranging the letters of a word or phrase to produce a new word or phrase, using all the original letters exactly once; for example, the word anagram can be rearranged into nag-a-ram.

Try re-arranging letters or components and see if anything memorable emerges. Visit http://www.nameacronym.net/ to use a simple anagram generator.

One particularly memorable form of anagram is the spoonerism, where you swap the initial syllables or letters of words to make new phrases. These are usually humorous, and this makes them easier to remember. Here are some examples:

"Is it kisstomary to cuss the bride?" (as opposed to "customary to kiss")
"The Lord is a shoving leopard." (instead of "a loving shepherd")
"A blushing crow." ("crushing blow")
"A well-boiled icicle" ("well-oiled bicycle")
"You were fighting a liar in the quadrangle." ("lighting a fire")
"Is the bean dizzy?" (as opposed to "is the dean busy?")

## 7. Stories

Make up quick stories or incidents involving the material you want to memorize. For larger chunks of information, the stories can get more elaborate. Structured stories are particularly good for remembering lists or other sequenced information. Have a look at https://en.wikipedia.org/wiki/Method_of_loci for a more advanced memory sequencing technique.

# Visual Metaphors

"LIMITS, LIKE FEAR, IS OFTEN AN ILLUSION." –MICHAEL JORDAN

What is a Metaphor?

A metaphor is a figure of speech that refers to one thing by mentioning another thing. Metaphors provide clarity and identify hidden similarities between two seemingly unrelated ideas. A visual metaphor is an image that creates a link between different ideas.

Visual metaphors help us use our understanding of the world to learn new concepts, skills, and ideas. Visual metaphors help us relate new material to what we already know. Visual metaphors must be clear and simple enough to spark a connection and understanding. Visual metaphors should use familiar things to help you be less fearful of new, complex, or challenging topics. Metaphors trigger a sense of familiarity so that you are more accepting of the new idea. Metaphors work best when you associate a familiar, easy to understand idea with a challenging, obscure, or abstract concept.

## How to make a visual metaphor

1. Brainstorm using the words of the concept. Use different fonts, colors, or shapes to represent parts of the concept.

2. Merge these images together

3. Show the process using arrows, accents, etc.

4. Think about the story line your metaphor projects.

## Examples of visual metaphors:

A skeleton used to show a framework of something.

A cloud showing an outline.

A bodybuilder whose muscles represent supporting ideas and details.

A sandwich where the meat, tomato, and lettuce represent supporting ideas.

A recipe card to show a process.

Your metaphor should be accurate. It should be complex enough to convey meaning, but simple and clear enough to be easily understood.

# Morphology
## "SCIENCE IS THE CAPTAIN, AND PRACTICE THE SOLDIERS." LEONARDO DA VINCI

Morphology is the study of the origin, roots, suffixes, and prefixes of the words. Understanding the meaning of prefixes, suffixes, and roots make it easier to decode the meaning of new vocabulary. Having the ability to decode using morphology increases text comprehension when initially reading as well.

The capability of identifying meaningful parts of words (morphemes), including prefixes, suffixes, and roots can be helpful. Identifying morphemes improves decoding accuracy and fluency. Reading speed improves when you can decode larger chunks of text quickly. When you can recognize morphemes in words, you will be better able to make sense of new words in context. Below are charts containing the most common prefixes, suffixes, and root words. Use them to help you decode your vocabulary terms.

**Prefixes**

| Prefix | Meaning | Example words and meanings | |
|---|---|---|---|
| a, ab, abs | away from | absent | not to be present, to give |
| | | abdicate | up an office or throne. |
| ad, a, ac, af, ag, an, ar, at, as | to, toward | Advance | To move forward |
| | | advantage | To have the upper hand |
| anti | against | Antidote | To repair poisoning |
| | | antisocial | refers to someone who's |
| | | antibiotic | not social |
| bi, bis | two | bicycle | two-wheeled cycle |
| | | binary | two number system |
| | | biweekly | every two weeks |
| circum, cir | around | circumnavigate | Travel around the world |
| | | circle | a figure that goes all |
| | | | around |
| com, con, co, col | with, together | Complete | To finish |
| | | Complement | To go along with |
| de | away from, down, the opposite of | depart | to go away from |
| | | detour | to go out of your way |
| dis, dif, di | apart | dislike | not to like |
| | | dishonest | not honest |
| | | distant | away |
| En-, em- | Cause to | Entrance | the way in. |
| epi | upon, on top of | epitaph | writing upon a tombstone |
| | | epilogue | speech at the end, on top |
| | | epidemic | of the rest |
| equ, equi | equal | equalize | to make equal |
| | | equitable | fair, equal |
| ex, e, ef | out, from | exit | to go out |
| | | eject | to throw out |
| | | exhale | to breathe out |
| Fore- | Before | Forewarned | To have prior warning |

| Prefix | Meaning | Example Words and Meanings | |
|---|---|---|---|
| in, il, ir, im, en | in, into | Infield | The inner playing field |
| | | Imbibe | to take part in |
| in, il, ig, ir, im | not | inactive | not active |
| | | ignorant | not knowing |
| | | irreversible | not reversible |
| | | irritate | to put into discomfort |
| inter | between, among | international | among nations |
| | | interact | to mix with |
| mal, male | bad, ill, wrong | malpractice | bad practice |
| | | malfunction | fail to function, bad function |
| Mid | Middle | Amidships | In the middle of a ship |
| mis | wrong, badly | misnomer | The wrong name |
| mono | one, alone, single | monocle | one lensed glasses |
| non | not, the reverse of | nonprofit | not making a profit |
| ob | in front, against, in front of, in the way of | Obsolete | No longer needed |
| omni | everywhere, all | omnipresent | always present, everywhere |
| | | omnipotent | all powerful |
| Over | On top | Overdose | Take too much medication |
| Pre | Before | Preview | Happens before a show. |
| per | through | Permeable | to pass through, |
| | | pervasive | all encompassing |
| poly | many | Polygamy | many spouses |
| | | polygon | figure with many sides |
| post | after | postpone | to do after |
| | | postmortem | after death |
| pre | before, earlier than | Predict | To know before |
| | | Preview | To view before release |
| pro | forward, going ahead of, supporting | proceed | to go forward |
| | | pro-war | supporting the war |
| | | promote | to raise or move forward |
| re | again, back | retell | to tell again |
| | | recall | to call back |
| | | reverse | to go back |
| se | apart | secede | to withdraw, become apart |
| | | seclude | to stay apart from others |
| Semi | Half | Semipermeable | Half-permeable |

| Prefix | Meaning | Example Words and Meanings | |
|---|---|---|---|
| Sub | under, less than | Submarine | under water |
| super | over, above, greater | superstar<br>superimpose | a start greater than her stars<br>to put over something else |
| trans | across | transcontinental<br>transverse | across the continent<br>to lie or go across |
| un, uni | one | unidirectional<br>unanimous<br>unilateral | having one direction<br>sharing one view<br>having one side |
| un | not | uninterested<br>unhelpful<br>unethical | not interested<br>not helpful<br>not ethical |

## Roots

| Root | Meaning | Example words & meanings | |
|---|---|---|---|
| act, ag | to do, to act | Agent<br>Activity | One who acts as a representative<br>Action |
| Aqua | Water | Aquamarine | The color of water |
| Aud | To hear | Auditorium | A place to hear music |
| apert | open | Aperture | An opening |
| bas | low | Basement<br>Basement | Something that is low, at the bottom<br>A room that is low |
| Bio | Living thing | Biological | Living matter |
| cap, capt, cip, cept, ceive | to take, to hold, to seize | Captive<br>Receive<br>Capable<br>Recipient | One who is held<br>To take<br>Able to take hold of things<br>One who takes hold or receives |
| ced, cede, ceed, cess | to go, to give in | Precede<br>Access<br>Proceed | To go before<br>Means of going to<br>To go forward |
| Cogn | Know | Cognitive | Ability to think |
| cred, credit | to believe | Credible<br>Incredible<br>Credit | Believable<br>Not believable<br>Belief, trust |
| curr, curs, cours | to run | Current<br>Precursory<br>Recourse | Now in progress, running<br>Running (going) before<br>To run for aid |
| Cycle | Circle | Lifecycle | The circle of life |
| dic, dict | to say | Dictionary<br>Indict | A book explaining words (sayings) |

| Root | Meaning | Examples and meanings | |
|---|---|---|---|
| duc, duct | to lead | Induce<br>Conduct<br>Aqueduct | To lead to action<br>To lead or guide<br>Pipe that leads water somewhere |
| equ | equal, even | Equality<br>Equanimity | Equal in social, political rights<br>Evenness of mind, tranquility |
| fac, fact, fic, fect, fy | to make, to do | Facile<br>Fiction<br>Factory<br>Affect | Easy to do<br>Something that is made up<br>Place that makes things<br>To make a change in |
| fer, ferr | to carry, bring | Defer<br>Referral | To carry away<br>Bring a source for help/information |
| Gen | Birth | Generate | To create something |
| graph | write | Monograph<br>Graphite | A writing on a particular subject<br>A form of carbon used for writing |
| Loc | Place | Location | A place |
| Mater | Mother | Maternity | Expecting birth |
| Mem | Recall | Memory | The recall experiences |
| mit, mis | to send | Admit<br>Missile | To send in<br>Something sent through the air |
| Nat | Born | Native | Born in a place |
| par | equal | Parity<br>Disparate | Equality<br>No equal, not alike |
| Ped | Foot | Podiatrist | Foot doctor |
| Photo | Light | Photograph | A picture |
| plic | to fold, to bend, to turn | Complicate<br>Implicate | To fold (mix) together<br>To fold in, to involve |
| pon, pos, posit, pose | to place | Component<br>Transpose<br>Compose<br>Deposit | A part placed together with others<br>A place across<br>To put many parts into place<br>To place for safekeeping |
| scrib, script | to write | Describe<br>Transcript<br>Subscription | To write about or tell about<br>A written copy<br>A written signature or document |
| sequ, secu | to follow | Sequence | In following order |

| Root | Meaning | Examples and Meanings | |
|---|---|---|---|
| Sign | Mark | Signal | to alert somebody |
| spec, spect, spic | to appear, to look, to see | Specimen<br>Aspect | An example to look at<br>One way to see something |
| sta, stat, sist, | to stand, or make stand | Constant | Standing with |
| stit, sisto | Stable, steady | Status<br>Stable<br>Desist | Social standing<br>Steady (standing)<br>To stand away from |
| Struct | To build | Construction | To build a thing |
| tact | to touch | Contact<br>Tactile | To touch together<br>To be able to be touched |
| ten, tent, tain | to hold | Tenable<br>Retentive<br>Maintain | Able to be held, holding<br>Holding<br>To keep or hold up |
| tend, tens, tent | to stretch | Extend<br>Tension | To stretch or draw out<br>Stretched |
| Therm | Temperature | Thermometer | Detects temperature |
| tract | to draw | Attract<br>Contract | To draw together<br>An agreement drawn up |
| ven, vent | to come | Convene<br>Advent | To come together<br>A coming |
| Vis | See | Invisible | Cannot be seen |
| ver, vert, vers | to turn | Avert<br>Revert<br>Reverse | To turn away<br>To turn back<br>To turn around |

## Crossword Puzzles

1. Using the Across and Down clues, write the correct words in the numbered grid below.

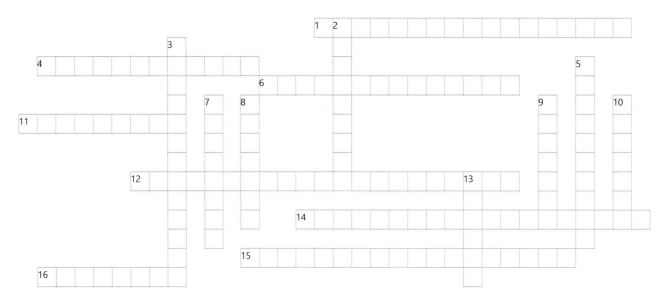

## ACROSS

1. Threatened by factors such as habitat loss, hunting, disease and climate change, and usually have declining populations or a very limited range.
4. Refers to genetically determined structures or attributes that have apparently lost most or all their ancestral function in a given species.
6. A pairing between two nucleotides in RNA molecules that does not follow Watson crick base pair rules
11. Also known as a macula adhaerens, is a cell structure specialized for cell to cell adhesion.
12. A laboratory process that determines the complete DNA sequence of an organism's genome at a single time.
14. The modern form of the metric system and is the most widely used system of measurement.
15. The spectrum of electromagnetic radiation that has passed through a medium that absorbed radiation of certain wavelengths.
16. A compound of chlorine with another element or group, especially a salt of the anion or an organic compound with chlorine bonded to an alkyl group.

## DOWN

2. A small dense spherical structure in the nucleus of a cell during interphase.
3. Virus that infects and multiplies within bacteria.
5. A mammalian blastula in which some differentiation of cells has occurred.
7. Single-cell microscopic organisms which lack a true nucleus. they represent one of the three domains.
8. Large biomolecules, or macromolecules, consisting of one or more long chains of amino acid residues.
9. A type of cell division that reduces the number of chromosomes in the parent cell by half and produces four gamete cells.
10. One of the four main nucleobases found in the nucleic acids DNA and RNA, the others being adenine, cytosine, and thymine.
13. A molecule with the same chemical formula as another molecule, but with a different chemical structure.

A. Bacteria
D. Isomer
G. Vestigiality
J. Absorption spectrum
M. Bacteriophage
P. Blastocyst

B. Guanine
E. Protein
H. Desmosome
K. Meiosis
N. Whole Genome Sequencing

C. Nucleolus
F. Endangered Species
I. Chloride
L. International System
O. Wobble Base Pair

2. Using the Across and Down clues, write the correct words in the numbered grid below.

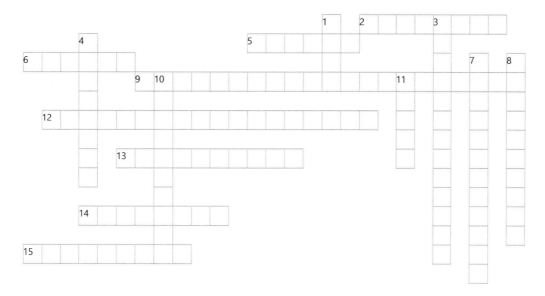

## ACROSS

2. An irregularly shaped region within the cell of a prokaryote that contains all or most of the genetic material, called gonophore.
5. The vascular tissue in plants that conducts sugars and other metabolic products downward from the leaves.
6. One of the four nucleobases in the nucleic acid of RNA that are represented by the letters a, g, c and u.
9. A chemical synapse formed by the contact between a motor neuron and a muscle fiber.
12. A chemical reaction in which the standard change in free energy is positive, and energy is absorbed
13. The branch of biology dealing with the functions and activities of living organisms and their parts, including all physical and chemical processes.
14. A steroidal prohormone of the major insect molting hormone is secreted from the prothoracic glands.
15. The third phase of mitosis, the process that separates duplicated genetic material carried in the nucleus of a parent cell into two identical daughter cells.

## DOWN

1. The structural and functional unit of all organisms.
3. A chemical entity that donates electrons to another compound.
4. The outermost layer of cells or tissue of an embryo in early development, or the parts derived from this, which include the epidermis, nerve tissue, and nephridia.
7. The variety of life in the world or in a habitat or ecosystem.
8. The study of insects.
10. A process by which the contents of a cell vacuole are released to the exterior through fusion of the vacuole membrane with the cell membrane.
11. A liquid by-product of the body secreted by the kidneys through a process called urination (or micturition) and excreted through the urethra.

A. Ectoderm
D. Entomology
G. Endergonic Reaction
J. Nucleoid
M. Exocytosis

B. Metaphase
E. Ecdysone
H. Physiology
K. Biodiversity
N. Electron Donor

C. Phloem
F. Uracil
I. Neuromuscular Junction
L. Urine
O. Cell

3. Using the Across and Down clues, write the correct words in the numbered grid below.

## ACROSS

2. Also known as selective breeding.
5. Cytosine, guanine, adenine (which can be found in DNA and RNA), thymine (found only in DNA), and uracil (found only in RNA).
8. The branch of morphology that deals with the structure of animals
9. A part of an organism that is typically self-contained and has a specific vital function, such as the heart or liver in humans.
10. Variations of genomes between members of species, or between groups of species thriving in different parts of the world as a result of genetic mutation.
11. The application of concepts and methods of biology to solve real world problems.
12. A process by which the contents of a cell vacuole are released to the exterior through fusion of the vacuole membrane with the cell membrane.
13. The study of the chemical elements and compounds necessary for plant growth, plant metabolism and their external supply.
14. The study of plants.
15. The application of the principles of biology to the study of physiological, genetic, and developmental mechanisms of behavior in humans and other animals.

## DOWN

1. A membrane-bound organelle which is present in all plant and fungal cells and some protist, animal and bacterial cells.
3. A compound of chlorine with another element or group, especially a salt of the anion or an organic compound with chlorine bonded to an alkyl group.
4. The study of insects.
6. A sequence of three nucleotides forming a unit of genetic code in a transfer RNA molecule, corresponding to a complementary codon in messenger RNA.
7. Means "falling off at maturity" or "tending to fall off", and it is typically used in order to refer to trees or shrubs that lose their leaves seasonally.

A. Nucleobase
E. Artificial Selection
I. Botany
M. Genetic Variation

B. Anatomy
F. Vacuole
J. Bioengineering
N. Organ

C. Psychobiology
G. Exocytosis
K. Plant Nutrition
O. Entomology

D. Anticodon
H. Chloride
L. Deciduous

4. Using the Across and Down clues, write the correct words in the numbered grid below.

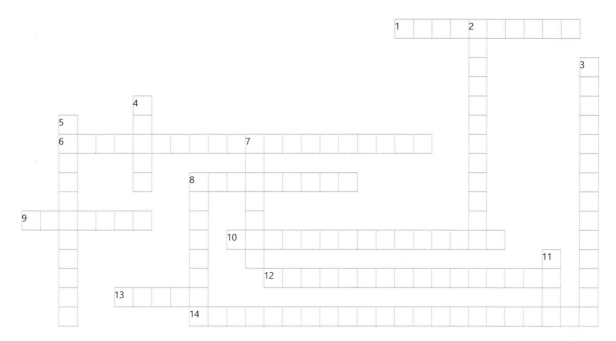

## ACROSS

1. A mammalian blastula in which some differentiation of cells has occurred.
6. A network of membranous tubules within the cytoplasm of a eukaryotic cell, continuous with the nuclear membrane.
8. A organism in which internal physiological sources of heat are of relatively small or quite negligible importance in controlling body temperature. "cold blooded".
9. The process in which a eukaryotic cell nucleus splits in two, followed by division of the parent cell into two daughter cells.
10. The collection of glands that produce hormones that regulate metabolism, growth and development, tissue function, sexual function, reproduction, sleep, and mood.
12. Known as chemical messengers, are endogenous chemicals that enable neurotransmission.
13. One of the proteins into which actomyosin can be split; can exist in either a globular or a fibrous form.
14. The site of oxidative phosphorylation in eukaryotes.

## DOWN

2. A steroid hormone from the androgen group and is found in humans and other vertebrates.
3. Refers to the provision of essential nutrients necessary to support human life and health.
4. A chemical substance that is insoluble in water and soluble in alcohol, ether, and chloroform. the basis for fats and oils.
5. The branch of zoology concerned with reptiles and amphibians.
7. Propagate (an organism or cell) to make an identical copy of.
8. A steroidal prohormone of the major insect molting hormone is secreted from the prothoracic glands.
11. Serves an important role in the metabolism of nitrogen-containing compounds by animals and is the main nitrogen-containing substance in the urine of mammals.

A. Blastocyst
D. Herpetology
G. Endocrine System
J. Ectotherm
M. Endoplasmic Reticulum

B. Ecdysone
E. Lipid
H. Human Nutrition
K. Mitosis
N. Neurotransmitter

C. Testosterone
F. Electron Transport Chain
I. Urea
L. Cloning
O. Actin

5. Using the Across and Down clues, write the correct words in the numbered grid below.

## ACROSS

1. A group of animals that have no backbone, unlike animals such as reptiles, amphibians, fish, birds and mammals who all have a backbone.
4. An electron shell is the outside part of an atom around the atomic nucleus. it is a group of atomic orbitals with the same value of the principal quantum number n.
5. A class of organic compounds containing an amino group and a carboxylic acid group
9. Usually characterized by a chemical change, and they yield one or more products, which usually have properties different from the reactants
10. A nucleotide derived from adenosine that occurs in muscle tissue; the major source of energy for cellular reactions.
11. Containing more than two homologous sets of chromosomes.
12. A membrane-bound organelle which is present in all plant and fungal cells and some protist, animal and bacterial cells.
13. The study of the evolutionary basis for animal behavior due to ecological pressures.

## DOWN

1. Refers to two solutions having the same osmotic pressure across a semipermeable membrane.
2. Helps keep blood sugar level from getting too high (hyperglycemia) or too low (hypoglycemia).
3. Component of the blood that functions in the immune system. also known as a leukocyte.
4. One of the three primary germ layers in the very early human embryo. the other two layers are the ectoderm (outside layer) and mesoderm (middle layer).
6. Often defined as the largest group of organisms in which two individuals can reproduce fertile offspring, typically using sexual reproduction.
7. An interdisciplinary science that applies the approaches and methods of physics to study biological systems.
8. A harmless pill, medicine, or procedure prescribed more for the psychological benefit to the patient than for any physiological effect.

A. Chemical reaction
D. Placebo
G. Isotonic Solution
J. Electron Shell
M. Biophysics

B. White Blood Cell
E. Polyploidy
H. Amino acid
K. Species
N. Invertebrate

C. Insulin
F. Adenosine Triphosphate
I. Endoderm
L. Vacuole
O. Behavioral ecology

6. Using the Across and Down clues, write the correct words in the numbered grid below.

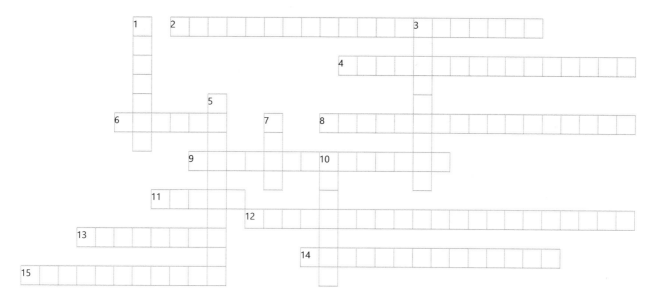

## ACROSS

2. The chemical name for DNA.
4. A chemical substance consisting of two or more different chemically bonded chemical elements, with a fixed ratio determining the composition.
6. A unit of mass (also known as an atomic mass unit, AMU), equal to the mass of a hydrogen atom.
8. When a nerve or muscle cell is at "rest", its membrane potential is called the resting membrane potential.
9. A pairing between two nucleotides in RNA molecules that does not follow Watson crick base pair rules
11. The vascular tissue in plants that conducts water and dissolved nutrients upward from the root and also helps to form the woody element in the stem.
12. A nucleotide derived from adenosine that occurs in muscle tissue; the major source of energy for cellular reactions.
13. One of the three primary germ layers in the very early human embryo. the other two layers are the ectoderm (outside layer) and mesoderm (middle layer).
14. The application of concepts and methods of biology to solve real world problems.
15. The "control room" for the cell. the nucleus gives out all the orders.

## DOWN

1. A lymphatic capillary that absorbs dietary fats in the villi of the small intestine.
3. The interaction of genes that are not alleles. The suppression of the effect of one such gene by another.
5. An inner layer of cells in the cortex of a root and of some stems, surrounding a vascular bundle.
7. A dark green to yellowish brown fluid, produced by the liver of most vertebrates, that aids the digestion of lipids in the small intestine.
10. Depending on free oxygen or air.

A. Aerobic
B. Lacteal
C. Membrane Potential
D. Cell nucleus
E. Epistasis
F. Wobble Base Pair
G. Deoxyribonucleic Acid
H. Chemical compound
I. Xylem
J. Bile
K. Endoderm
L. Endodermis
M. Adenosine Triphosphate
N. Dalton
O. Bioengineering

7. Using the Across and Down clues, write the correct words in the numbered grid below.

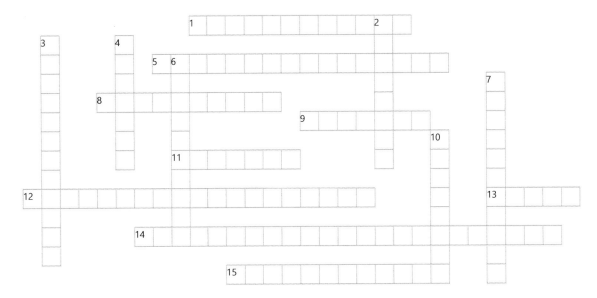

## ACROSS

1. The study and analysis of the patterns, causes, and effects of health and disease conditions in defined populations.
5. The genetic contribution of an individual to the next generation's gene pool relative to the average for the population.
8. A mammalian blastula in which some differentiation of cells has occurred.
9. A system of physical units-based on the meter, kilogram, second, ampere, kelvin, candela, and mole, together with a set of prefixes.
11. Describes a genetically distinct geographic variety, population or race within a species, which is adapted to specific environmental conditions.
12. The modern form of the metric system and is the most widely used system of measurement.
13. One of the proteins into which actomyosin can be split; can exist in either a globular or a fibrous form.
14. A gradient of electrochemical potential, usually for an ion that can move across a membrane.
15. The form of rna in which genetic information transcribed from dna as a sequence of bases is transferred to a ribosome.

## DOWN

2. A cluster (functional group) of nerve cell bodies in a centralized nervous system.
3. The system of immune responses of an organism against its own healthy cells and tissues.
4. The branch of biology that relates to the animal kingdom, including the structure, embryology, evolution, classification, habits, and distribution of all animals.
6. The part of an enzyme or antibody where the chemical reaction occurs
7. The branch of biology that deals with classification and nomenclature; taxonomy.
10. Single-cell microscopic organisms which lack a true nucleus. they represent one of the three domains.

| | | |
|---|---|---|
| A. International System | B. Active site | C. Zoology |
| D. Ganglion | E. Systematics | F. Darwinian Fitness |
| G. Bacteria | H. Blastocyst | I. Actin |
| J. Epidemiology | K. Ecotype | L. Autoimmunity |
| M. Messenger RNA | N. Electrochemical Gradient | O. SI units |

8. Using the Across and Down clues, write the correct words in the numbered grid below.

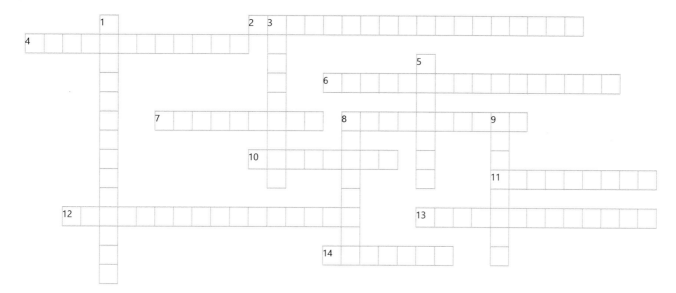

## ACROSS

2. Type of reproduction in which cells from two parents unite to form the first cell of a new organism.
4. The electrons in the outermost occupied shell (or shells) determine the chemical properties of the atom; it is called the valence shell.
6. Refers to two solutions having the same osmotic pressure across a semipermeable membrane.
7. Also known as a macula adhaerens, is a cell structure specialized for cell to cell adhesion.
8. Stereoisomers that are non-superimposable mirror images. a molecule with 1 chiral carbon atom exists as 2 stereoisomers termed enantiomers.
10. A cluster (functional group) of nerve cell bodies in a centralized nervous system.
11. The interaction of genes that are not alleles. The suppression of the effect of one such gene by another.
12. The energy that an atomic system must acquire before a process (such as an emission or reaction) can occur.
13. An electron shell is the outside part of an atom around the atomic nucleus. it is a group of atomic orbitals with the same value of the principal quantum number n.
14. A fluid or air-filled cavity or sac.

## DOWN

1. The double helix is unwound and each strand acts as a template for the next strand. bases are matched to synthesize the new partner strands.
3. The female gametophyte of a seed plant, within which the embryo develops.
5. The branch of morphology that deals with the structure of animals
8. A plant that grows harmlessly upon another plant and derives its moisture and nutrients from the air, rain, and sometimes from debris accumulating around it.
9. An organ or cell that acts in response to a stimulus.

A. Vesicle
E. DNA Replication
I. Activation energy
M. Epiphyte

B. Ganglion
F. Desmosome
J. Effector
N. Epistasis

C. Valence shell
G. Sexual Reproduction
K. Embryo Sac
O. Isotonic Solution

D. Enantiomer
H. Anatomy
L. Electron Shell

9. Using the Across and Down clues, write the correct words in the numbered grid below.

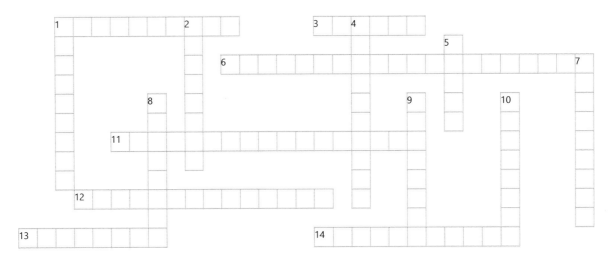

## ACROSS

1. Stereoisomers that are non-superimposable mirror images. a molecule with 1 chiral carbon atom exists as 2 stereoisomers termed enantiomers.
3. One of the four nucleobases in the nucleic acid of RNA that are represented by the letters a, g, c and u.
6. A network of membranous tubules within the cytoplasm of a eukaryotic cell, continuous with the nuclear membrane.
11. The independent evolution of similar traits, starting from a similar ancestral condition.
12. Evolutionary change within a species or small group of organisms, especially over a short period.
13. The study of viruses-submicroscopic, parasitic particles of genetic material contained in a protein coat and virus -like agents.
14. An organic lipid molecule that is biosynthesized by all animal cells because it is an essential structural component of all animal cell membranes.

## DOWN

1. The female gametophyte of a seed plant, within which the embryo develops.
2. The smallest particle in a chemical element or compound that has the chemical properties of that element or compound.
4. A process in which one substance permeates another; a fluid permeates or is dissolved by a liquid or solid.
5. A human embryo after eight weeks of development.
7. The third phase of mitosis, the process that separates duplicated genetic material carried in the nucleus of a parent cell into two identical daughter cells.
8. The inactive x chromosome in a female somatic cell, rendered inactive in a process called lyonization
9. The study of heredity
10. The stock of different genes in an interbreeding population.

A. Gene Pool
B. Barr body
C. Enantiomer
D. Microevolution
E. Cholesterol
F. Endoplasmic Reticulum
G. Embryo Sac
H. Absorption
I. Metaphase
J. Parallel Evolution
K. Genetics
L. Virology
M. Uracil
N. Fetus
O. Molecule

10. Using the Across and Down clues, write the correct words in the numbered grid below.

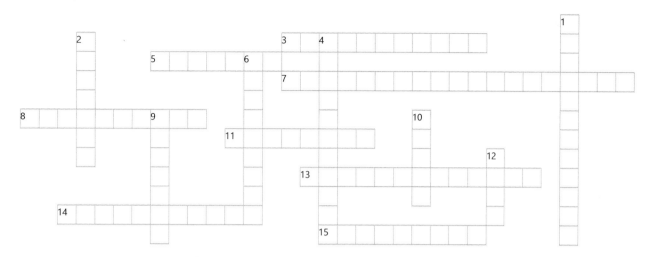

## ACROSS

3. The ecological region at the lowest level of a body of water such as an ocean or a lake.
5. The branch of morphology that deals with the structure of animals
7. A form of intermediate inheritance in which one allele for a specific trait is not completely expressed over its paired allele.
8. An inner layer of cells in the cortex of a root and of some stems, surrounding a vascular bundle.
11. A cluster (functional group) of nerve cell bodies in a centralized nervous system.
13. Nutrients that provide calories or energy. nutrients are substances needed for growth, metabolism, and for other body functions.
14. Density is mass per volume.
15. Also known as a macula adhaerens, is a cell structure specialized for cell to cell adhesion.

## DOWN

1. The study of parasites, their hosts, and the relationship between them.
2. Study of living organisms.
4. A complex organic substance present in living cells, especially DNA or RNA, whose molecules consist of many nucleotides linked in a long chain.
6. The study of mammals.
9. A molecule that can be bonded to other identical molecules to form a polymer.
10. A biological agent that reproduces inside the cells of living hosts.
12. The structural and functional unit of all organisms.

A. Monomer
D. Biology
G. Virus
J. Anatomy
M. Cell

B. Ganglion
E. Macronutrient
H. Desmosome
K. Mammalogy
N. Nucleic Acid

C. Mass Density
F. Parasitology
I. Incomplete Dominance
L. Endodermis
O. Benthic zone

11. Using the Across and Down clues, write the correct words in the numbered grid below.

## ACROSS

1. An enzyme that synthesizes short RNA sequences called primers.
3. Any of various molecules that can accept one or two electrons from one molecule and donating them to another in the process of electron transport.
5. Any of the elongated contractile threads found in striated muscle cells.
6. A sub-field of ecology that deals with the dynamics of species populations and how these populations interact with the environment.
11. The site of oxidative phosphorylation in eukaryotes.
12. Refers to the provision of essential nutrients necessary to support human life and health.
13. The double helix is unwound and each strand acts as a template for the next strand. bases are matched to synthesize the new partner strands.
14. The haploid set of chromosomes in a gamete or microorganism, or in each cell of a multicellular organism.

## DOWN

1. The study of the history of life on earth as reflected in the fossil record. fossils are the remains or traces of organisms.
2. An evolutionary theory that explains the origin of eukaryotic cells from prokaryotes.
4. Any organism whose cells contain a nucleus and other organelles enclosed within membranes.
7. A complex organic substance present in living cells, especially DNA or RNA, whose molecules consist of many nucleotides linked in a long chain.
8. The inactive x chromosome in a female somatic cell, rendered inactive in a process called lyonization
9. The nucleotide triplets of DNA and RNA molecules that carry genetic information in living cells.
10. The branch of biology dealing with the functions and activities of living organisms and their parts, including all physical and chemical processes.

A. Symbiogenesis
D. Human Nutrition
G. Nucleic Acid
J. Genetic Code
M. Electron Transport Chain

B. Barr body
E. Population Ecology
H. Myofibril
K. Physiology
N. Paleontology

C. DNA Replication
F. Electron Carrier
I. Genome
L. Primase
O. Eukaryote

12. Using the Across and Down clues, write the correct words in the numbered grid below.

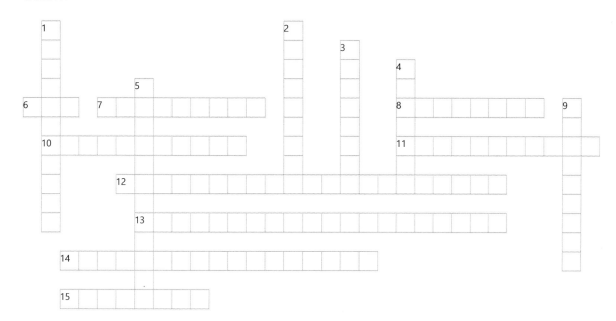

## ACROSS

6. The hereditary material in humans and almost all other organisms.
7. A branch of physical science that studies the composition, structure, properties and change of matter.
8. The fibrous connective tissue that connects bones to other bones.
10. An organic lipid molecule that is biosynthesized by all animal cells because it is an essential structural component of all animal cell membranes.
11. Density is mass per volume.
12. The principle, originated by Gregor Mendel, stating that when two or more characteristics are inherited, individual hereditary factors assort independently.
13. The branch of biology concerned with the relations between organisms and their environment.
14. When a nerve or muscle cell is at "rest", its membrane potential is called the resting membrane potential.
15. A heterocyclic compound of carbon, nitrogen, oxygen, and hydrogen. it forms ions and salts known as urates and acid urates, such as ammonium acid urate.

## DOWN

1. The "control room" for the cell. the nucleus gives out all the orders.
2. A sequence of three nucleotides forming a unit of genetic code in a transfer RNA molecule, corresponding to a complementary codon in messenger RNA.
3. The study of heredity
4. A large molecule, or macromolecule, composed of many repeated subunits.
5. The form of rna in which genetic information transcribed from dna as a sequence of bases is transferred to a ribosome.
9. The third phase of mitosis, the process that separates duplicated genetic material carried in the nucleus of a parent cell into two identical daughter cells.

A. Ligament
D. DNA
G. Cholesterol
J. Chemistry
M. Messenger RNA

B. Environmental Biology
E. Genetics
H. Polymer
K. Anticodon
N. Uric acid

C. Independent Assortment
F. Membrane Potential
I. Mass Density
L. Cell nucleus
O. Metaphase

13. Using the Across and Down clues, write the correct words in the numbered grid below.

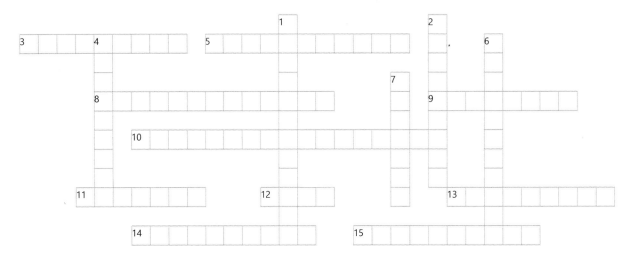

## ACROSS

3. The complete transfer of valence electron(s) between atoms. it is a type of chemical bond that generates two oppositely charged ions.
5. The ecological region at the lowest level of a body of water such as an ocean or a lake.
8. The study of the transformation of energy in living organisms.
9. The intersection of the three medians of the triangle (each median connecting a vertex with the midpoint of the opposite side).
10. A graphical representation designed to show the biomass or bio productivity at each trophic level in a given ecosystem.
11. A type of cell division that reduces the number of chromosomes in the parent cell by half and produces four gamete cells.
12. The yellow internal part of a bird's egg, which is surrounded by the white, is rich in protein and fat, and nourishes the developing embryo.
13. An interaction of living things and non-living things in a physical environment.
14. Organic molecules that serve as the monomers, or subunits, of nucleic acids like DNA (deoxyribonucleic acid) and RNA (ribonucleic acid).
15. A mammalian blastula in which some differentiation of cells has occurred.

## DOWN

1. A lasting attraction between atoms that enables the formation of chemical compounds.
2. A sequence of three nucleotides forming a unit of genetic code in a transfer RNA molecule, corresponding to a complementary codon in messenger RNA.
4. Any member of two classes of chemical compounds derived from carbonic acid or carbon dioxide.
6. Known as fish science, is the branch of biology devoted to the study of fish.
7. One of the four nucleobases in the nucleic acid of DNA that are represented by the letters g–c–a–t.

A. Carbonate
E. Ichthyology
I. Blastocyst
M. Centroid

B. Anticodon
F. Ionic Bond
J. Bioenergetics
N. Benthic zone

C. Meiosis
G. Yolk
K. Thymine
O. Chemical bond

D. Nucleotide
H. Ecosystem
L. Ecological Pyramid

14. Using the Across and Down clues, write the correct words in the numbered grid below.

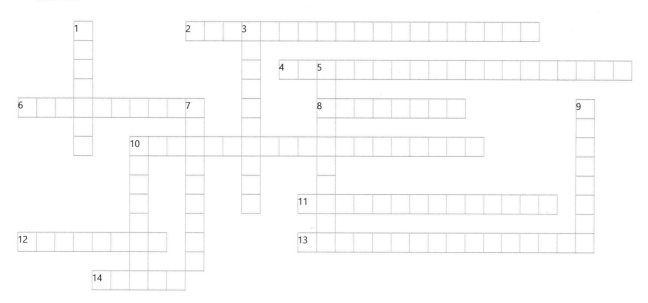

## ACROSS

2. The state in which both reactants and products are present in concentrations which have no further tendency to change with time.
4. A succession of letters that indicate the order of nucleotides within a DNA (using GACT or RNA (GACU) molecule.
6. In cell biology, an organelle that is the main place where cell microtubules get organized. they occur only in plant and animal cells.
8. The fibrous connective tissue that connects bones to other bones.
10. An evolutionary theory that explains the origin of eukaryotic cells from prokaryotes.
11. A pairing between two nucleotides in RNA molecules that does not follow Watson crick base pair rules
12. A short branched extension of a nerve cell, along which impulses received from other cells at synapses are transmitted to the cell body
13. An interdisciplinary branch of biology and engineering.
14. The vascular tissue in plants that conducts water and dissolved nutrients upward from the root and also helps to form the woody element in the stem.

## DOWN

1. A place for animals, people and plants and non-living things
3. The total number of protons and neutrons (together known as nucleons) in an atomic nucleus
5. The theory that all living things are made up of cells.
7. An interaction of living things and non-living things in a physical environment.
9. The study of viruses-submicroscopic, parasitic particles of genetic material contained in a protein coat and virus -like agents.
10. The region of an embryo or seedling stem above the cotyledon.

A. Cell theory
B. Mass Number
C. Endosymbiotic Theory
D. Nucleic Acid Sequence
E. Chemical equilibrium
F. Xylem
G. Wobble Base Pair
H. Ecosystem
I. Virology
J. Ligament
K. Dendrite
L. Epicotyl
M. Habitat
N. Centrosome
O. Synthetic Biology

15. Using the Across and Down clues, write the correct words in the numbered grid below.

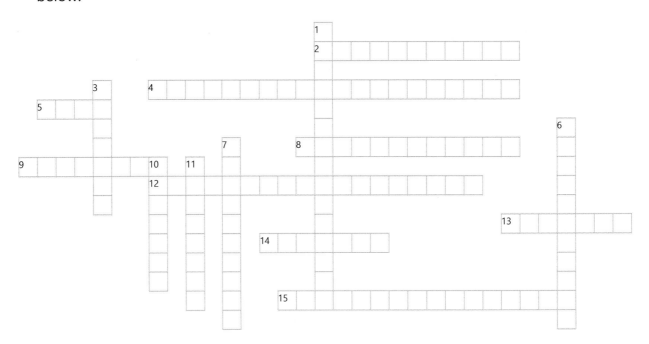

## ACROSS

2. Another term for adrenaline.
4. A network of membranous tubules within the cytoplasm of a eukaryotic cell, continuous with the nuclear membrane.
5. The si unit of measurement used to measure the number of things, usually atoms or molecules.
8. The branch of science that explores the chemical processes within and related to living organisms.
9. An individual animal, plant, or single-celled life form.
12. A type of microscope that uses a beam of electrons to create an image of the specimen. it is capable of much higher magnifications.
13. A fluid or air-filled cavity or sac.
14. Describes a genetically distinct geographic variety, population or race within a species, which is adapted to specific environmental conditions.
15. Variations of genomes between members of species, or between groups of species thriving in different parts of the world as a result of genetic mutation.

## DOWN

1. A microbially facilitated process of nitrate reduction that may ultimately produce molecular nitrogen.
3. The midsection of the small intestine of many higher vertebrates like mammals, birds, reptiles. it is present between the duodenum and the ileum.
6. The ecological region at the lowest level of a body of water such as an ocean or a lake.
7. A class of drug used to kill bacteria.
10. A type of cell division that reduces the number of chromosomes in the parent cell by half and produces four gamete cells.
11. The study of heredity

A. Mole
D. Benthic zone
G. Genetics
J. Genetic Variation
M. Denitrification

B. Epinephrine
E. Electron Microscope
H. Organism
K. Biochemistry
N. Meiosis

C. Antibiotic
F. Jejunum
I. Ecotype
L. Vesicle
O. Endoplasmic Reticulum

16. Using the Across and Down clues, write the correct words in the numbered grid below.

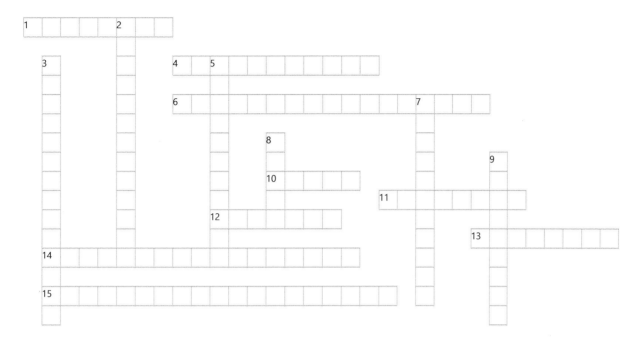

## ACROSS

1. The fibrous connective tissue that connects bones to other bones.
4. Known as fish science, is the branch of biology devoted to the study of fish.
6. Threatened by factors such as habitat loss, hunting, disease and climate change, and usually have declining populations or a very limited range.
10. A chemical substance that is insoluble in water and soluble in alcohol, ether, and chloroform. the basis for fats and oils.
11. A heterocyclic compound of carbon, nitrogen, oxygen, and hydrogen. it forms ions and salts known as urates and acid urates, such as ammonium acid urate.
12. Organic matter derived from living, or recently living organisms.
13. The smallest particle in a chemical element or compound that has the chemical properties of that element or compound.
14. The study of populations of organisms, especially the regulation of population size, life history traits such as clutch size, and extinction.
15. The modern form of the metric system and is the most widely used system of measurement.

## DOWN

2. An electron shell is the outside part of an atom around the atomic nucleus. it is a group of atomic orbitals with the same value of the principal quantum number n.
3. A pairing between two nucleotides in RNA molecules that does not follow Watson crick base pair rules
5. In organic chemistry, a hydrocarbon is an organic compound consisting entirely of hydrogen and carbon.
7. The branch of biology that studies the effects of low temperatures on living things within earth's cryosphere or in science.
8. The vascular tissue in plants that conducts water and dissolved nutrients upward from the root and also helps to form the woody element in the stem.
9. A class of organic compounds containing an amino group and a carboxylic acid group

| | |
|---|---|
| A. Ligament | B. Wobble Base Pair |
| E. Lipid | F. Endangered Species |
| I. Biomass | J. Hydrocarbon |
| M. Uric acid | N. Cryobiology |

| | |
|---|---|
| C. Amino acid | D. Electron Shell |
| G. Population Biology | H. Xylem |
| K. Molecule | L. International System |
| O. Ichthyology | |

17. Using the Across and Down clues, write the correct words in the numbered grid below.

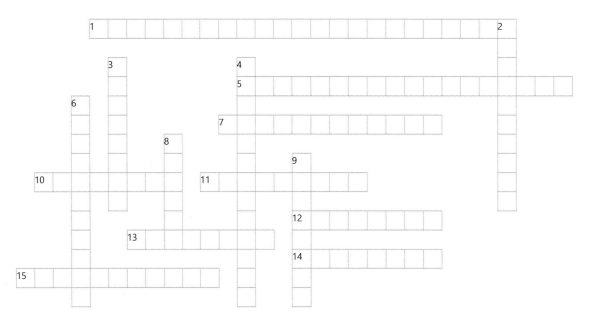

## ACROSS

1. A technique used in molecular biology to amplify a single copy or a few copies of a piece of DNA across several orders of magnitude.
5. A label frequently used to describe various forms of cross-disciplinary and multitaxon research.
7. The study of cells of the nervous system and the organization of these cells into functional circuits that process information and mediate behavior.
10. The region of an embryo or seedling stem above the cotyledon.
11. Any member of two classes of chemical compounds derived from carbonic acid or carbon dioxide.
12. An individual animal, plant, or single-celled life form.
13. A short branched extension of a nerve cell, along which impulses received from other cells at synapses are transmitted to the cell body
14. The primary female sex hormone. it is responsible for the development and regulation of the female reproductive system and secondary sex characteristics.
15. The branch of biology that studies the effects of low temperatures on living things within earth's cryosphere or in science.

## DOWN

2. Cytosine, guanine, adenine (which can be found in DNA and RNA), thymine (found only in DNA), and uracil (found only in RNA).
3. An organ or cell that acts in response to a stimulus.
4. The study of the transformation of energy in living organisms.
6. The act of transferring pollen grains from the male anther of a flower to the female stigma.
8. A unit of mass (also known as an atomic mass unit, AMU), equal to the mass of a hydrogen atom.
9. One of the three primary germ layers in the very early human embryo. the other two layers are the ectoderm (outside layer) and mesoderm (middle layer).

A. Endoderm
D. Dendrite
G. Polymerase Chain Reaction
J. Integrative Biology
M. Organism

B. Cryobiology
E. Carbonate
H. Dalton
K. Bioenergetics
N. Effector

C. Epicotyl
F. Neurobiology
I. Estrogen
L. Pollination
O. Nucleobase

18. Using the Across and Down clues, write the correct words in the numbered grid below.

## ACROSS

3. The study of plant nutrition and growth especially to increase crop yield
5. The dilatation of blood vessels, which decreases blood pressure.
7. The subfield of biology that studies the evolutionary processes that produced the diversity of life on earth starting from a single origin of life.
10. When two genes are close together on the same chromosome, they do not assort independently.
12. The collection of glands that produce hormones that regulate metabolism, growth and development, tissue function, sexual function, reproduction, sleep, and mood.
13. The energy that an atomic system must acquire before a process (such as an emission or reaction) can occur.
14. The si unit of measurement used to measure the number of things, usually atoms or molecules.
15. A steroid hormone from the androgen group and is found in humans and other vertebrates.

## DOWN

1. A measure of the potential energy in water as well as the difference between the potential in a water sample and pure water.
2. Work to convert light energy of the sun into sugars that can be used by cells.
4. The study of the structure and function of biological systems by means of the methods of "mechanics."
6. The continuation of the spinal cord within the skull, forming the lowest part of the brainstem and containing control centers for the heart and lungs.
8. The yellow internal part of a bird's egg, which is surrounded by the white, is rich in protein and fat, and nourishes the developing embryo.
9. The stock of different genes in an interbreeding population.
11. The process in which a eukaryotic cell nucleus splits in two, followed by division of the parent cell into two daughter cells.

A. Water Potential
B. Medulla
C. Testosterone
D. Mitosis
E. Evolutionary Biology
F. Activation energy
G. Chloroplast
H. Biomechanics
I. Yolk
J. Vasodilation
K. Gene Pool
L. Endocrine System
M. Linked Genes
N. Agrobiology
O. Mole

19. Using the Across and Down clues, write the correct words in the numbered grid below.

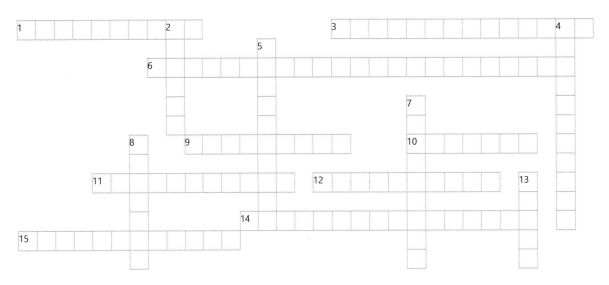

## ACROSS

1. A process by which the contents of a cell vacuole are released to the exterior through fusion of the vacuole membrane with the cell membrane.
3. Refers to the provision of essential nutrients necessary to support human life and health.
6. A technique used in molecular biology to amplify a single copy or a few copies of a piece of DNA across several orders of magnitude.
9. The tendency of a crossbred individual to show qualities superior to those of both parents.
10. Organic matter derived from living, or recently living organisms.
11. An organic lipid molecule that is biosynthesized by all animal cells because it is an essential structural component of all animal cell membranes.
12. An interdisciplinary science that applies the approaches and methods of physics to study biological systems.
14. Known as chemical messengers, are endogenous chemicals that enable neurotransmission.
15. The study of the distribution of species and ecosystems in geographic space and through time.

## DOWN

2. A molecule with the same chemical formula as another molecule, but with a different chemical structure.
4. A branch of zoology that concerns the study of birds.
5. A microscopic single celled organism that has no distinct nucleus
7. The female gametophyte of a seed plant, within which the embryo develops.
8. Study of living organisms.
13. A biological agent that reproduces inside the cells of living hosts.

A. Biology
D. Heterosis
G. Exocytosis
J. Embryo Sac
M. Human Nutrition

B. Biogeography
E. Polymerase Chain Reaction
H. Biomass
K. Biophysics
N. Virus

C. Cholesterol
F. Prokaryote
I. Ornithology
L. Neurotransmitter
O. Isomer

20. Using the Across and Down clues, write the correct words in the numbered grid below.

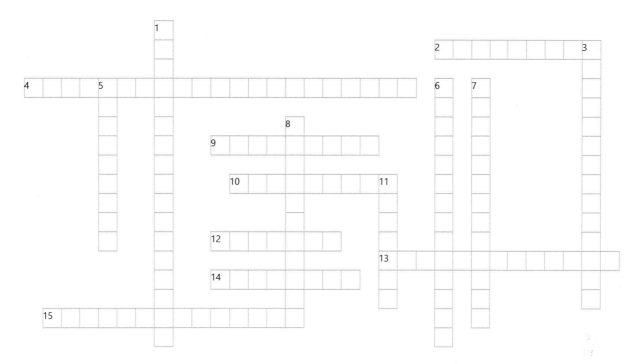

## ACROSS

2. A class of organic compounds containing an amino group and a carboxylic acid group
4. The application of engineering principles and design concepts to medicine and biology for healthcare purposes (e.g. diagnostic or therapeutic).
9. The tendency of a crossbred individual to show qualities superior to those of both parents.
10. A organism in which internal physiological sources of heat are of relatively small or quite negligible importance in controlling body temperature. "cold blooded".
12. The branch of morphology that deals with the structure of animals
13. An evolutionary theory that explains the origin of eukaryotic cells from prokaryotes.
14. Organisms that produce an egg composed of shell and membranes that creates a protected environment in which the embryo can develop out of water
15. The science of diagnosing and managing plant diseases.

## DOWN

1. The amount of work needed to move a unit charge from a reference point to a specific point against an electric field.
3. The double helix is unwound and each strand acts as a template for the next strand. bases are matched to synthesize the new partner strands.
5. The interaction of genes that are not alleles. The suppression of the effect of one such gene by another.
6. An epithelial tissue that secretes mucus and that lines many body cavities and tubular organs including the gut and respiratory passages.
7. A chemical entity that donates electrons to another compound.
8. The branch of biology that studies the effects of low temperatures on living things within earth's cryosphere or in science.
11. The process in which a eukaryotic cell nucleus splits in two, followed by division of the parent cell into two daughter cells.

A. Heterosis
D. Phytopathology
G. Electron Donor
J. Cryobiology
M. Symbiogenesis

B. Mitosis
E. Mucous Membrane
H. DNA Replication
K. Anatomy
N. Amino acid

C. Biomedical engineering
F. Amniotes
I. Electric Potential
L. Ectotherm
O. Epistasis

21. Using the Across and Down clues, write the correct words in the numbered grid below.

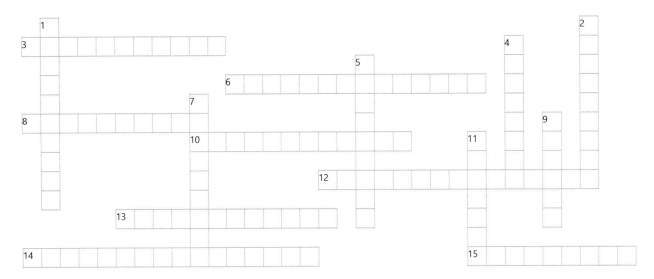

## ACROSS

3. The branch of biology that studies the effects of low temperatures on living things within earth's cryosphere or in science.
6. The double helix is unwound and each strand acts as a template for the next strand. bases are matched to synthesize the new partner strands.
8. the sequence of reactions by which most living cells generate energy during the process of aerobic respiration.
10. A lasting attraction between atoms that enables the formation of chemical compounds.
12. The role and position a species has in its environment; how it meets its needs for food and shelter, how it survives, and how it reproduces.
13. Giving birth to one of its kind, sexually or asexually.
14. Known as chemical messengers, are endogenous chemicals that enable neurotransmission.
15. An interaction of living things and non-living things in a physical environment.

## DOWN

1. A microscopic single celled organism that has no distinct nucleus
2. A colorless cell which circulates in the blood and body fluids and is involved in counteracting foreign substances and disease; a white (blood) cell.
4. A cluster (functional group) of nerve cell bodies in a centralized nervous system.
5. The study of the microscopic anatomy of cells and tissues of plants and animals.
7. Means "falling off at maturity" or "tending to fall off", and it is typically used in order to refer to trees or shrubs that lose their leaves seasonally.
9. One of the four nucleobases in the nucleic acid of RNA that are represented by the letters a, g, c and u.
11. One of the four main nucleobases found in the nucleic acids DNA and RNA, the others being adenine, cytosine, and thymine.

A. Deciduous
E. Krebs Cycle
I. Chemical bond
M. Cryobiology

B. Ecological Niche
F. Neurotransmitter
J. Leukocyte
N. DNA Replication

C. Guanine
G. Prokaryote
K. Ecosystem
O. Ganglion

D. Histology
H. Uracil
L. Reproduction

22. Using the Across and Down clues, write the correct words in the numbered grid below.

## ACROSS

4. The study of the transformation of energy in living organisms.
5. Adaptation to a new climate (a new temperature or altitude or environment).
7. A pairing between two nucleotides in RNA molecules that does not follow Watson crick base pair rules
9. The branch of biology that studies the development of gametes (sex cells), fertilization, and development of embryos and fetuses.
10. A molecule that can be bonded to other identical molecules to form a polymer.
11. A human embryo after eight weeks of development.
12. The branch of biology that deals with classification and nomenclature; taxonomy.
13. The science of drug action on biological systems.
14. The collection of glands that produce hormones that regulate metabolism, growth and development, tissue function, sexual function, reproduction, sleep, and mood.

## DOWN

1. The outermost layer of cells or tissue of an embryo in early development, or the parts derived from this, which include the epidermis, nerve tissue, and nephridia.
2. An individual animal, plant, or single-celled life form.
3. A complex organic substance present in living cells, especially DNA or RNA, whose molecules consist of many nucleotides linked in a long chain.
4. A mammalian blastula in which some differentiation of cells has occurred.
6. The branch of biology concerned with the effects of outer space on living organisms and the search for extraterrestrial life
8. An organ or cell that acts in response to a stimulus.

A. Embryology
E. Bioenergetics
I. Systematics
M. Fetus
B. Astrobiology
F. Wobble Base Pair
J. Pharmacology
N. Nucleic Acid
C. Endocrine System
G. Organism
K. Acclimatization
O. Blastocyst
D. Effector
H. Monomer
L. Ectoderm

23. Using the Across and Down clues, write the correct words in the numbered grid below.

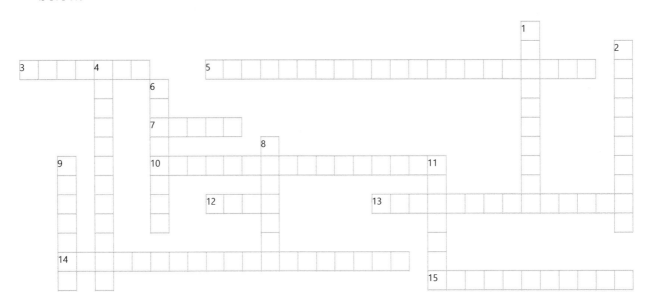

## ACROSS

3. A harmless pill, medicine, or procedure prescribed more for the psychological benefit to the patient than for any physiological effect.
5. The application of engineering principles and design concepts to medicine and biology for healthcare purposes (e.g. diagnostic or therapeutic).
7. A distinct juvenile form many animals undergo before metamorphosis into adults. animals with indirect development such as insects, amphibians, or cnidarians.
10. The study and discussion of chemical reactions with respect to reaction rates.
12. The si unit of measurement used to measure the number of things, usually atoms or molecules.
13. The application of concepts and methods of biology to solve real world problems.
14. Also known as selective breeding.
15. A monosaccharide. its name indicates that it is a deoxy sugar, meaning that it is derived from the sugar ribose by loss of an oxygen atom.

## DOWN

1. A threadlike strand of DNA in the cell nucleus that carries the genes in a linear order.
2. The branch of biology dealing with the functions and activities of living organisms and their parts, including all physical and chemical processes.
4. Variations in a phenotype among individuals carrying a genotype.
6. The smallest particle in a chemical element or compound that has the chemical properties of that element or compound.
8. Refers to the number of elements to which it can connect.
9. A form of terrestrial locomotion where an organism moves by means of its two rear limbs or legs.
11. An organic compound with four rings arranged in a specific configuration. examples include the dietary lipid cholesterol and the sex hormones.

A. Larva
B. Valence
C. Artificial Selection
D. Bipedal
E. Chemical kinetics
F. Molecule
G. Physiology
H. Expressivity
I. Deoxyribose
J. Chromosome
K. Bioengineering
L. Mole
M. Steroid
N. Placebo
O. Biomedical engineering

24. Using the Across and Down clues, write the correct words in the numbered grid below.

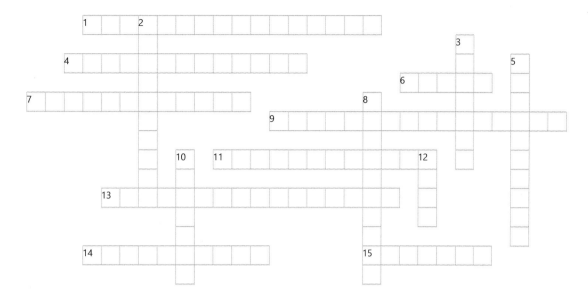

## ACROSS

1. A chemical entity that accepts electrons transferred to it from another compound.
4. The scientific study of organisms in the ocean or other marine bodies of water.
6. The vascular tissue in plants that conducts water and dissolved nutrients upward from the root and also helps to form the woody element in the stem.
7. A process in which proteins or nucleic acids lose the quaternary structure, tertiary structure and secondary structure which is present in their native state.
9. A branch of science concerning biological activity at the molecular level.
11. Refers to genetically determined structures or attributes that have apparently lost most or all their ancestral function in a given species.
13. Usually characterized by a chemical change, and they yield one or more products, which usually have properties different from the reactants
14. Stereoisomers that are non-superimposable mirror images. a molecule with 1 chiral carbon atom exists as 2 stereoisomers termed enantiomers.
15. A system of physical units-based on the meter, kilogram, second, ampere, kelvin, candela, and mole, together with a set of prefixes.

## DOWN

2. In cell biology, an organelle that is the main place where cell microtubules get organized. they occur only in plant and animal cells.
3. One of the two purine nucleobases (the other being guanine) used in forming nucleotides of the nucleic acids.
5. The study of insects.
8. Cytosine, guanine, adenine (which can be found in DNA and RNA), thymine (found only in DNA), and uracil (found only in RNA).
10. A type of cell division that reduces the number of chromosomes in the parent cell by half and produces four gamete cells.
12. The yellow internal part of a bird's egg, which is surrounded by the white, is rich in protein and fat, and nourishes the developing embryo.

A. Electron Acceptor
E. Entomology
I. Centrosome
M. Meiosis

B. Molecular biology
F. Vestigiality
J. Denaturation
N. SI units

C. Yolk
G. Nucleobase
K. Chemical reaction
O. Adenine

D. Xylem
H. Enantiomer
L. Marine Biology

25. Using the Across and Down clues, write the correct words in the numbered grid below.

## ACROSS

2. A part of an organism that is typically self-contained and has a specific vital function, such as the heart or liver in humans.
5. The study of the structure and function of biological systems by means of the methods of "mechanics."
6. The study of viruses-submicroscopic, parasitic particles of genetic material contained in a protein coat and virus-like agents.
7. The study of the evolutionary basis for animal behavior due to ecological pressures.
8. The intersection of the three medians of the triangle (each median connecting a vertex with the midpoint of the opposite side).
9. Organisms that produce an egg composed of shell and membranes that creates a protected environment in which the embryo can develop out of water
11. The first step of gene expression, in which a segment of DNA is copied into RNA (mRNA) by the enzyme RNA polymerase.
12. The dilatation of blood vessels, which decreases blood pressure.
13. RNA consisting of folded molecules that transport amino acids from the cytoplasm of a cell to a ribosome.
14. The branch of biology that deals with classification and nomenclature; taxonomy.

## DOWN

1. The stock of different genes in an interbreeding population.
3. One of the four main nucleobases found in the nucleic acids DNA and RNA, the others being adenine, cytosine, and thymine.
4. The study and analysis of the patterns, causes, and effects of health and disease conditions in defined populations.
5. The branch of science that explores the chemical processes within and related to living organisms.
10. Hadronic subatomic particles composed of one quark and one antiquark, bound together by the strong interaction.

A. Biomechanics
E. Guanine
I. Transcription
M. Systematics

B. Vasodilation
F. Epidemiology
J. Biochemistry
N. Transfer RNA

C. Behavioral ecology
G. Meson
K. Gene Pool
O. Centroid

D. Virology
H. Organ
L. Amniotes

26. Using the Across and Down clues, write the correct words in the numbered grid below.

## ACROSS

6. Any of various molecules that can accept one or two electrons from one molecule and donating them to another in the process of electron transport.
8. The total number of protons and neutrons (together known as nucleons) in an atomic nucleus
10. The study of the evolutionary basis for animal behavior due to ecological pressures.
11. Organic matter derived from living, or recently living organisms.
12. The process in which a eukaryotic cell nucleus splits in two, followed by division of the parent cell into two daughter cells.
13. The practice of cultivating land, growing food, and raising stock.
14. The local voltage change across the cell wall as a nerve impulse is transmitted.
15. A complex organic substance present in living cells, especially DNA or RNA, whose molecules consist of many nucleotides linked in a long chain.

## DOWN

1. Of or pertaining to the throat.
2. A form of terrestrial locomotion where an organism moves by means of its two rear limbs or legs.
3. The branch of biology dealing with the functions and activities of living organisms and their parts, including all physical and chemical processes.
4. Known as fish science, is the branch of biology devoted to the study of fish.
5. Single-cell microscopic organisms which lack a true nucleus. they represent one of the three domains.
7. the sequence of reactions by which most living cells generate energy during the process of aerobic respiration.
9. A cluster (functional group) of nerve cell bodies in a centralized nervous system.

A. Action potential      B. Nucleic Acid      C. Krebs Cycle      D. Electron Carrier
E. Gular                 F. Physiology        G. Mitosis          H. Mass Number
I. Ganglion              J. Biomass           K. Bipedal          L. Bacteria
M. Ichthyology           N. Behavioral ecology   O. Agriculture

27. Using the Across and Down clues, write the correct words in the numbered grid below.

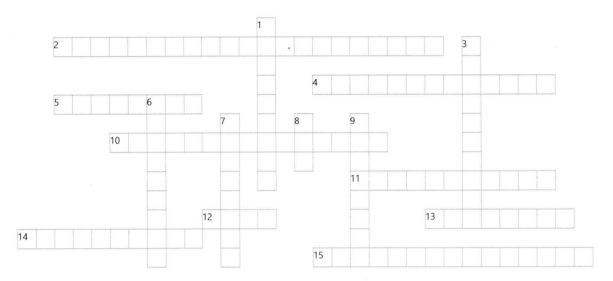

## ACROSS

2. The principle, originated by Gregor Mendel, stating that when two or more characteristics are inherited, individual hereditary factors assort independently.
4. Nutrients that provide calories or energy. nutrients are substances needed for growth, metabolism, and for other body functions.
5. One of the three primary germ layers in the very early human embryo. the other two layers are the ectoderm (outside layer) and mesoderm (middle layer).
10. The role and position a species has in its environment; how it meets its needs for food and shelter, how it survives, and how it reproduces.
11. A branch of zoology that concerns the study of birds.
12. A gene is a locus (or region) of DNA that encodes a functional RNA or protein product and is the molecular unit of heredity.
13. A subatomic particle with a negative elementary electric charge.
14. A microscopic single celled organism that has no distinct nucleus
15. Any of various molecules that can accept one or two electrons from one molecule and donating them to another in the process of electron transport.

## DOWN

1. Any member of two classes of chemical compounds derived from carbonic acid or carbon dioxide.
3. A threadlike strand of DNA in the cell nucleus that carries the genes in a linear order.
6. The change in genetic composition of a population over successive generations, which may be caused by natural selection, inbreeding, hybridization, or mutation.
7. The fibrous connective tissue that connects bones to other bones.
8. The hereditary material in humans and almost all other organisms.
9. A compound of chlorine with another element or group, especially a salt of the anion or an organic compound with chlorine bonded to an alkyl group.

A. Macronutrient
D. Independent Assortment
G. Endoderm
J. DNA
M. Ecological Niche

B. Chloride
E. Ornithology
H. Prokaryote
K. Gene
N. Ligament

C. Chromosome
F. Electron
I. Carbonate
L. Evolution
O. Electron Carrier

28. Using the Across and Down clues, write the correct words in the numbered grid below.

## ACROSS

2. A straightforward extension of Lewis structures. states that electrons in a covalent bond reside in a region that is the overlap of individual atomic orbitals.
3. The female gametophyte of a seed plant, within which the embryo develops.
4. The yellow colored photosynthetic pigments.
7. A form of terrestrial locomotion where an organism moves by means of its two rear limbs or legs.
8. Variations of genomes between members of species, or between groups of species thriving in different parts of the world as a result of genetic mutation.
9. Also known as a macula adhaerens, is a cell structure specialized for cell to cell adhesion.
10. One cell dividing into two identical daughter cells.
11. Propagate (an organism or cell) to make an identical copy of.
12. The site of oxidative phosphorylation in eukaryotes.
13. A sub-field of ecology that deals with the dynamics of species populations and how these populations interact with the environment.
14. The subfield of biology that studies the evolutionary processes that produced the diversity of life on earth starting from a single origin of life.

## DOWN

1. A large molecule, or macromolecule, composed of many repeated subunits.
3. Any of various molecules that can accept one or two electrons from one molecule and donating them to another in the process of electron transport.
5. A harmless pill, medicine, or procedure prescribed more for the psychological benefit to the patient than for any physiological effect.
6. The study of the history of life on earth as reflected in the fossil record. fossils are the remains or traces of organisms.
8. Of or pertaining to the throat.

A. Gular
D. Desmosome
G. Valence bond theory
J. Paleontology
M. Binary fission
P. Population Ecology

B. Polymer
E. Evolutionary Biology
H. Genetic Variation
K. Bipedal
N. Cloning

C. Electron Carrier
F. Electron Transport Chain
I. Placebo
L. Embryo Sac
O. Xanthophyll

29. Using the Across and Down clues, write the correct words in the numbered grid below.

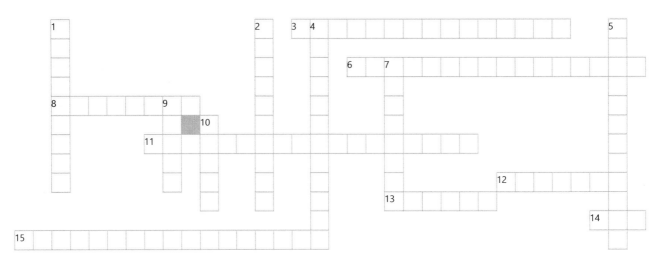

## ACROSS

3. The collection of glands that produce hormones that regulate metabolism, growth and development, tissue function, sexual function, reproduction, sleep, and mood.
6. The study and discussion of chemical reactions with respect to reaction rates.
8. A branch of medicine that deals with the prevention, diagnosis and treatment of cancer.
11. A type of microscope that uses a beam of electrons to create an image of the specimen. it is capable of much higher magnifications.
12. A lymphatic capillary that absorbs dietary fats in the villi of the small intestine.
13. Biological molecules (proteins) that act as catalysts and help complex reactions occur everywhere in life.
14. The female reproductive cell (gamete) in oogamous organisms.
15. The study of the evolutionary basis for animal behavior due to ecological pressures.

## DOWN

1. A colorless cell which circulates in the blood and body fluids and is involved in counteracting foreign substances and disease; a white (blood) cell.
2. A process by which the contents of a cell vacuole are released to the exterior through fusion of the vacuole membrane with the cell membrane.
4. The study of cells of the nervous system and the organization of these cells into functional circuits that process information and mediate behavior.
5. The study of microscopic organisms, such as bacteria, viruses, archaea, fungi and protozoa.
7. A steroidal prohormone of the major insect molting hormone is secreted from the prothoracic glands.
9. Of or pertaining to the throat.
10. One of the proteins into which actomyosin can be split; can exist in either a globular or a fibrous form.

A. Actin
E. Lacteal
I. Endocrine System
M. Leukocyte

B. Chemical kinetics
F. Behavioral ecology
J. Oncology
N. Electron Microscope

C. Egg
G. Exocytosis
K. Gular
O. Neurobiology

D. Ecdysone
H. Enzyme
L. Microbiology

30. Using the Across and Down clues, write the correct words in the numbered grid below.

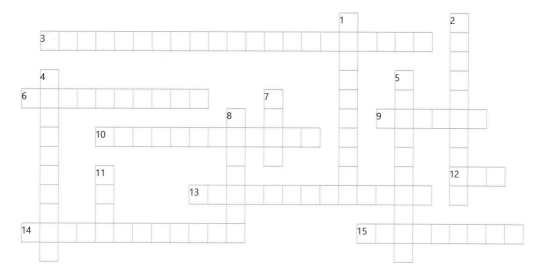

## ACROSS

3. A chemical synapse formed by the contact between a motor neuron and a muscle fiber.
6. An inner layer of cells in the cortex of a root and of some stems, surrounding a vascular bundle.
9. Any particle that is made from quarks, antiquarks and gluons.
10. The science of drug action on biological systems.
12. The hereditary material in humans and almost all other organisms.
13. The study of the transformation of energy in living organisms.
14. The study of the distribution of species and ecosystems in geographic space and through time.
15. Also known as a macula adhaerens, is a cell structure specialized for cell to cell adhesion.

## DOWN

1. Animals, like flatworms and jellyfish, that have no body cavity (coelom).
2. Organic molecules that serve as the monomers, or subunits, of nucleic acids like DNA (deoxyribonucleic acid) and RNA (ribonucleic acid).
4. A class of drug used to kill bacteria.
5. A mammalian blastula in which some differentiation of cells has occurred.
7. Any part of a gene that will become a part of the final mature RNA produced by that gene after introns have been removed by RNA splicing.
8. The branch of biology that relates to the animal kingdom, including the structure, embryology, evolution, classification, habits, and distribution of all animals.
11. A dark green to yellowish brown fluid, produced by the liver of most vertebrates, that aids the digestion of lipids in the small intestine.

| | | |
|---|---|---|
| A. Endodermis | B. DNA | C. Blastocyst |
| D. Exon | E. Acoelomate | F. Pharmacology |
| G. Biogeography | H. Desmosome | I. Bioenergetics |
| J. Bile | K. Hadron | L. Neuromuscular Junction |
| M. Zoology | N. Nucleotide | O. Antibiotic |

1. Using the Across and Down clues, write the correct words in the numbered grid below.

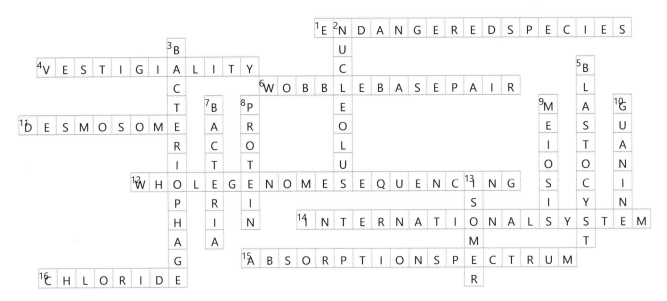

## ACROSS

1. Threatened by factors such as habitat loss, hunting, disease and climate change, and usually have declining populations or a very limited range.
4. Refers to genetically determined structures or attributes that have apparently lost most or all their ancestral function in a given species.
6. A pairing between two nucleotides in RNA molecules that does not follow Watson crick base pair rules
11. Also known as a macula adhaerens, is a cell structure specialized for cell to cell adhesion.
12. A laboratory process that determines the complete DNA sequence of an organism's genome at a single time.
14. The modern form of the metric system and is the most widely used system of measurement.
15. The spectrum of electromagnetic radiation that has passed through a medium that absorbed radiation of certain wavelengths.
16. A compound of chlorine with another element or group, especially a salt of the anion or an organic compound with chlorine bonded to an alkyl group.

## DOWN

2. A small dense spherical structure in the nucleus of a cell during interphase.
3. Virus that infects and multiplies within bacteria.
5. A mammalian blastula in which some differentiation of cells has occurred.
7. Single-cell microscopic organisms which lack a true nucleus. they represent one of the three domains.
8. Large biomolecules, or macromolecules, consisting of one or more long chains of amino acid residues.
9. A type of cell division that reduces the number of chromosomes in the parent cell by half and produces four gamete cells.
10. One of the four main nucleobases found in the nucleic acids DNA and RNA, the others being adenine, cytosine, and thymine.
13. A molecule with the same chemical formula as another molecule, but with a different chemical structure.

A. Bacteria
D. Isomer
G. Vestigiality
J. Absorption spectrum
M. Bacteriophage
P. Blastocyst

B. Guanine
E. Protein
H. Desmosome
K. Meiosis
N. Whole Genome Sequencing

C. Nucleolus
F. Endangered Species
I. Chloride
L. International System
O. Wobble Base Pair

2. Using the Across and Down clues, write the correct words in the numbered grid below.

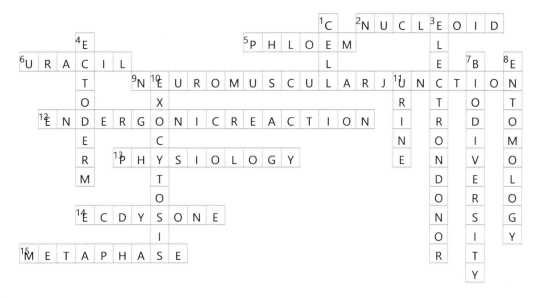

## ACROSS

2. An irregularly shaped region within the cell of a prokaryote that contains all or most of the genetic material, called gonophore.
5. The vascular tissue in plants that conducts sugars and other metabolic products downward from the leaves.
6. One of the four nucleobases in the nucleic acid of RNA that are represented by the letters a, g, c and u.
9. A chemical synapse formed by the contact between a motor neuron and a muscle fiber.
12. A chemical reaction in which the standard change in free energy is positive, and energy is absorbed
13. The branch of biology dealing with the functions and activities of living organisms and their parts, including all physical and chemical processes.
14. A steroidal prohormone of the major insect molting hormone is secreted from the prothoracic glands.
15. The third phase of mitosis, the process that separates duplicated genetic material carried in the nucleus of a parent cell into two identical daughter cells.

## DOWN

1. The structural and functional unit of all organisms.
3. A chemical entity that donates electrons to another compound.
4. The outermost layer of cells or tissue of an embryo in early development, or the parts derived from this, which include the epidermis, nerve tissue, and nephridia.
7. The variety of life in the world or in a habitat or ecosystem.
8. The study of insects.
10. A process by which the contents of a cell vacuole are released to the exterior through fusion of the vacuole membrane with the cell membrane.
11. A liquid by-product of the body secreted by the kidneys through a process called urination (or micturition) and excreted through the urethra.

A. Ectoderm
D. Entomology
G. Endergonic Reaction
J. Nucleoid
M. Exocytosis

B. Metaphase
E. Ecdysone
H. Physiology
K. Biodiversity
N. Electron Donor

C. Phloem
F. Uracil
I. Neuromuscular Junction
L. Urine
O. Cell

3. Using the Across and Down clues, write the correct words in the numbered grid below.

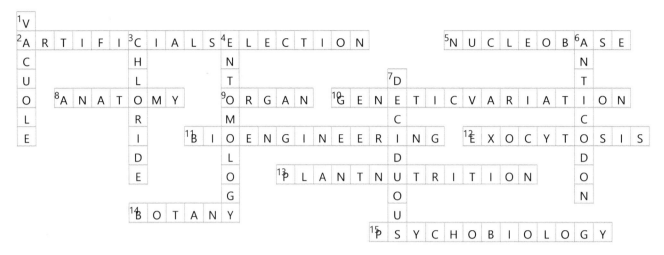

## ACROSS

2. Also known as selective breeding.
5. Cytosine, guanine, adenine (which can be found in DNA and RNA), thymine (found only in DNA), and uracil (found only in RNA).
8. The branch of morphology that deals with the structure of animals
9. A part of an organism that is typically self-contained and has a specific vital function, such as the heart or liver in humans.
10. Variations of genomes between members of species, or between groups of species thriving in different parts of the world as a result of genetic mutation.
11. The application of concepts and methods of biology to solve real world problems.
12. A process by which the contents of a cell vacuole are released to the exterior through fusion of the vacuole membrane with the cell membrane.
13. The study of the chemical elements and compounds necessary for plant growth, plant metabolism and their external supply.
14. The study of plants.
15. The application of the principles of biology to the study of physiological, genetic, and developmental mechanisms of behavior in humans and other animals.

## DOWN

1. A membrane-bound organelle which is present in all plant and fungal cells and some protist, animal and bacterial cells.
3. A compound of chlorine with another element or group, especially a salt of the anion or an organic compound with chlorine bonded to an alkyl group.
4. The study of insects.
6. A sequence of three nucleotides forming a unit of genetic code in a transfer RNA molecule, corresponding to a complementary codon in messenger RNA.
7. Means "falling off at maturity" or "tending to fall off", and it is typically used in order to refer to trees or shrubs that lose their leaves seasonally.

A. Nucleobase
E. Artificial Selection
I. Botany
M. Genetic Variation

B. Anatomy
F. Vacuole
J. Bioengineering
N. Organ

C. Psychobiology
G. Exocytosis
K. Plant Nutrition
O. Entomology

D. Anticodon
H. Chloride
L. Deciduous

4. Using the Across and Down clues, write the correct words in the numbered grid below.

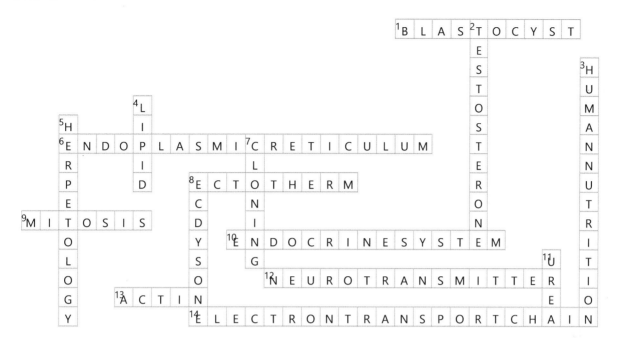

## ACROSS

1. A mammalian blastula in which some differentiation of cells has occurred.
6. A network of membranous tubules within the cytoplasm of a eukaryotic cell, continuous with the nuclear membrane.
8. A organism in which internal physiological sources of heat are of relatively small or quite negligible importance in controlling body temperature. "cold blooded".
9. The process in which a eukaryotic cell nucleus splits in two, followed by division of the parent cell into two daughter cells.
10. The collection of glands that produce hormones that regulate metabolism, growth and development, tissue function, sexual function, reproduction, sleep, and mood.
12. Known as chemical messengers, are endogenous chemicals that enable neurotransmission.
13. One of the proteins into which actomyosin can be split; can exist in either a globular or a fibrous form.
14. The site of oxidative phosphorylation in eukaryotes.

## DOWN

2. A steroid hormone from the androgen group and is found in humans and other vertebrates.
3. Refers to the provision of essential nutrients necessary to support human life and health.
4. A chemical substance that is insoluble in water and soluble in alcohol, ether, and chloroform. the basis for fats and oils.
5. The branch of zoology concerned with reptiles and amphibians.
7. Propagate (an organism or cell) to make an identical copy of.
8. A steroidal prohormone of the major insect molting hormone is secreted from the prothoracic glands.
11. Serves an important role in the metabolism of nitrogen-containing compounds by animals and is the main nitrogen-containing substance in the urine of mammals.

A. Blastocyst
B. Ecdysone
C. Testosterone
D. Herpetology
E. Lipid
F. Electron Transport Chain
G. Endocrine System
H. Human Nutrition
I. Urea
J. Ectotherm
K. Mitosis
L. Cloning
M. Endoplasmic Reticulum
N. Neurotransmitter
O. Actin

5. Using the Across and Down clues, write the correct words in the numbered grid below.

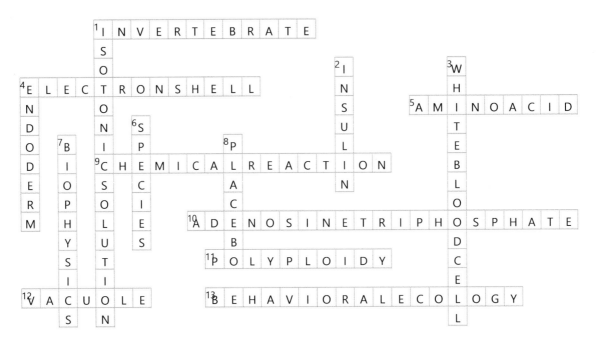

## ACROSS

1. A group of animals that have no backbone, unlike animals such as reptiles, amphibians, fish, birds and mammals who all have a backbone.
4. An electron shell is the outside part of an atom around the atomic nucleus. it is a group of atomic orbitals with the same value of the principal quantum number n.
5. A class of organic compounds containing an amino group and a carboxylic acid group
9. Usually characterized by a chemical change, and they yield one or more products, which usually have properties different from the reactants
10. A nucleotide derived from adenosine that occurs in muscle tissue; the major source of energy for cellular reactions.
11. Containing more than two homologous sets of chromosomes.
12. A membrane-bound organelle which is present in all plant and fungal cells and some protist, animal and bacterial cells.
13. The study of the evolutionary basis for animal behavior due to ecological pressures.

## DOWN

1. Refers to two solutions having the same osmotic pressure across a semipermeable membrane.
2. Helps keep blood sugar level from getting too high (hyperglycemia) or too low (hypoglycemia).
3. Component of the blood that functions in the immune system. also known as a leukocyte.
4. One of the three primary germ layers in the very early human embryo. the other two layers are the ectoderm (outside layer) and mesoderm (middle layer).
6. Often defined as the largest group of organisms in which two individuals can reproduce fertile offspring, typically using sexual reproduction.
7. An interdisciplinary science that applies the approaches and methods of physics to study biological systems.
8. A harmless pill, medicine, or procedure prescribed more for the psychological benefit to the patient than for any physiological effect.

A. Chemical reaction
D. Placebo
G. Isotonic Solution
J. Electron Shell
M. Biophysics
B. White Blood Cell
E. Polyploidy
H. Amino acid
K. Species
N. Invertebrate
C. Insulin
F. Adenosine Triphosphate
I. Endoderm
L. Vacuole
O. Behavioral ecology

6. Using the Across and Down clues, write the correct words in the numbered grid below.

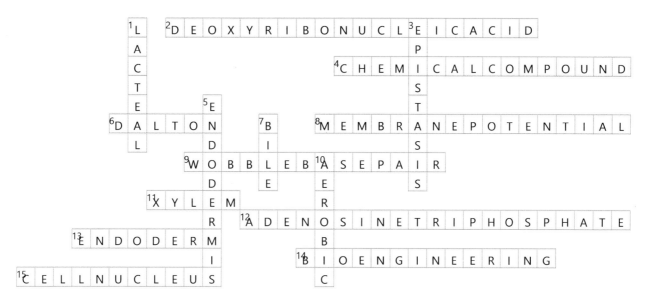

## ACROSS

2. The chemical name for DNA.
4. A chemical substance consisting of two or more different chemically bonded chemical elements, with a fixed ratio determining the composition.
6. A unit of mass (also known as an atomic mass unit, AMU), equal to the mass of a hydrogen atom.
8. When a nerve or muscle cell is at "rest", its membrane potential is called the resting membrane potential.
9. A pairing between two nucleotides in RNA molecules that does not follow Watson crick base pair rules
11. The vascular tissue in plants that conducts water and dissolved nutrients upward from the root and also helps to form the woody element in the stem.
12. A nucleotide derived from adenosine that occurs in muscle tissue; the major source of energy for cellular reactions.
13. One of the three primary germ layers in the very early human embryo. the other two layers are the ectoderm (outside layer) and mesoderm (middle layer).
14. The application of concepts and methods of biology to solve real world problems.
15. The "control room" for the cell. the nucleus gives out all the orders.

## DOWN

1. A lymphatic capillary that absorbs dietary fats in the villi of the small intestine.
3. The interaction of genes that are not alleles. The suppression of the effect of one such gene by another.
5. An inner layer of cells in the cortex of a root and of some stems, surrounding a vascular bundle.
7. A dark green to yellowish brown fluid, produced by the liver of most vertebrates, that aids the digestion of lipids in the small intestine.
10. Depending on free oxygen or air.

A. Aerobic
D. Cell nucleus
G. Deoxyribonucleic Acid
J. Bile
M. Adenosine Triphosphate

B. Lacteal
E. Epistasis
H. Chemical compound
K. Endoderm
N. Dalton

C. Membrane Potential
F. Wobble Base Pair
I. Xylem
L. Endodermis
O. Bioengineering

7. Using the Across and Down clues, write the correct words in the numbered grid below.

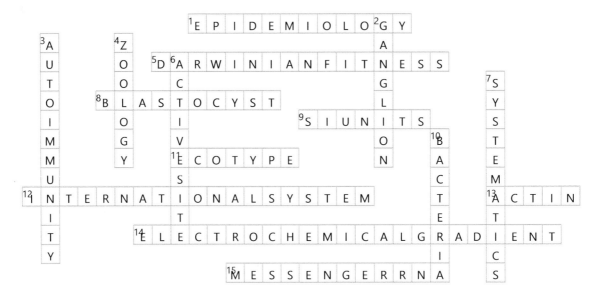

## ACROSS

1. The study and analysis of the patterns, causes, and effects of health and disease conditions in defined populations.
5. The genetic contribution of an individual to the next generation's gene pool relative to the average for the population.
8. A mammalian blastula in which some differentiation of cells has occurred.
9. A system of physical units-based on the meter, kilogram, second, ampere, kelvin, candela, and mole, together with a set of prefixes.
11. Describes a genetically distinct geographic variety, population or race within a species, which is adapted to specific environmental conditions.
12. The modern form of the metric system and is the most widely used system of measurement.
13. One of the proteins into which actomyosin can be split; can exist in either a globular or a fibrous form.
14. A gradient of electrochemical potential, usually for an ion that can move across a membrane.
15. The form of rna in which genetic information transcribed from dna as a sequence of bases is transferred to a ribosome.

## DOWN

2. A cluster (functional group) of nerve cell bodies in a centralized nervous system.
3. The system of immune responses of an organism against its own healthy cells and tissues.
4. The branch of biology that relates to the animal kingdom, including the structure, embryology, evolution, classification, habits, and distribution of all animals.
6. The part of an enzyme or antibody where the chemical reaction occurs
7. The branch of biology that deals with classification and nomenclature; taxonomy.
10. Single-cell microscopic organisms which lack a true nucleus. they represent one of the three domains.

A. International System
D. Ganglion
G. Bacteria
J. Epidemiology
M. Messenger RNA

B. Active site
E. Systematics
H. Blastocyst
K. Ecotype
N. Electrochemical Gradient

C. Zoology
F. Darwinian Fitness
I. Actin
L. Autoimmunity
O. SI units

8. Using the Across and Down clues, write the correct words in the numbered grid below.

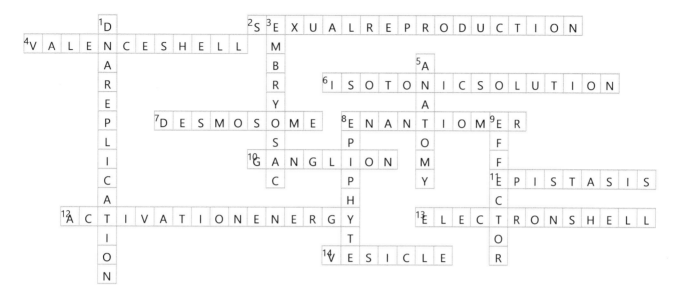

## ACROSS

2. Type of reproduction in which cells from two parents unite to form the first cell of a new organism.
4. The electrons in the outermost occupied shell (or shells) determine the chemical properties of the atom; it is called the valence shell.
6. Refers to two solutions having the same osmotic pressure across a semipermeable membrane.
7. Also known as a macula adhaerens, is a cell structure specialized for cell to cell adhesion.
8. Stereoisomers that are non-superimposable mirror images. a molecule with 1 chiral carbon atom exists as 2 stereoisomers termed enantiomers.
10. A cluster (functional group) of nerve cell bodies in a centralized nervous system.
11. The interaction of genes that are not alleles. The suppression of the effect of one such gene by another.
12. The energy that an atomic system must acquire before a process (such as an emission or reaction) can occur.
13. An electron shell is the outside part of an atom around the atomic nucleus. it is a group of atomic orbitals with the same value of the principal quantum number n.
14. A fluid or air-filled cavity or sac.

## DOWN

1. The double helix is unwound and each strand acts as a template for the next strand. bases are matched to synthesize the new partner strands.
3. The female gametophyte of a seed plant, within which the embryo develops.
5. The branch of morphology that deals with the structure of animals
8. A plant that grows harmlessly upon another plant and derives its moisture and nutrients from the air, rain, and sometimes from debris accumulating around it.
9. An organ or cell that acts in response to a stimulus.

A. Vesicle
E. DNA Replication
I. Activation energy
M. Epiphyte

B. Ganglion
F. Desmosome
J. Effector
N. Epistasis

C. Valence shell
G. Sexual Reproduction
K. Embryo Sac
O. Isotonic Solution

D. Enantiomer
H. Anatomy
L. Electron Shell

9. Using the Across and Down clues, write the correct words in the numbered grid below.

```
 1E  N  A  N  T  I  O 2M  E  R        3U  R 4A  C  I  L
 M              O                        B        5F
 B              L     6E  N  D  O  P  L  A  S  M  I  C  R  E  T  I  C  U  L  U 7M
 R              E                        O              T                    E
 Y          8B  C                        R     9G  U        10G              T
 O          A  U                         P     E  S        E                 A
 S       11P  A  R  A  L  L  E  L  E  V  O  L  U  T  I  O  N     N           P
 A          R  E                         I     E           E                 H
 C          B                            O     T           P                 A
       12M  I  C  R  O  E  V  O  L  U  T  I  O  N     N     O                 S
           D                             N     I           O                 E
 13V  I  R  O  L  O  G  Y                      C        14C  H  O  L  E  S  T  E  R  O  L
```

## ACROSS

1. Stereoisomers that are non-superimposable mirror images. a molecule with 1 chiral carbon atom exists as 2 stereoisomers termed enantiomers.
3. One of the four nucleobases in the nucleic acid of RNA that are represented by the letters a, g, c and u.
6. A network of membranous tubules within the cytoplasm of a eukaryotic cell, continuous with the nuclear membrane.
11. The independent evolution of similar traits, starting from a similar ancestral condition.
12. Evolutionary change within a species or small group of organisms, especially over a short period.
13. The study of viruses-submicroscopic, parasitic particles of genetic material contained in a protein coat and virus -like agents.
14. An organic lipid molecule that is biosynthesized by all animal cells because it is an essential structural component of all animal cell membranes.

## DOWN

1. The female gametophyte of a seed plant, within which the embryo develops.
2. The smallest particle in a chemical element or compound that has the chemical properties of that element or compound.
4. A process in which one substance permeates another; a fluid permeates or is dissolved by a liquid or solid.
5. A human embryo after eight weeks of development.
7. The third phase of mitosis, the process that separates duplicated genetic material carried in the nucleus of a parent cell into two identical daughter cells.
8. The inactive x chromosome in a female somatic cell, rendered inactive in a process called lyonization
9. The study of heredity
10. The stock of different genes in an interbreeding population.

A. Gene Pool
D. Microevolution
G. Embryo Sac
J. Parallel Evolution
M. Uracil

B. Barr body
E. Cholesterol
H. Absorption
K. Genetics
N. Fetus

C. Enantiomer
F. Endoplasmic Reticulum
I. Metaphase
L. Virology
O. Molecule

10. Using the Across and Down clues, write the correct words in the numbered grid below.

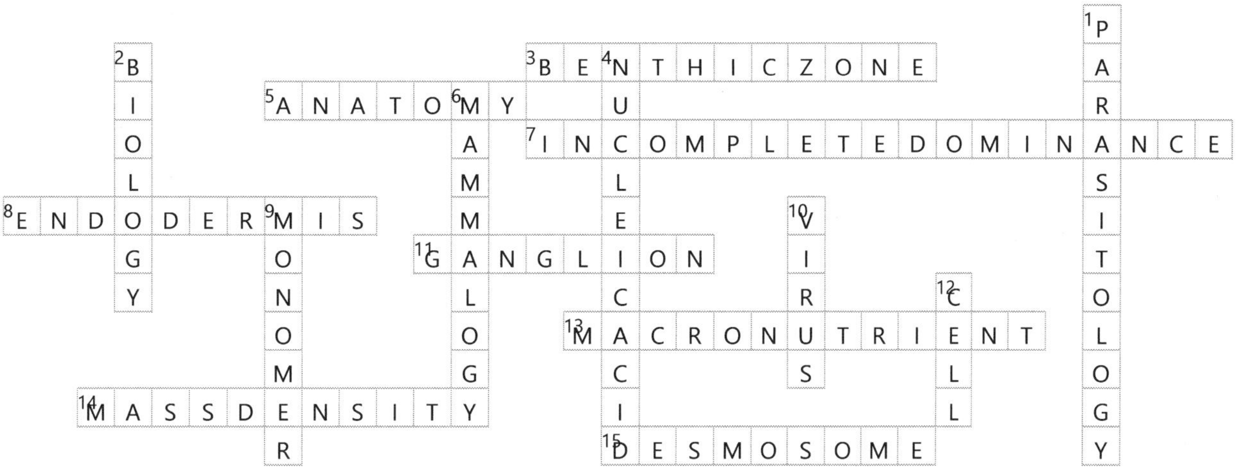

1 PARASITOLOGY
2 BIOLOGY
3 BENTHICZONE
4 NUCLEICACID
5 ANATOMY
6 MAMMALOGY
7 INCOMPLETEDOMINANCE
8 ENDODERMIS
9 MONOMER
10 VIRUS
11 GANGLION
12 CELL
13 MACRONUTRIENT
14 MASSDENSITY
15 DESMOSOME


## ACROSS

3. The ecological region at the lowest level of a body of water such as an ocean or a lake.
5. The branch of morphology that deals with the structure of animals
7. A form of intermediate inheritance in which one allele for a specific trait is not completely expressed over its paired allele.
8. An inner layer of cells in the cortex of a root and of some stems, surrounding a vascular bundle.
11. A cluster (functional group) of nerve cell bodies in a centralized nervous system.
13. Nutrients that provide calories or energy. nutrients are substances needed for growth, metabolism, and for other body functions.
14. Density is mass per volume.
15. Also known as a macula adhaerens, is a cell structure specialized for cell to cell adhesion.

## DOWN

1. The study of parasites, their hosts, and the relationship between them.
2. Study of living organisms.
4. A complex organic substance present in living cells, especially DNA or RNA, whose molecules consist of many nucleotides linked in a long chain.
6. The study of mammals.
9. A molecule that can be bonded to other identical molecules to form a polymer.
10. A biological agent that reproduces inside the cells of living hosts.
12. The structural and functional unit of all organisms.

| | | |
|---|---|---|
| A. Monomer | B. Ganglion | C. Mass Density |
| D. Biology | E. Macronutrient | F. Parasitology |
| G. Virus | H. Desmosome | I. Incomplete Dominance |
| J. Anatomy | K. Mammalogy | L. Endodermis |
| M. Cell | N. Nucleic Acid | O. Benthic zone |

11. Using the Across and Down clues, write the correct words in the numbered grid below.

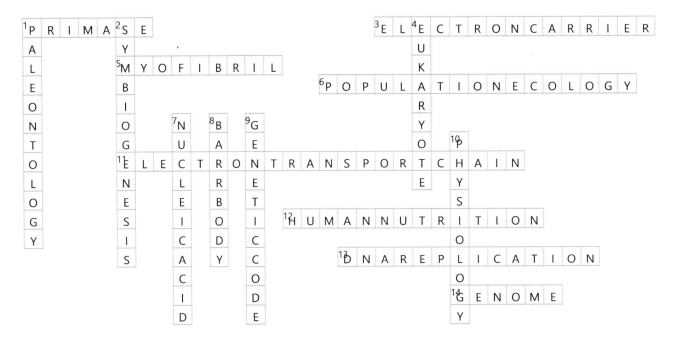

## ACROSS

1. An enzyme that synthesizes short RNA sequences called primers.
3. Any of various molecules that can accept one or two electrons from one molecule and donating them to another in the process of electron transport.
5. Any of the elongated contractile threads found in striated muscle cells.
6. A sub-field of ecology that deals with the dynamics of species populations and how these populations interact with the environment.
11. The site of oxidative phosphorylation in eukaryotes.
12. Refers to the provision of essential nutrients necessary to support human life and health.
13. The double helix is unwound and each strand acts as a template for the next strand. bases are matched to synthesize the new partner strands.
14. The haploid set of chromosomes in a gamete or microorganism, or in each cell of a multicellular organism.

## DOWN

1. The study of the history of life on earth as reflected in the fossil record. fossils are the remains or traces of organisms.
2. An evolutionary theory that explains the origin of eukaryotic cells from prokaryotes.
4. Any organism whose cells contain a nucleus and other organelles enclosed within membranes.
7. A complex organic substance present in living cells, especially DNA or RNA, whose molecules consist of many nucleotides linked in a long chain.
8. The inactive x chromosome in a female somatic cell, rendered inactive in a process called lyonization
9. The nucleotide triplets of DNA and RNA molecules that carry genetic information in living cells.
10. The branch of biology dealing with the functions and activities of living organisms and their parts, including all physical and chemical processes.

A. Symbiogenesis
D. Human Nutrition
G. Nucleic Acid
J. Genetic Code
M. Electron Transport Chain

B. Barr body
E. Population Ecology
H. Myofibril
K. Physiology
N. Paleontology

C. DNA Replication
F. Electron Carrier
I. Genome
L. Primase
O. Eukaryote

12. Using the Across and Down clues, write the correct words in the numbered grid below.

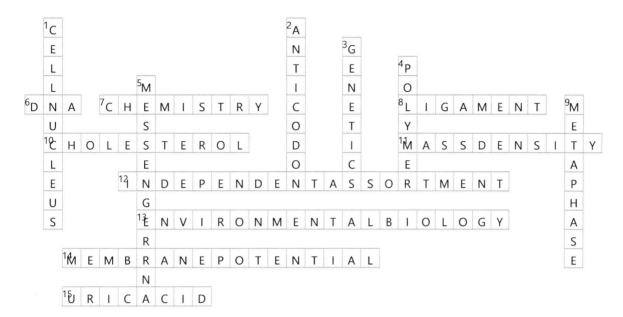

## ACROSS

6. The hereditary material in humans and almost all other organisms.
7. A branch of physical science that studies the composition, structure, properties and change of matter.
8. The fibrous connective tissue that connects bones to other bones.
10. An organic lipid molecule that is biosynthesized by all animal cells because it is an essential structural component of all animal cell membranes.
11. Density is mass per volume.
12. The principle, originated by Gregor Mendel, stating that when two or more characteristics are inherited, individual hereditary factors assort independently.
13. The branch of biology concerned with the relations between organisms and their environment.
14. When a nerve or muscle cell is at "rest", its membrane potential is called the resting membrane potential.
15. A heterocyclic compound of carbon, nitrogen, oxygen, and hydrogen. it forms ions and salts known as urates and acid urates, such as ammonium acid urate.

## DOWN

1. The "control room" for the cell. the nucleus gives out all the orders.
2. A sequence of three nucleotides forming a unit of genetic code in a transfer RNA molecule, corresponding to a complementary codon in messenger RNA.
3. The study of heredity
4. A large molecule, or macromolecule, composed of many repeated subunits.
5. The form of rna in which genetic information transcribed from dna as a sequence of bases is transferred to a ribosome.
9. The third phase of mitosis, the process that separates duplicated genetic material carried in the nucleus of a parent cell into two identical daughter cells.

A. Ligament
D. DNA
G. Cholesterol
J. Chemistry
M. Messenger RNA

B. Environmental Biology
E. Genetics
H. Polymer
K. Anticodon
N. Uric acid

C. Independent Assortment
F. Membrane Potential
I. Mass Density
L. Cell nucleus
O. Metaphase

13. Using the Across and Down clues, write the correct words in the numbered grid below.

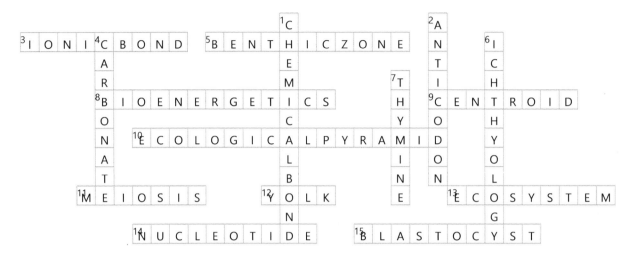

## ACROSS

3. The complete transfer of valence electron(s) between atoms. it is a type of chemical bond that generates two oppositely charged ions.
5. The ecological region at the lowest level of a body of water such as an ocean or a lake.
8. The study of the transformation of energy in living organisms.
9. The intersection of the three medians of the triangle (each median connecting a vertex with the midpoint of the opposite side).
10. A graphical representation designed to show the biomass or bio productivity at each trophic level in a given ecosystem.
11. A type of cell division that reduces the number of chromosomes in the parent cell by half and produces four gamete cells.
12. The yellow internal part of a bird's egg, which is surrounded by the white, is rich in protein and fat, and nourishes the developing embryo.
13. An interaction of living things and non-living things in a physical environment.
14. Organic molecules that serve as the monomers, or subunits, of nucleic acids like DNA (deoxyribonucleic acid) and RNA (ribonucleic acid).
15. A mammalian blastula in which some differentiation of cells has occurred.

## DOWN

1. A lasting attraction between atoms that enables the formation of chemical compounds.
2. A sequence of three nucleotides forming a unit of genetic code in a transfer RNA molecule, corresponding to a complementary codon in messenger RNA.
4. Any member of two classes of chemical compounds derived from carbonic acid or carbon dioxide.
6. Known as fish science, is the branch of biology devoted to the study of fish.
7. One of the four nucleobases in the nucleic acid of DNA that are represented by the letters g–c–a–t.

| | | | |
|---|---|---|---|
| A. Carbonate | B. Anticodon | C. Meiosis | D. Nucleotide |
| E. Ichthyology | F. Ionic Bond | G. Yolk | H. Ecosystem |
| I. Blastocyst | J. Bioenergetics | K. Thymine | L. Ecological Pyramid |
| M. Centroid | N. Benthic zone | O. Chemical bond | |

14. Using the Across and Down clues, write the correct words in the numbered grid below.

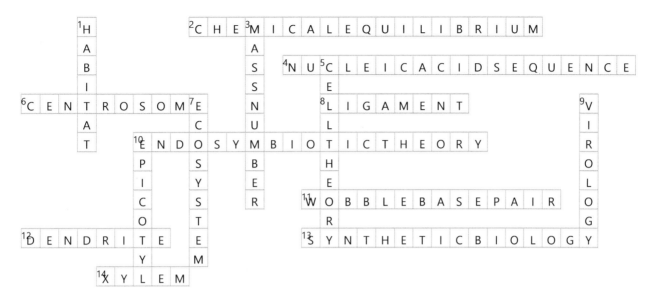

## ACROSS

2. The state in which both reactants and products are present in concentrations which have no further tendency to change with time.
4. A succession of letters that indicate the order of nucleotides within a DNA (using GACT or RNA (GACU) molecule.
6. In cell biology, an organelle that is the main place where cell microtubules get organized. they occur only in plant and animal cells.
8. The fibrous connective tissue that connects bones to other bones.
10. An evolutionary theory that explains the origin of eukaryotic cells from prokaryotes.
11. A pairing between two nucleotides in RNA molecules that does not follow Watson crick base pair rules
12. A short branched extension of a nerve cell, along which impulses received from other cells at synapses are transmitted to the cell body
13. An interdisciplinary branch of biology and engineering.
14. The vascular tissue in plants that conducts water and dissolved nutrients upward from the root and also helps to form the woody element in the stem.

## DOWN

1. A place for animals, people and plants and non-living things
3. The total number of protons and neutrons (together known as nucleons) in an atomic nucleus
5. The theory that all living things are made up of cells.
7. An interaction of living things and non-living things in a physical environment.
9. The study of viruses-submicroscopic, parasitic particles of genetic material contained in a protein coat and virus-like agents.
10. The region of an embryo or seedling stem above the cotyledon.

A. Cell theory
D. Nucleic Acid Sequence
G. Wobble Base Pair
J. Ligament
M. Habitat

B. Mass Number
E. Chemical equilibrium
H. Ecosystem
K. Dendrite
N. Centrosome

C. Endosymbiotic Theory
F. Xylem
I. Virology
L. Epicotyl
O. Synthetic Biology

15. Using the Across and Down clues, write the correct words in the numbered grid below.

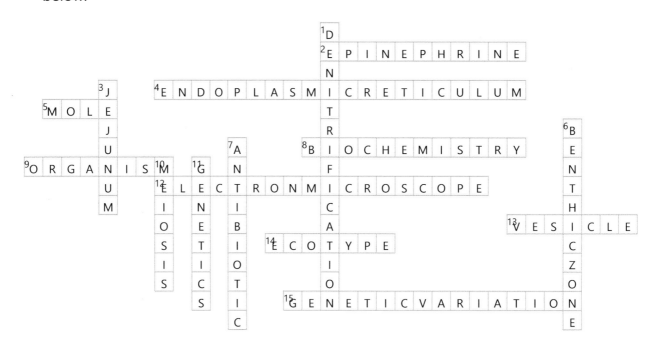

## ACROSS

2. Another term for adrenaline.
4. A network of membranous tubules within the cytoplasm of a eukaryotic cell, continuous with the nuclear membrane.
5. The si unit of measurement used to measure the number of things, usually atoms or molecules.
8. The branch of science that explores the chemical processes within and related to living organisms.
9. An individual animal, plant, or single-celled life form.
12. A type of microscope that uses a beam of electrons to create an image of the specimen. it is capable of much higher magnifications.
13. A fluid or air-filled cavity or sac.
14. Describes a genetically distinct geographic variety, population or race within a species, which is adapted to specific environmental conditions.
15. Variations of genomes between members of species, or between groups of species thriving in different parts of the world as a result of genetic mutation.

## DOWN

1. A microbially facilitated process of nitrate reduction that may ultimately produce molecular nitrogen.
3. The midsection of the small intestine of many higher vertebrates like mammals, birds, reptiles. it is present between the duodenum and the ileum.
6. The ecological region at the lowest level of a body of water such as an ocean or a lake.
7. A class of drug used to kill bacteria.
10. A type of cell division that reduces the number of chromosomes in the parent cell by half and produces four gamete cells.
11. The study of heredity

A. Mole
D. Benthic zone
G. Genetics
J. Genetic Variation
M. Denitrification

B. Epinephrine
E. Electron Microscope
H. Organism
K. Biochemistry
N. Meiosis

C. Antibiotic
F. Jejunum
I. Ecotype
L. Vesicle
O. Endoplasmic Reticulum

16. Using the Across and Down clues, write the correct words in the numbered grid below.

```
¹L I G A M ²E N T
          L
  ³W      E       ⁴I C ⁵H T H Y O L O G Y
   O      C          Y
   B      T       ⁶E N D A N G E R E D S P E ⁷C I E S
   B      R          R                      R
   L      O          O       ⁸X             Y
   E      N          C        Y             O          ⁹A
   B      S          A      ¹⁰L I P I D      B          M
   A      H          R        E          ¹¹U R I C A C I D
   S      E          R        E             O          N
   E      L        ¹²B I O M A S S          L        ¹³M O L E C U L E
 ¹⁴P O P U L A T I O N B I O L O G Y        O          A
   A                                        G          C
 ¹⁵I N T E R N A T I O N A L S Y S T E M    Y          I
   R                                                   D
```

## ACROSS

1. The fibrous connective tissue that connects bones to other bones.
4. Known as fish science, is the branch of biology devoted to the study of fish.
6. Threatened by factors such as habitat loss, hunting, disease and climate change, and usually have declining populations or a very limited range.
10. A chemical substance that is insoluble in water and soluble in alcohol, ether, and chloroform. the basis for fats and oils.
11. A heterocyclic compound of carbon, nitrogen, oxygen, and hydrogen. it forms ions and salts known as urates and acid urates, such as ammonium acid urate.
12. Organic matter derived from living, or recently living organisms.
13. The smallest particle in a chemical element or compound that has the chemical properties of that element or compound.
14. The study of populations of organisms, especially the regulation of population size, life history traits such as clutch size, and extinction.
15. The modern form of the metric system and is the most widely used system of measurement.

## DOWN

2. An electron shell is the outside part of an atom around the atomic nucleus. it is a group of atomic orbitals with the same value of the principal quantum number n.
3. A pairing between two nucleotides in RNA molecules that does not follow Watson crick base pair rules
5. In organic chemistry, a hydrocarbon is an organic compound consisting entirely of hydrogen and carbon.
7. The branch of biology that studies the effects of low temperatures on living things within earth's cryosphere or in science.
8. The vascular tissue in plants that conducts water and dissolved nutrients upward from the root and also helps to form the woody element in the stem.
9. A class of organic compounds containing an amino group and a carboxylic acid group

A. Ligament
E. Lipid
I. Biomass
M. Uric acid

B. Wobble Base Pair
F. Endangered Species
J. Hydrocarbon
N. Cryobiology

C. Amino acid
G. Population Biology
K. Molecule
O. Ichthyology

D. Electron Shell
H. Xylem
L. International System

17. Using the Across and Down clues, write the correct words in the numbered grid below.

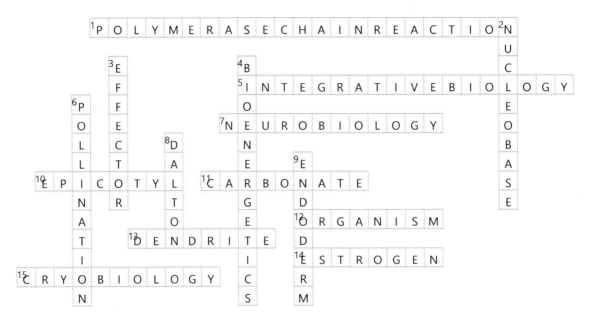

## ACROSS

1. A technique used in molecular biology to amplify a single copy or a few copies of a piece of DNA across several orders of magnitude.
5. A label frequently used to describe various forms of cross-disciplinary and multitaxon research.
7. The study of cells of the nervous system and the organization of these cells into functional circuits that process information and mediate behavior.
10. The region of an embryo or seedling stem above the cotyledon.
11. Any member of two classes of chemical compounds derived from carbonic acid or carbon dioxide.
12. An individual animal, plant, or single-celled life form.
13. A short branched extension of a nerve cell, along which impulses received from other cells at synapses are transmitted to the cell body
14. The primary female sex hormone. it is responsible for the development and regulation of the female reproductive system and secondary sex characteristics.
15. The branch of biology that studies the effects of low temperatures on living things within earth's cryosphere or in science.

## DOWN

2. Cytosine, guanine, adenine (which can be found in DNA and RNA), thymine (found only in DNA), and uracil (found only in RNA).
3. An organ or cell that acts in response to a stimulus.
4. The study of the transformation of energy in living organisms.
6. The act of transferring pollen grains from the male anther of a flower to the female stigma.
8. A unit of mass (also known as an atomic mass unit, AMU), equal to the mass of a hydrogen atom.
9. One of the three primary germ layers in the very early human embryo. the other two layers are the ectoderm (outside layer) and mesoderm (middle layer).

A. Endoderm
D. Dendrite
G. Polymerase Chain Reaction
J. Integrative Biology
M. Organism

B. Cryobiology
E. Carbonate
H. Dalton
K. Bioenergetics
N. Effector

C. Epicotyl
F. Neurobiology
I. Estrogen
L. Pollination
O. Nucleobase

18. Using the Across and Down clues, write the correct words in the numbered grid below.

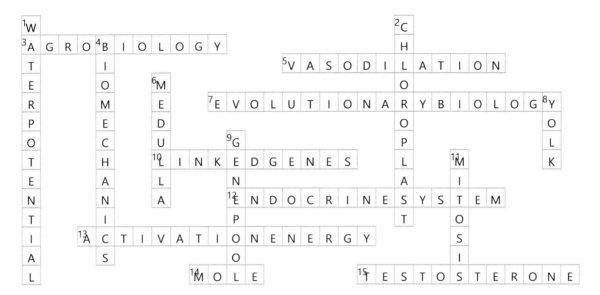

## ACROSS

3. The study of plant nutrition and growth especially to increase crop yield
5. The dilatation of blood vessels, which decreases blood pressure.
7. The subfield of biology that studies the evolutionary processes that produced the diversity of life on earth starting from a single origin of life.
10. When two genes are close together on the same chromosome, they do not assort independently.
12. The collection of glands that produce hormones that regulate metabolism, growth and development, tissue function, sexual function, reproduction, sleep, and mood.
13. The energy that an atomic system must acquire before a process (such as an emission or reaction) can occur.
14. The si unit of measurement used to measure the number of things, usually atoms or molecules.
15. A steroid hormone from the androgen group and is found in humans and other vertebrates.

## DOWN

1. A measure of the potential energy in water as well as the difference between the potential in a water sample and pure water.
2. Work to convert light energy of the sun into sugars that can be used by cells.
4. The study of the structure and function of biological systems by means of the methods of "mechanics."
6. The continuation of the spinal cord within the skull, forming the lowest part of the brainstem and containing control centers for the heart and lungs.
8. The yellow internal part of a bird's egg, which is surrounded by the white, is rich in protein and fat, and nourishes the developing embryo.
9. The stock of different genes in an interbreeding population.
11. The process in which a eukaryotic cell nucleus splits in two, followed by division of the parent cell into two daughter cells.

| | | | |
|---|---|---|---|
| A. Water Potential | B. Medulla | C. Testosterone | D. Mitosis |
| E. Evolutionary Biology | F. Activation energy | G. Chloroplast | H. Biomechanics |
| I. Yolk | J. Vasodilation | K. Gene Pool | L. Endocrine System |
| M. Linked Genes | N. Agrobiology | O. Mole | |

19. Using the Across and Down clues, write the correct words in the numbered grid below.

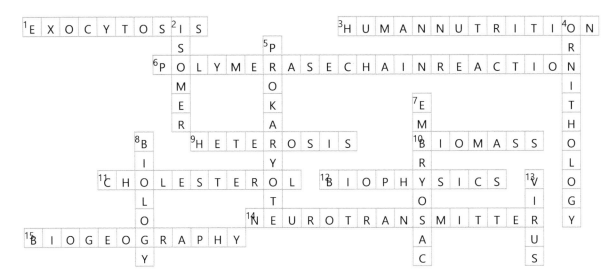

## ACROSS

1. A process by which the contents of a cell vacuole are released to the exterior through fusion of the vacuole membrane with the cell membrane.
3. Refers to the provision of essential nutrients necessary to support human life and health.
6. A technique used in molecular biology to amplify a single copy or a few copies of a piece of DNA across several orders of magnitude.
9. The tendency of a crossbred individual to show qualities superior to those of both parents.
10. Organic matter derived from living, or recently living organisms.
11. An organic lipid molecule that is biosynthesized by all animal cells because it is an essential structural component of all animal cell membranes.
12. An interdisciplinary science that applies the approaches and methods of physics to study biological systems.
14. Known as chemical messengers, are endogenous chemicals that enable neurotransmission.
15. The study of the distribution of species and ecosystems in geographic space and through time.

## DOWN

2. A molecule with the same chemical formula as another molecule, but with a different chemical structure.
4. A branch of zoology that concerns the study of birds.
5. A microscopic single celled organism that has no distinct nucleus
7. The female gametophyte of a seed plant, within which the embryo develops.
8. Study of living organisms.
13. A biological agent that reproduces inside the cells of living hosts.

A. Biology
D. Heterosis
G. Exocytosis
J. Embryo Sac
M. Human Nutrition

B. Biogeography
E. Polymerase Chain Reaction
H. Biomass
K. Biophysics
N. Virus

C. Cholesterol
F. Prokaryote
I. Ornithology
L. Neurotransmitter
O. Isomer

20. Using the Across and Down clues, write the correct words in the numbered grid below.

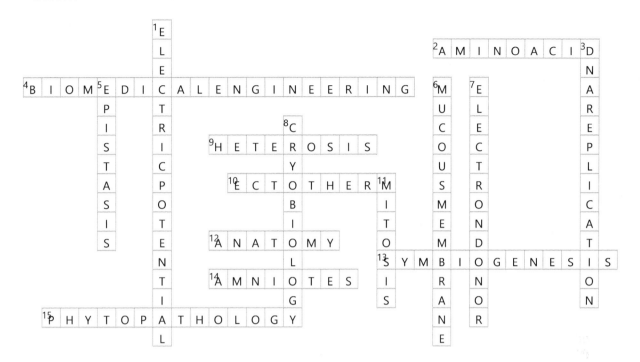

## ACROSS

2. A class of organic compounds containing an amino group and a carboxylic acid group
4. The application of engineering principles and design concepts to medicine and biology for healthcare purposes (e.g. diagnostic or therapeutic).
9. The tendency of a crossbred individual to show qualities superior to those of both parents.
10. A organism in which internal physiological sources of heat are of relatively small or quite negligible importance in controlling body temperature. "cold blooded".
12. The branch of morphology that deals with the structure of animals
13. An evolutionary theory that explains the origin of eukaryotic cells from prokaryotes.
14. Organisms that produce an egg composed of shell and membranes that creates a protected environment in which the embryo can develop out of water
15. The science of diagnosing and managing plant diseases.

## DOWN

1. The amount of work needed to move a unit charge from a reference point to a specific point against an electric field.
3. The double helix is unwound and each strand acts as a template for the next strand. bases are matched to synthesize the new partner strands.
5. The interaction of genes that are not alleles. The suppression of the effect of one such gene by another.
6. An epithelial tissue that secretes mucus and that lines many body cavities and tubular organs including the gut and respiratory passages.
7. A chemical entity that donates electrons to another compound.
8. The branch of biology that studies the effects of low temperatures on living things within earth's cryosphere or in science.
11. The process in which a eukaryotic cell nucleus splits in two, followed by division of the parent cell into two daughter cells.

A. Heterosis
D. Phytopathology
G. Electron Donor
J. Cryobiology
M. Symbiogenesis

B. Mitosis
E. Mucous Membrane
H. DNA Replication
K. Anatomy
N. Amino acid

C. Biomedical engineering
F. Amniotes
I. Electric Potential
L. Ectotherm
O. Epistasis

21. Using the Across and Down clues, write the correct words in the numbered grid below.

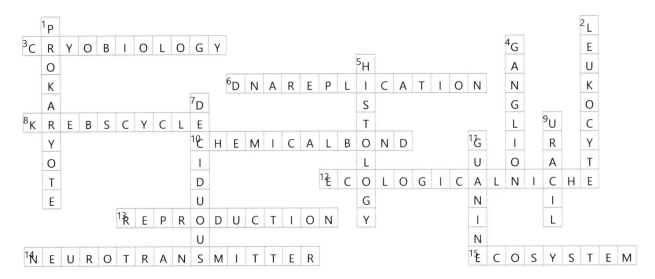

## ACROSS

3. The branch of biology that studies the effects of low temperatures on living things within earth's cryosphere or in science.
6. The double helix is unwound and each strand acts as a template for the next strand. bases are matched to synthesize the new partner strands.
8. the sequence of reactions by which most living cells generate energy during the process of aerobic respiration.
10. A lasting attraction between atoms that enables the formation of chemical compounds.
12. The role and position a species has in its environment; how it meets its needs for food and shelter, how it survives, and how it reproduces.
13. Giving birth to one of its kind, sexually or asexually.
14. Known as chemical messengers, are endogenous chemicals that enable neurotransmission.
15. An interaction of living things and non-living things in a physical environment.

## DOWN

1. A microscopic single celled organism that has no distinct nucleus
2. A colorless cell which circulates in the blood and body fluids and is involved in counteracting foreign substances and disease; a white (blood) cell.
4. A cluster (functional group) of nerve cell bodies in a centralized nervous system.
5. The study of the microscopic anatomy of cells and tissues of plants and animals.
7. Means "falling off at maturity" or "tending to fall off", and it is typically used in order to refer to trees or shrubs that lose their leaves seasonally.
9. One of the four nucleobases in the nucleic acid of RNA that are represented by the letters a, g, c and u.
11. One of the four main nucleobases found in the nucleic acids DNA and RNA, the others being adenine, cytosine, and thymine.

A. Deciduous
E. Krebs Cycle
I. Chemical bond
M. Cryobiology

B. Ecological Niche
F. Neurotransmitter
J. Leukocyte
N. DNA Replication

C. Guanine
G. Prokaryote
K. Ecosystem
O. Ganglion

D. Histology
H. Uracil
L. Reproduction

22. Using the Across and Down clues, write the correct words in the numbered grid below.

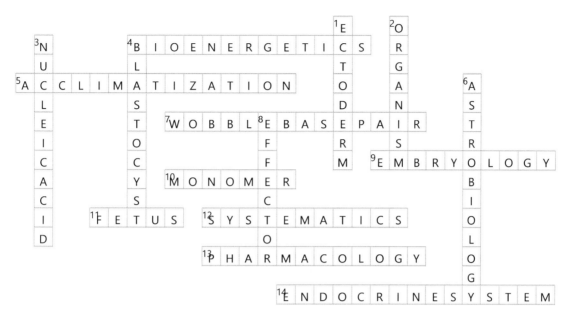

## ACROSS

4. The study of the transformation of energy in living organisms.
5. Adaptation to a new climate (a new temperature or altitude or environment).
7. A pairing between two nucleotides in RNA molecules that does not follow Watson crick base pair rules
9. The branch of biology that studies the development of gametes (sex cells), fertilization, and development of embryos and fetuses.
10. A molecule that can be bonded to other identical molecules to form a polymer.
11. A human embryo after eight weeks of development.
12. The branch of biology that deals with classification and nomenclature; taxonomy.
13. The science of drug action on biological systems.
14. The collection of glands that produce hormones that regulate metabolism, growth and development, tissue function, sexual function, reproduction, sleep, and mood.

## DOWN

1. The outermost layer of cells or tissue of an embryo in early development, or the parts derived from this, which include the epidermis, nerve tissue, and nephridia.
2. An individual animal, plant, or single-celled life form.
3. A complex organic substance present in living cells, especially DNA or RNA, whose molecules consist of many nucleotides linked in a long chain.
4. A mammalian blastula in which some differentiation of cells has occurred.
6. The branch of biology concerned with the effects of outer space on living organisms and the search for extraterrestrial life
8. An organ or cell that acts in response to a stimulus.

A. Embryology
B. Astrobiology
C. Endocrine System
D. Effector
E. Bioenergetics
F. Wobble Base Pair
G. Organism
H. Monomer
I. Systematics
J. Pharmacology
K. Acclimatization
L. Ectoderm
M. Fetus
N. Nucleic Acid
O. Blastocyst

23. Using the Across and Down clues, write the correct words in the numbered grid below.

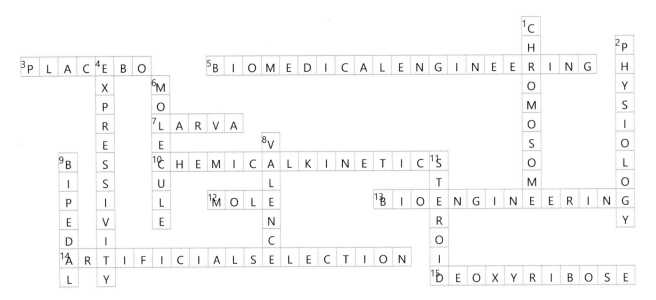

## ACROSS

3. A harmless pill, medicine, or procedure prescribed more for the psychological benefit to the patient than for any physiological effect.
5. The application of engineering principles and design concepts to medicine and biology for healthcare purposes (e.g. diagnostic or therapeutic).
7. A distinct juvenile form many animals undergo before metamorphosis into adults. animals with indirect development such as insects, amphibians, or cnidarians.
10. The study and discussion of chemical reactions with respect to reaction rates.
12. The si unit of measurement used to measure the number of things, usually atoms or molecules.
13. The application of concepts and methods of biology to solve real world problems.
14. Also known as selective breeding.
15. A monosaccharide. its name indicates that it is a deoxy sugar, meaning that it is derived from the sugar ribose by loss of an oxygen atom.

## DOWN

1. A threadlike strand of DNA in the cell nucleus that carries the genes in a linear order.
2. The branch of biology dealing with the functions and activities of living organisms and their parts, including all physical and chemical processes.
4. Variations in a phenotype among individuals carrying a genotype.
6. The smallest particle in a chemical element or compound that has the chemical properties of that element or compound.
8. Refers to the number of elements to which it can connect.
9. A form of terrestrial locomotion where an organism moves by means of its two rear limbs or legs.
11. An organic compound with four rings arranged in a specific configuration. examples include the dietary lipid cholesterol and the sex hormones.

A. Larva
D. Bipedal
G. Physiology
J. Chromosome
M. Steroid

B. Valence
E. Chemical kinetics
H. Expressivity
K. Bioengineering
N. Placebo

C. Artificial Selection
F. Molecule
I. Deoxyribose
L. Mole
O. Biomedical engineering

24. Using the Across and Down clues, write the correct words in the numbered grid below.

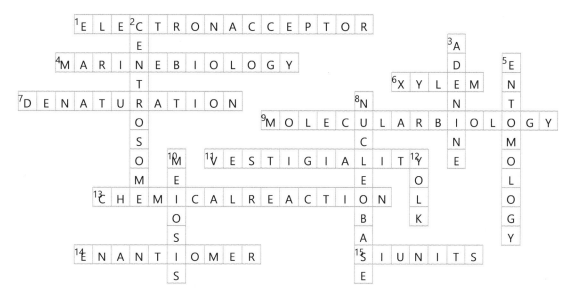

## ACROSS

1. A chemical entity that accepts electrons transferred to it from another compound.
4. The scientific study of organisms in the ocean or other marine bodies of water.
6. The vascular tissue in plants that conducts water and dissolved nutrients upward from the root and also helps to form the woody element in the stem.
7. A process in which proteins or nucleic acids lose the quaternary structure, tertiary structure and secondary structure which is present in their native state.
9. A branch of science concerning biological activity at the molecular level.
11. Refers to genetically determined structures or attributes that have apparently lost most or all their ancestral function in a given species.
13. Usually characterized by a chemical change, and they yield one or more products, which usually have properties different from the reactants
14. Stereoisomers that are non-superimposable mirror images. a molecule with 1 chiral carbon atom exists as 2 stereoisomers termed enantiomers.
15. A system of physical units-based on the meter, kilogram, second, ampere, kelvin, candela, and mole, together with a set of prefixes.

## DOWN

2. In cell biology, an organelle that is the main place where cell microtubules get organized. they occur only in plant and animal cells.
3. One of the two purine nucleobases (the other being guanine) used in forming nucleotides of the nucleic acids.
5. The study of insects.
8. Cytosine, guanine, adenine (which can be found in DNA and RNA), thymine (found only in DNA), and uracil (found only in RNA).
10. A type of cell division that reduces the number of chromosomes in the parent cell by half and produces four gamete cells.
12. The yellow internal part of a bird's egg, which is surrounded by the white, is rich in protein and fat, and nourishes the developing embryo.

A. Electron Acceptor
E. Entomology
I. Centrosome
M. Meiosis

B. Molecular biology
F. Vestigiality
J. Denaturation
N. SI units

C. Yolk
G. Nucleobase
K. Chemical reaction
O. Adenine

D. Xylem
H. Enantiomer
L. Marine Biology

25. Using the Across and Down clues, write the correct words in the numbered grid below.

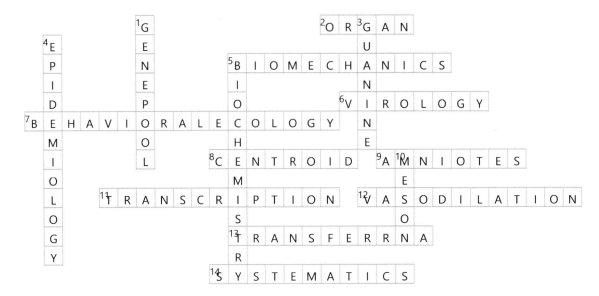

## ACROSS

2. A part of an organism that is typically self-contained and has a specific vital function, such as the heart or liver in humans.
5. The study of the structure and function of biological systems by means of the methods of "mechanics."
6. The study of viruses-submicroscopic, parasitic particles of genetic material contained in a protein coat and virus-like agents.
7. The study of the evolutionary basis for animal behavior due to ecological pressures.
8. The intersection of the three medians of the triangle (each median connecting a vertex with the midpoint of the opposite side).
9. Organisms that produce an egg composed of shell and membranes that creates a protected environment in which the embryo can develop out of water
11. The first step of gene expression, in which a segment of DNA is copied into RNA (mRNA) by the enzyme RNA polymerase.
12. The dilatation of blood vessels, which decreases blood pressure.
13. RNA consisting of folded molecules that transport amino acids from the cytoplasm of a cell to a ribosome.
14. The branch of biology that deals with classification and nomenclature; taxonomy.

## DOWN

1. The stock of different genes in an interbreeding population.
3. One of the four main nucleobases found in the nucleic acids DNA and RNA, the others being adenine, cytosine, and thymine.
4. The study and analysis of the patterns, causes, and effects of health and disease conditions in defined populations.
5. The branch of science that explores the chemical processes within and related to living organisms.
10. Hadronic subatomic particles composed of one quark and one antiquark, bound together by the strong interaction.

A. Biomechanics    B. Vasodilation    C. Behavioral ecology    D. Virology
E. Guanine    F. Epidemiology    G. Meson    H. Organ
I. Transcription    J. Biochemistry    K. Gene Pool    L. Amniotes
M. Systematics    N. Transfer RNA    O. Centroid

26. Using the Across and Down clues, write the correct words in the numbered grid below.

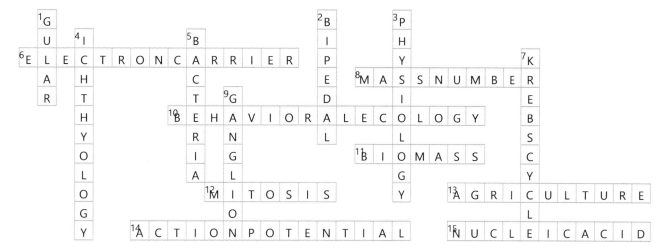

## ACROSS

6. Any of various molecules that can accept one or two electrons from one molecule and donating them to another in the process of electron transport.
8. The total number of protons and neutrons (together known as nucleons) in an atomic nucleus
10. The study of the evolutionary basis for animal behavior due to ecological pressures.
11. Organic matter derived from living, or recently living organisms.
12. The process in which a eukaryotic cell nucleus splits in two, followed by division of the parent cell into two daughter cells.
13. The practice of cultivating land, growing food, and raising stock.
14. The local voltage change across the cell wall as a nerve impulse is transmitted.
15. A complex organic substance present in living cells, especially DNA or RNA, whose molecules consist of many nucleotides linked in a long chain.

## DOWN

1. Of or pertaining to the throat.
2. A form of terrestrial locomotion where an organism moves by means of its two rear limbs or legs.
3. The branch of biology dealing with the functions and activities of living organisms and their parts, including all physical and chemical processes.
4. Known as fish science, is the branch of biology devoted to the study of fish.
5. Single-cell microscopic organisms which lack a true nucleus. they represent one of the three domains.
7. the sequence of reactions by which most living cells generate energy during the process of aerobic respiration.
9. A cluster (functional group) of nerve cell bodies in a centralized nervous system.

A. Action potential       B. Nucleic Acid       C. Krebs Cycle       D. Electron Carrier
E. Gular                  F. Physiology         G. Mitosis           H. Mass Number
I. Ganglion               J. Biomass            K. Bipedal           L. Bacteria
M. Ichthyology            N. Behavioral ecology O. Agriculture

27. Using the Across and Down clues, write the correct words in the numbered grid below.

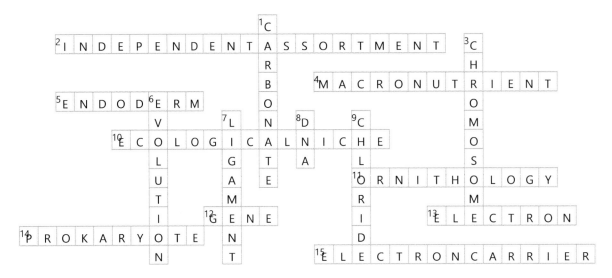

## ACROSS

2. The principle, originated by Gregor Mendel, stating that when two or more characteristics are inherited, individual hereditary factors assort independently.
4. Nutrients that provide calories or energy. nutrients are substances needed for growth, metabolism, and for other body functions.
5. One of the three primary germ layers in the very early human embryo. the other two layers are the ectoderm (outside layer) and mesoderm (middle layer).
10. The role and position a species has in its environment; how it meets its needs for food and shelter, how it survives, and how it reproduces.
11. A branch of zoology that concerns the study of birds.
12. A gene is a locus (or region) of DNA that encodes a functional RNA or protein product and is the molecular unit of heredity.
13. A subatomic particle with a negative elementary electric charge.
14. A microscopic single celled organism that has no distinct nucleus
15. Any of various molecules that can accept one or two electrons from one molecule and donating them to another in the process of electron transport.

## DOWN

1. Any member of two classes of chemical compounds derived from carbonic acid or carbon dioxide.
3. A threadlike strand of DNA in the cell nucleus that carries the genes in a linear order.
6. The change in genetic composition of a population over successive generations, which may be caused by natural selection, inbreeding, hybridization, or mutation.
7. The fibrous connective tissue that connects bones to other bones.
8. The hereditary material in humans and almost all other organisms.
9. A compound of chlorine with another element or group, especially a salt of the anion or an organic compound with chlorine bonded to an alkyl group.

A. Macronutrient
B. Chloride
C. Chromosome
D. Independent Assortment
E. Ornithology
F. Electron
G. Endoderm
H. Prokaryote
I. Carbonate
J. DNA
K. Gene
L. Evolution
M. Ecological Niche
N. Ligament
O. Electron Carrier

28. Using the Across and Down clues, write the correct words in the numbered grid below.

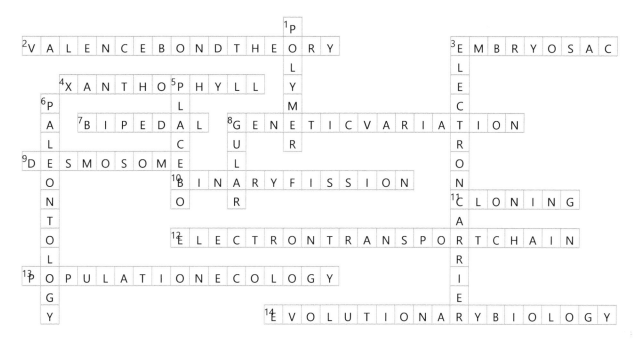

## ACROSS

2. A straightforward extension of Lewis structures. states that electrons in a covalent bond reside in a region that is the overlap of individual atomic orbitals.
3. The female gametophyte of a seed plant, within which the embryo develops.
4. The yellow colored photosynthetic pigments.
7. A form of terrestrial locomotion where an organism moves by means of its two rear limbs or legs.
8. Variations of genomes between members of species, or between groups of species thriving in different parts of the world as a result of genetic mutation.
9. Also known as a macula adhaerens, is a cell structure specialized for cell to cell adhesion.
10. One cell dividing into two identical daughter cells.
11. Propagate (an organism or cell) to make an identical copy of.
12. The site of oxidative phosphorylation in eukaryotes.
13. A sub-field of ecology that deals with the dynamics of species populations and how these populations interact with the environment.
14. The subfield of biology that studies the evolutionary processes that produced the diversity of life on earth starting from a single origin of life.

## DOWN

1. A large molecule, or macromolecule, composed of many repeated subunits.
3. Any of various molecules that can accept one or two electrons from one molecule and donating them to another in the process of electron transport.
5. A harmless pill, medicine, or procedure prescribed more for the psychological benefit to the patient than for any physiological effect.
6. The study of the history of life on earth as reflected in the fossil record. fossils are the remains or traces of organisms.
8. Of or pertaining to the throat.

A. Gular
D. Desmosome
G. Valence bond theory
J. Paleontology
M. Binary fission
P. Population Ecology

B. Polymer
E. Evolutionary Biology
H. Genetic Variation
K. Bipedal
N. Cloning

C. Electron Carrier
F. Electron Transport Chain
I. Placebo
L. Embryo Sac
O. Xanthophyll

29. Using the Across and Down clues, write the correct words in the numbered grid below.

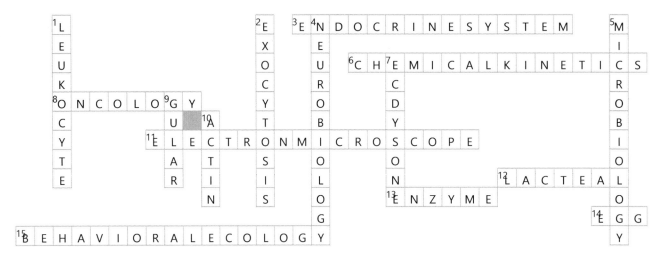

## ACROSS

3. The collection of glands that produce hormones that regulate metabolism, growth and development, tissue function, sexual function, reproduction, sleep, and mood.
6. The study and discussion of chemical reactions with respect to reaction rates.
8. A branch of medicine that deals with the prevention, diagnosis and treatment of cancer.
11. A type of microscope that uses a beam of electrons to create an image of the specimen. it is capable of much higher magnifications.
12. A lymphatic capillary that absorbs dietary fats in the villi of the small intestine.
13. Biological molecules (proteins) that act as catalysts and help complex reactions occur everywhere in life.
14. The female reproductive cell (gamete) in oogamous organisms.
15. The study of the evolutionary basis for animal behavior due to ecological pressures.

## DOWN

1. A colorless cell which circulates in the blood and body fluids and is involved in counteracting foreign substances and disease; a white (blood) cell.
2. A process by which the contents of a cell vacuole are released to the exterior through fusion of the vacuole membrane with the cell membrane.
4. The study of cells of the nervous system and the organization of these cells into functional circuits that process information and mediate behavior.
5. The study of microscopic organisms, such as bacteria, viruses, archaea, fungi and protozoa.
7. A steroidal prohormone of the major insect molting hormone is secreted from the prothoracic glands.
9. Of or pertaining to the throat.
10. One of the proteins into which actomyosin can be split; can exist in either a globular or a fibrous form.

A. Actin
E. Lacteal
I. Endocrine System
M. Leukocyte
B. Chemical kinetics
F. Behavioral ecology
J. Oncology
N. Electron Microscope
C. Egg
G. Exocytosis
K. Gular
O. Neurobiology
D. Ecdysone
H. Enzyme
L. Microbiology

30. Using the Across and Down clues, write the correct words in the numbered grid below.

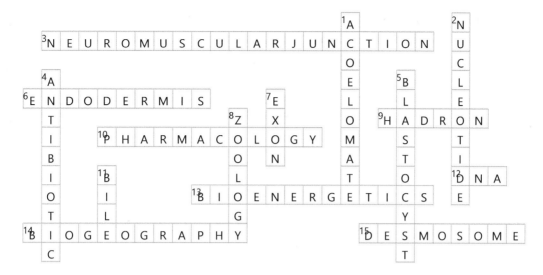

## ACROSS

3. A chemical synapse formed by the contact between a motor neuron and a muscle fiber.
6. An inner layer of cells in the cortex of a root and of some stems, surrounding a vascular bundle.
9. Any particle that is made from quarks, antiquarks and gluons.
10. The science of drug action on biological systems.
12. The hereditary material in humans and almost all other organisms.
13. The study of the transformation of energy in living organisms.
14. The study of the distribution of species and ecosystems in geographic space and through time.
15. Also known as a macula adhaerens, is a cell structure specialized for cell to cell adhesion.

## DOWN

1. Animals, like flatworms and jellyfish, that have no body cavity (coelom).
2. Organic molecules that serve as the monomers, or subunits, of nucleic acids like DNA (deoxyribonucleic acid) and RNA (ribonucleic acid).
4. A class of drug used to kill bacteria.
5. A mammalian blastula in which some differentiation of cells has occurred.
7. Any part of a gene that will become a part of the final mature RNA produced by that gene after introns have been removed by RNA splicing.
8. The branch of biology that relates to the animal kingdom, including the structure, embryology, evolution, classification, habits, and distribution of all animals.
11. A dark green to yellowish brown fluid, produced by the liver of most vertebrates, that aids the digestion of lipids in the small intestine.

A. Endodermis
D. Exon
G. Biogeography
J. Bile
M. Zoology

B. DNA
E. Acoelomate
H. Desmosome
K. Hadron
N. Nucleotide

C. Blastocyst
F. Pharmacology
I. Bioenergetics
L. Neuromuscular Junction
O. Antibiotic

## Multiple Choice

From the words provided for each clue, provide the letter of the word which best matches the clue.

1. _____ Large superfamily of motor proteins that move along actin filaments, while hydrolyzing ATP.
   A. Reproduction   B. Chemical reaction   C. Myosin   D. Whole Genome Sequencing

2. _____ Nutrients that provide calories or energy. nutrients are substances needed for growth, metabolism, and for other body functions.
   A. Membrane Potential   B. Psychobiology   C. Macronutrient   D. Mucous Membrane

3. _____ The modern form of the metric system and is the most widely used system of measurement.
   A. Epidemiology   B. Meiosis   C. International System   D. Endergonic Reaction

4. _____ The stock of different genes in an interbreeding population.
   A. Translation   B. Mole   C. Prokaryote   D. Gene Pool

5. _____ A process in nature in which organisms possessing certain genotypic characteristics that make them better adjusted to an environment tend to survive.
   A. Agriculture   B. Valence shell   C. Bacteria   D. Natural Selection

6. _____ The female reproductive cell (gamete) in oogamous organisms.
   A. Abscisic acid   B. Independent Assortment   C. Egg   D. Endangered Species

7. _____ A dark green to yellowish brown fluid, produced by the liver of most vertebrates, that aids the digestion of lipids in the small intestine.
   A. Food Chain   B. Mass Density   C. Acid precipitation   D. Bile

8. _____ Component of the blood that functions in the immune system. also known as a leukocyte.
   A. Chemical bond   B. White Blood Cell   C. Messenger RNA   D. Bioinformatics

9. _____ The branch of biology that studies the development of gametes (sex cells), fertilization, and development of embryos and fetuses.
   A. International System   B. Stem cell   C. Embryology   D. Darwinian Fitness

10. _____ The science of diagnosing and managing plant diseases.
    A. Stem cell   B. Biogeography   C. Neurotransmitter   D. Phytopathology

11. _____ An epithelial tissue that secretes mucus and that lines many body cavities and tubular organs including the gut and respiratory passages.
    A. Exon   B. Lacteal   C. Mucous Membrane   D. Evolutionary Biology

12. _____ An enzyme that synthesizes short RNA sequences called primers.
    A. Ecological Efficiency   B. Primase   C. Endergonic Reaction   D. Dendrite

13. _____ Of or pertaining to the throat.
    A. Biodiversity   B. Cloning   C. Valence electron   D. Gular

14. _____ The application of the principles of biology to the study of physiological, genetic, and developmental mechanisms of behavior in humans and other animals.
    A. Population Ecology   B. Fetus   C. Myosin   D. Psychobiology

15. _____ A sub-field of ecology that deals with the dynamics of species populations and how these populations interact with the environment.
    A. Meiosis   B. Population Ecology   C. Immune Response   D. Nucleotide

16. _____ Study of living organisms.
A. Biology   B. Ionic Bond   C. Mole   D. Biodiversity

17. _____ The study of mammals.
A. Mass Balance   B. Evolutionary Biology   C. Mammalogy   D. Centrosome

18. _____ A microscopic single celled organism that has no distinct nucleus
A. Uterus   B. Parasitology   C. Population Genetics   D. Prokaryote

19. _____ Refers to genetically determined structures or attributes that have apparently lost most or all their ancestral function in a given species.
A. Vestigiality   B. Valence shell   C. Endemism   D. Organism

20. _____ A technique used in molecular biology to amplify a single copy or a few copies of a piece of DNA across several orders of magnitude.
A. Polymerase Chain Reaction   B. Chromosome   C. Enantiomer   D. Polyploidy

21. _____ One of the proteins into which actomyosin can be split; can exist in either a globular or a fibrous form.
A. Action potential   B. Chromosome   C. Actin   D. Gene

22. _____ The study of plant nutrition and growth especially to increase crop yield
A. Agrobiology   B. T Cell   C. Virology   D. Electron Acceptor

23. _____ Animals, like flatworms and jellyfish, that have no body cavity (coelom).
A. Endosperm   B. Epidemiology   C. Lacteal   D. Acoelomate

24. _____ Any of various molecules that can accept one or two electrons from one molecule and donating them to another in the process of electron transport.
A. Isomer   B. Bionics   C. Electron Carrier   D. Cryobiology

25. _____ Glands that secrete their products, hormones, directly into the blood rather than through a duct.
A. Membrane Potential   B. Endemism   C. Endocrine Gland   D. Ecological Niche

26. _____ A part of an organism that is typically self-contained and has a specific vital function, such as the heart or liver in humans.
A. Organ   B. Carbonate   C. Lipoprotein   D. Darwinian Fitness

27. _____ Stereoisomers that are non-superimposable mirror images. a molecule with 1 chiral carbon atom exists as 2 stereoisomers termed enantiomers.
A. Mucous Membrane   B. Enantiomer   C. Zoology   D. Mole

28. _____ The study of organic particles, such as bacteria, fungal spores, very small insects, pollen grains and viruses, which are passively transported by the air.
A. Ecotype   B. Biomechanics   C. Anatomy   D. Aerobiology

29. _____ The study of viruses-submicroscopic, parasitic particles of genetic material contained in a protein coat and virus-like agents.
A. Translation   B. Parasitology   C. Myosin   D. Virology

30. _____ Biological molecules (proteins) that act as catalysts and help complex reactions occur everywhere in life.
A. Ethology   B. Enzyme   C. Acid precipitation   D. Electron Microscope

31. _____ A molecule that can be bonded to other identical molecules to form a polymer.
A. Stem cell   B. Monomer   C. Hydrocarbon   D. Parasitology

32. _____ The study of the structure and function of biological systems by means of the methods of "mechanics."
A. Messenger RNA   B. Aerobic   C. Chromosome   D. Biomechanics

33. _____ A organism in which internal physiological sources of heat are of relatively small or quite negligible importance in controlling body temperature. "cold blooded".
A. External Fertilization   B. Ectotherm   C. Metaphase   D. Acoelomate

34. _____ A type of microscope that uses a beam of electrons to create an image of the specimen. it is capable of much higher magnifications.
A. Valence band   B. Agriculture   C. Wood   D. Electron Microscope

35. _____ A very large molecule, such as protein, commonly created by polymerization of smaller subunits (monomers).
A. Enzyme   B. Ecotype   C. Macromolecule   D. Independent Assortment

36. _____ The application of computer technology to the management of biological information.
A. Absorption   B. Active Transport   C. Bioinformatics   D. Enantiomer

37. _____ A colorless cell which circulates in the blood and body fluids and is involved in counteracting foreign substances and disease; a white (blood) cell.
A. External Fertilization   B. Leukocyte   C. Membrane Potential   D. Mucous Membrane

38. _____ How your body recognizes and defends itself against bacteria, viruses, and substances that appear foreign and harmful.
A. Population Genetics   B. Genetics   C. Antibiotic   D. Immune Response

39. _____ Threatened by factors such as habitat loss, hunting, disease and climate change, and usually have declining populations or a very limited range.
A. Endotherm   B. Endangered Species   C. Ethology   D. Bacteria

40. _____ Helps keep blood sugar level from getting too high (hyperglycemia) or too low (hypoglycemia).
A. Insulin   B. Desmosome   C. Enantiomer   D. Plasmolysis

41. _____ A class of drug used to kill bacteria.
A. Plasmolysis   B. Mass Density   C. Antibiotic   D. Enzyme

42. _____ A hierarchical series of organisms each dependent on the next as a source of food.
A. Valence band   B. Carbonate   C. SI units   D. Food Chain

43. _____ A group of cytokines (secreted proteins and signal molecules) that were first seen to be expressed by white blood cells (leukocytes)
A. Nucleic Acid Sequence   B. Interleukin   C. Evolutionary Biology   D. Astrobiology

44. _____ One of the four main nucleobases found in the nucleic acids DNA and RNA, the others being adenine, cytosine, and thymine.
A. Guanine   B. Dehydration Reaction   C. Darwinian Fitness   D. Ganglion

45. _____ A chemical synapse formed by the contact between a motor neuron and a muscle fiber.
A. Neuromuscular Junction   B. Electron Microscope   C. Anatomy   D. Zoology

46. _____ An inner layer of cells in the cortex of a root and of some stems, surrounding a vascular bundle.
A. Deciduous   B. Biodiversity   C. Endodermis   D. Plant Nutrition

47. _____ The study of populations of organisms, especially the regulation of population size, life history traits such as clutch size, and extinction.
A. Chloride   B. Amino acid   C. Population Biology   D. Endergonic Reaction

48. _____ The "control room" for the cell. the nucleus gives out all the orders.
A. Aerobic   B. Ethology   C. Action potential   D. Cell nucleus

49. _____ The study of the distribution of species and ecosystems in geographic space and through time.
A. Biogeography   B. Parallel Evolution   C. Active Transport   D. Bile

50. _____ Sperm units with egg in the open, rather than inside the body of the parents
A. Abscisic acid   B. Ionic Bond   C. Bionics   D. External Fertilization

51. _____ The hereditary material in humans and almost all other organisms.
A. Zygote   B. Endotherm   C. DNA   D. Cell theory

52. _____ A gradient of electrochemical potential, usually for an ion that can move across a membrane.
A. Hydrocarbon   B. Electrochemical Gradient   C. Independent Assortment   D. Psychobiology

53. _____ The variety of life in the world or in a habitat or ecosystem.
A. Biodiversity   B. Ecotype   C. Endemic Species   D. Mammalogy

54. _____ The highest range of electron energies in which electrons are normally present at absolute zero temperature.
A. Valence band   B. Bile   C. Psychobiology   D. Ethology

55. _____ Rain containing acids that form in the atmosphere when industrial gas emissions (especially sulfur dioxide and nitrogen oxides) combine with water.
A. Amino acid   B. Absorption   C. Endergonic Reaction   D. Acid precipitation

56. _____ An undifferentiated cell of a multicellular organism that can give rise to indefinitely more cells of the same type.
A. Stem cell   B. Ecosystem   C. Endergonic Reaction   D. Amniotes

57. _____ A measure of the tendency of an atom to attract a bonding pair of electrons. the Pauling scale is the most commonly used.
A. Population Biology   B. Chemical equilibrium   C. Physiology   D. Electronegativity

58. _____ Any member of two classes of chemical compounds derived from carbonic acid or carbon dioxide.
A. Chemical kinetics   B. Membrane Potential   C. Symbiogenesis   D. Carbonate

59. _____ Any of the elongated contractile threads found in striated muscle cells.
A. Myofibril   B. Endemism   C. Neuromuscular Junction   D. Mitosis

60. _____ Also known as a macula adhaerens, is a cell structure specialized for cell to cell adhesion.
A. Chemical equilibrium   B. Actin   C. Active Transport   D. Desmosome

61. _____ The study of parasites, their hosts, and the relationship between them.
A. Agrobiology   B. Ion   C. Biomechanics   D. Parasitology

62. _____ The branch of biology concerned with the relations between organisms and their environment.
A. Embryo Sac   B. Organ   C. Endocrine System   D. Environmental Biology

63. _____ Usually defined as a chemical reaction that involves the loss of a water molecule from the reacting molecule.
A. Translation   B. Dehydration Reaction   C. Deoxyribose   D. Phytopathology

64. _____ A molecule with the same chemical formula as another molecule, but with a different chemical structure.
A. Biomechanics   B. Microevolution   C. Whole Genome Sequencing   D. Isomer

65. _____ Giving birth to one of its kind, sexually or asexually.
A. Neurotransmitter   B. Amino acid   C. Reproduction   D. Active site

66. _____ A lymphatic capillary that absorbs dietary fats in the villi of the small intestine.
A. Synthetic Biology   B. Lacteal   C. Molecular biology   D. DNA

67. _____ A type of cell division that reduces the number of chromosomes in the parent cell by half and produces four gamete cells.
A. Gular   B. Organ   C. Interleukin   D. Meiosis

68. _____ The process of reversing the charge across a cell membrane (usually a neuron), so causing an action potential.
A. Interleukin   B. Active site   C. SI units   D. Depolarization

69. _____ The organ in the lower body of a woman or female mammal where offspring are conceived and in which they gestate before birth; the womb.
A. Nucleolus   B. White Blood Cell   C. Uterus   D. Basal body

70. _____ A measure of the potential energy in water as well as the difference between the potential in a water sample and pure water.
A. DNA   B. Water Potential   C. Endocrine System   D. Active site

71. _____ A cluster (functional group) of nerve cell bodies in a centralized nervous system.
A. Ectoderm   B. Epiphyte   C. Lacteal   D. Ganglion

72. _____ An organelle formed from a centriole, and a short cylindrical array of microtubules.
A. Basal body   B. Immune Response   C. Cell theory   D. Microevolution

73. _____ The female gametophyte of a seed plant, within which the embryo develops.
A. Polyploidy   B. Agrobiology   C. Embryo Sac   D. Membrane Potential

74. _____ Depending on free oxygen or air.
A. Interleukin   B. Denitrification   C. Microevolution   D. Aerobic

75. _____ The subfield of biology that studies the evolutionary processes that produced the diversity of life on earth starting from a single origin of life.
A. Parasitology   B. Cryobiology   C. Evolutionary Biology   D. Hadron

76. _____ An application of conservation of mass to the analysis of physical systems.
A. Organism   B. Lepton   C. Mole   D. Mass Balance

77. _____ A compound of chlorine with another element or group, especially a salt of the anion or an organic compound with chlorine bonded to an alkyl group.
A. Biology   B. Evolutionary Biology   C. T Cell   D. Chloride

78. _____ The branch of morphology that deals with the structure of animals
A. Anatomy   B. Water Potential   C. Cryobiology   D. Ecosystem

79. _____ An elementary, half-integer spin particle that does not undergo strong interactions.
A. Zygote   B. Mass Number   C. Lepton   D. Electron Donor

80. _____ In organic chemistry, a hydrocarbon is an organic compound consisting entirely of hydrogen and carbon.
A. Myosin   B. Hydrocarbon   C. Prokaryote   D. Agrobiology

81. _____ The genetic contribution of an individual to the next generation's gene pool relative to the average for the population.
A. Ecotype   B. Darwinian Fitness   C. Endemism   D. Electron

82. _____ Means "falling off at maturity" or "tending to fall off", and it is typically used in order to refer to trees or shrubs that lose their leaves seasonally.
A. Uterus   B. Protein   C. Deciduous   D. Vestigiality

83. _____ A microbially facilitated process of nitrate reduction that may ultimately produce molecular nitrogen.
A. Whole Genome Sequencing   B. Denitrification   C. Zygote   D. Ionic Bond

84. ____ A chemical reaction in which the standard change in free energy is positive, and energy is absorbed
A. B cell   B. Endergonic Reaction   C. Absorption   D. Microevolution

85. ____ One of the three primary germ layers in the very early human embryo. the other two layers are the ectoderm (outside layer) and mesoderm (middle layer).
A. Osmosis   B. Endoderm   C. Denitrification   D. Virology

86. ____ Single-cell microscopic organisms which lack a true nucleus. they represent one of the three domains.
A. Macromolecule   B. Valence electron   C. Agrobiology   D. Bacteria

87. ____ The inner layer of the stems of woody plants; composed of xylem.
A. Wood   B. Denitrification   C. Effector Cell   D. Aerobic

88. ____ The branch of biology concerned with the effects of outer space on living organisms and the search for extraterrestrial life
A. Active Transport   B. Valence   C. Physiology   D. Astrobiology

89. ____ The form of rna in which genetic information transcribed from dna as a sequence of bases is transferred to a ribosome.
A. Deciduous   B. Ecosystem   C. Biocatalysts   D. Messenger RNA

90. ____ A form of active transport in which a cell transports molecules into the cell.
A. Dehydration Reaction   B. Genetics   C. Reproduction   D. Endocytosis

91. ____ A tissue produced inside the seeds of most of the flowering plants around the time of fertilization.
A. Stem cell   B. Messenger RNA   C. Endosperm   D. Effector Cell

92. ____ Virus that infects and multiplies within bacteria.
A. Darwinian Fitness   B. Parasitology   C. Bacteriophage   D. Electron Microscope

93. ____ In cell biology, an organelle that is the main place where cell microtubules get organized. they occur only in plant and animal cells.
A. Centrosome   B. Agrobiology   C. Endosperm   D. Myosin

94. ____ The branch of biology that studies the effects of low temperatures on living things within earth's cryosphere or in science.
A. Darwinian Fitness   B. Facultative Anaerobe   C. Cryobiology   D. Electron

95. ____ Density is mass per volume.
A. Ecological Efficiency   B. Mass Density   C. Active site   D. Myosin

96. ____ Catalysis in living systems. in biological processes, natural catalysts, such as protein enzymes, perform chemical transformations on organic compounds.
A. Lepton   B. Bacteriophage   C. Ganglion   D. Biocatalysts

97. ____ A laboratory process that determines the complete DNA sequence of an organism's genome at a single time.
A. Chemical bond   B. Ectoderm   C. Active Transport   D. Whole Genome Sequencing

98. ____ The study and analysis of the patterns, causes, and effects of health and disease conditions in defined populations.
A. Epidemiology   B. Plasmolysis   C. Whole Genome Sequencing   D. Parasitology

99. ____ An atom or molecule with a net electric charge due to the loss or gain of one or more electrons.
A. Ion   B. Population Biology   C. Gene   D. Jejunum

100. ___ The principle, originated by Gregor Mendel, stating that when two or more characteristics are inherited, individual hereditary factors assort independently.
A. Centrosome   B. Enantiomer   C. Independent Assortment   D. Endemic Species

From the words provided for each clue, provide the letter of the word which best matches the clue.

101. ___ Work to convert light energy of the sun into sugars that can be used by cells.
A. Primase   B. Cloning   C. DNA   D. Chloroplast

102. ___ The primary female sex hormone. it is responsible for the development and regulation of the female reproductive system and secondary sex characteristics.
A. Pollination   B. Jejunum   C. Estrogen   D. Herpetology

103. ___ Any of various molecules that can accept one or two electrons from one molecule and donating them to another in the process of electron transport.
A. Barr body   B. Electron Carrier   C. Bacteriophage   D. Epinephrine

104. ___ The act of transferring pollen grains from the male anther of a flower to the female stigma.
A. Myosin   B. Pollination   C. Macrophage   D. Internal Fertilization

105. ___ Describes the efficiency with which energy is transferred from one trophic level to the next.
A. Herpetology   B. Ecological Efficiency   C. Chemistry   D. Epinephrine

106. ___ The double helix is unwound and each strand acts as a template for the next strand. bases are matched to synthesize the new partner strands.
A. DNA Replication   B. Gene   C. SI units   D. Sexual Reproduction

107. ___ A threadlike strand of DNA in the cell nucleus that carries the genes in a linear order.
A. Chromosome   B. Heterosis   C. Entomology   D. Translation

108. ___ Also known as a macula adhaerens, is a cell structure specialized for cell to cell adhesion.
A. Pathobiology   B. Marine Biology   C. Desmosome   D. Medulla

109. ___ A class of drug used to kill bacteria.
A. Environmental Biology   B. Molecular biology   C. Antibiotic   D. Myofibril

110. ___ A form of terrestrial locomotion where an organism moves by means of its two rear limbs or legs.
A. Pathobiology   B. Abscisic acid   C. Bipedal   D. Plasmolysis

111. ___ An interaction of living things and non-living things in a physical environment.
A. Uracil   B. Molecule   C. Macroevolution   D. Ecosystem

112. ___ The study of heredity
A. Herpetology   B. Genetics   C. Mass Balance   D. DNA Sequencing

113. ___ Known as chemical messengers, are endogenous chemicals that enable neurotransmission.
A. Metaphase   B. Marine Biology   C. Vesicle   D. Neurotransmitter

114. ___ A biological agent that reproduces inside the cells of living hosts.
A. Interleukin   B. Virus   C. Biomechanics   D. Urine

115. ___ The study of populations of organisms, especially the regulation of population size, life history traits such as clutch size, and extinction.
A. Biochemistry   B. Bacteria   C. Evolution   D. Population Biology

116. _____ The study of the evolutionary basis for animal behavior due to ecological pressures.
A. Behavioral ecology   B. Habitat   C. Bile   D. Chromosome

117. _____ The science of drug action on biological systems.
A. Pharmacology   B. Ichthyology   C. Endangered Species   D. Marine Biology

118. _____ A group of cytokines (secreted proteins and signal molecules) that were first seen to be expressed by white blood cells (leukocytes)
A. Jejunum   B. Active Transport   C. Monomer   D. Interleukin

119. _____ Catalysis in living systems. in biological processes, natural catalysts, such as protein enzymes, perform chemical transformations on organic compounds.
A. Chromosome   B. Cryobiology   C. Absorption spectrum   D. Biocatalysts

120. _____ Biological molecules (proteins) that act as catalysts and help complex reactions occur everywhere in life.
A. Endocrine System   B. Wobble Base Pair   C. Abyssal zone   D. Enzyme

121. _____ An interdisciplinary branch of biology and engineering.
A. Synthetic Biology   B. Gene Pool   C. Lipid   D. Ecological Niche

122. _____ An application of conservation of mass to the analysis of physical systems.
A. Nucleic Acid Sequence   B. Mass Balance   C. Deoxyribonucleic Acid   D. Synthetic Biology

123. _____ Contraction of the protoplast of a plant cell as a result of loss of water from the cell.
A. Endocrine Gland   B. Plasmolysis   C. Deoxyribonucleic Acid   D. External Fertilization

124. _____ The total number of protons and neutrons (together known as nucleons) in an atomic nucleus
A. Endodermis   B. Mass Number   C. Desmosome   D. Valence electron

125. _____ The smallest particle in a chemical element or compound that has the chemical properties of that element or compound.
A. Macroevolution   B. Translation   C. Antibiotic   D. Molecule

126. _____ An undifferentiated cell of a multicellular organism that can give rise to indefinitely more cells of the same type.
A. Stem cell   B. Mammalogy   C. Astrobiology   D. Barr body

127. _____ One of the four nucleobases in the nucleic acid of RNA that are represented by the letters a, g, c and u.
A. Mass Balance   B. Ecological Pyramid   C. Desmosome   D. Uracil

128. _____ A unit of concentration measuring the number of moles of a solute per liter of solution.
A. Ecological Efficiency   B. Pollination   C. Molarity   D. Desmosome

129. _____ Of or pertaining to the throat.
A. Interleukin   B. Gular   C. Chemical kinetics   D. Gene Pool

130. _____ A gradient of electrochemical potential, usually for an ion that can move across a membrane.
A. Gular   B. Acoelomate   C. Electrochemical Gradient   D. Virus

131. _____ A compound of chlorine with another element or group, especially a salt of the anion or an organic compound with chlorine bonded to an alkyl group.
A. Chloride   B. Action potential   C. Linked Genes   D. Deciduous

132. _____ The scientific study of organisms in the ocean or other marine bodies of water.
A. Behavioral ecology   B. Marine Biology   C. Zygote   D. Medulla

133. _____ Giving birth to one of its kind, sexually or asexually.
A. Messenger RNA   B. Reproduction   C. Endemic Species   D. Mass Balance

134. _____ The collection of glands that produce hormones that regulate metabolism, growth and development, tissue function, sexual function, reproduction, sleep, and mood.
A. Molecular biology   B. Lipid   C. Gular   D. Endocrine System

135. _____ A succession of letters that indicate the order of nucleotides within a DNA (using GACT or RNA (GACU) molecule.
A. Electronegativity   B. Nucleic Acid Sequence   C. Bacteria   D. Protein

136. _____ The science of diagnosing and managing plant diseases.
A. Gene Pool   B. Phloem   C. Bioengineering   D. Phytopathology

137. _____ Organisms that produce an egg composed of shell and membranes that creates a protected environment in which the embryo can develop out of water
A. Amniotes   B. Absorption spectrum   C. Ecdysone   D. Bioengineering

138. _____ A measure of the potential energy in water as well as the difference between the potential in a water sample and pure water.
A. Primase   B. T Cell   C. Water Potential   D. Integrative Biology

139. _____ A fluid or air-filled cavity or sac.
A. Cloning   B. Lipid   C. Vesicle   D. Hermaphrodite

140. _____ One of the four main nucleobases found in the nucleic acids DNA and RNA, the others being adenine, cytosine, and thymine.
A. Guanine   B. SI units   C. Amniotes   D. Electric Potential

141. _____ The study or practice of pathology with greater emphasis on the biological than on the medical aspects.
A. Pathobiology   B. Active Transport   C. B cell   D. Chromosome

142. _____ The si unit of measurement used to measure the number of things, usually atoms or molecules.
A. Medulla   B. Mole   C. Xanthophyll   D. Osmosis

143. _____ Large biomolecules, or macromolecules, consisting of one or more long chains of amino acid residues.
A. Protein   B. Herpetology   C. Population Biology   D. Macronutrient

144. _____ The branch of biology that studies the development of gametes (sex cells), fertilization, and development of embryos and fetuses.
A. Pollination   B. Prokaryote   C. DNA   D. Embryology

145. _____ A type of cell division that reduces the number of chromosomes in the parent cell by half and produces four gamete cells.
A. T Cell   B. Neurotransmitter   C. Electron Acceptor   D. Meiosis

146. _____ A type of microscope that uses a beam of electrons to create an image of the specimen. it is capable of much higher magnifications.
A. Electron Microscope   B. Zygote   C. Biology   D. Immune Response

147. _____ Threatened by factors such as habitat loss, hunting, disease and climate change, and usually have declining populations or a very limited range.
A. Artificial Selection   B. Predation   C. Cryobiology   D. Endangered Species

148. _____ One of the three primary germ layers in the very early human embryo. the other two layers are the ectoderm (outside layer) and mesoderm (middle layer).
A. Prokaryote   B. Reproduction   C. Epinephrine   D. Endoderm

149. ____ The midsection of the small intestine of many higher vertebrates like mammals, birds, reptiles. it is present between the duodenum and the ileum.
A. Monomer   B. Jejunum   C. Psychobiology   D. Translation

150. ____ The collective term for all possible frequencies of electromagnetic radiation.
A. Electromagnetic Spectrum   B. Hermaphrodite   C. Mole   D. Chemical bond

151. ____ The application of the principles of biology to the study of physiological, genetic, and developmental mechanisms of behavior in humans and other animals.
A. Linked Genes   B. Psychobiology   C. Entomology   D. Physiology

152. ____ Plasma cells, also called plasma b cells, plasmocytes, plasmacytes, or effector b cells, are white blood cells that secrete large volumes of antibodies.
A. Effector Cell   B. DNA Replication   C. Desmosome   D. Predation

153. ____ Conducted or conducting outwards or away from something (for nerves, the central nervous system; for blood vessels, the organ supplied).
A. Efferent   B. Arachnology   C. Evolution   D. Neuromuscular Junction

154. ____ An electrically excitable cell that processes and transmits information through electrical and chemical signals.
A. Transfer RNA   B. Neuron   C. Uracil   D. Vacuole

155. ____ The study of the structure and function of biological systems by means of the methods of "mechanics."
A. Prokaryote   B. Biomechanics   C. Astrobiology   D. Herpetology

156. ____ A organism in which internal physiological sources of heat are of relatively small or quite negligible importance in controlling body temperature. "cold blooded".
A. Ecosystem   B. Ectotherm   C. Chemistry   D. Embryo Sac

157. ____ When two genes are close together on the same chromosome, they do not assort independently.
A. Hermaphrodite   B. Bioengineering   C. Darwinian Fitness   D. Linked Genes

158. ____ The branch of science that explores the chemical processes within and related to living organisms.
A. Biochemistry   B. Metaphase   C. Cell   D. Electron Carrier

159. ____ The study of the history of life on earth as reflected in the fossil record. fossils are the remains or traces of organisms.
A. Ecdysone   B. Messenger RNA   C. Chemistry   D. Paleontology

160. ____ A microscopic single celled organism that has no distinct nucleus
A. Prokaryote   B. T Cell   C. Chromosome   D. Barr body

161. ____ An electron that is associated with an atom, and that can participate in the formation of a chemical bond.
A. Ecosystem   B. Valence electron   C. DNA   D. Hermaphrodite

162. ____ Any of the elongated contractile threads found in striated muscle cells.
A. Myofibril   B. Paleontology   C. Human Nutrition   D. SI units

163. ____ The scientific study of nature and of earth's biodiversity with the aim of protecting species, their habitats, and ecosystems from excessive rates of extinction.
A. Testosterone   B. Conservation Biology   C. Electromagnetic Spectrum   D. Eukaryote

164. ____ The interaction of genes that are not alleles. The suppression of the effect of one such gene by another.
A. Gene Pool   B. Efferent   C. Chromosome   D. Epistasis

165. ____ A molecule that can be bonded to other identical molecules to form a polymer.
A. Antibiotic   B. Mole   C. Molecule   D. Monomer

166. Scientific study of spiders, scorpions, pseudo-scorpions, and harvestmen.
A. Valence bond theory   B. Xanthophyll   C. Arachnology   D. Artificial Selection

167. Depending on free oxygen or air.
A. Aerobic   B. Bacteriophage   C. Messenger RNA   D. Asexual Reproduction

168. The study and discussion of chemical reactions with respect to reaction rates.
A. Osmosis   B. SI units   C. Chemical kinetics   D. Electron Microscope

169. Any organism whose cells contain a nucleus and other organelles enclosed within membranes.
A. Virology   B. Gular   C. Electron   D. Eukaryote

170. One of the proteins into which actomyosin can be split; can exist in either a globular or a fibrous form.
A. Water Potential   B. Benthic zone   C. Actin   D. Phenotype

171. Means "falling off at maturity" or "tending to fall off", and it is typically used in order to refer to trees or shrubs that lose their leaves seasonally.
A. Valence band   B. Deoxyribonucleic Acid   C. Deciduous   D. Bacteria

172. A pairing between two nucleotides in RNA molecules that does not follow Watson crick base pair rules
A. Bipedal   B. Herpetology   C. Wobble Base Pair   D. Plasmolysis

173. In organic chemistry, a hydrocarbon is an organic compound consisting entirely of hydrogen and carbon.
A. Chloroplast   B. Hydrocarbon   C. Metaphase   D. Cloning

174. The amount of work needed to move a unit charge from a reference point to a specific point against an electric field.
A. Integrative Biology   B. Mass Number   C. Chemical kinetics   D. Electric Potential

175. Type of reproduction in which cells from two parents unite to form the first cell of a new organism.
A. Ichthyology   B. Metaphase   C. Sexual Reproduction   D. Pharmacology

176. Hadronic subatomic particles composed of one quark and one antiquark, bound together by the strong interaction.
A. Genetic Code   B. Histology   C. Cholesterol   D. Meson

177. Organism with both male and female reproductive organs.
A. Genetics   B. Cell   C. Hermaphrodite   D. Electron Donor

178. The branch of biology dealing with the functions and activities of living organisms and their parts, including all physical and chemical processes.
A. Biomechanics   B. Physiology   C. Prokaryote   D. Hermaphrodite

179. An inner layer of cells in the cortex of a root and of some stems, surrounding a vascular bundle.
A. Endodermis   B. Messenger RNA   C. Uracil   D. Electron Acceptor

180. Known as fish science, is the branch of biology devoted to the study of fish.
A. Ichthyology   B. Zygote   C. Dalton   D. Electron

181. Study of living organisms.
A. Chemical compound   B. Arachnology   C. Denaturation   D. Biology

182. The nucleotide triplets of DNA and RNA molecules that carry genetic information in living cells.
A. Adenine   B. Biochemistry   C. Antibiotic   D. Genetic Code

183. _____ An animal that is dependent on or capable of the internal generation of heat; a warm
A. Molecule   B. Desmosome   C. Endotherm   D. Chloride

184. _____ Any part of a gene that will become a part of the final mature RNA produced by that gene after introns have
been removed by RNA splicing.
A. Amniotes   B. Antibiotic   C. Mass Balance   D. Exon

185. _____ One of the two purine nucleobases (the other being guanine) used in forming nucleotides of the nucleic acids.
A. Adenine   B. Heterosis   C. Molecule   D. Macronutrient

186. _____ The intersection of the three medians of the triangle (each median connecting a vertex with the midpoint of the
opposite side).
A. Centroid   B. Darwinian Fitness   C. Epistasis   D. Biocatalysts

187. _____ The highest range of electron energies in which electrons are normally present at absolute zero temperature.
A. Action potential   B. Valence band   C. Efferent   D. Interleukin

188. _____ The vascular tissue in plants that conducts sugars and other metabolic products downward from the leaves.
A. Mitosis   B. Molecular biology   C. Phloem   D. Biomechanics

189. _____ The branch of zoology concerned with reptiles and amphibians.
A. Herpetology   B. Neuron   C. Bacteria   D. Incomplete Dominance

190. _____ A place for animals, people and plants and non-living things
A. Physiology   B. Wobble Base Pair   C. Habitat   D. Amniotes

191. _____ An organic compound with four rings arranged in a specific configuration. examples include the dietary lipid
cholesterol and the sex hormones.
A. Chemical bond   B. Integrative Biology   C. Steroid   D. Antibiotic

192. _____ The hereditary material in humans and almost all other organisms.
A. Chemistry   B. DNA   C. Prokaryote   D. Linked Genes

193. _____ A subatomic particle with a negative elementary electric charge.
A. Ichthyology   B. T Cell   C. Electron   D. Embryology

194. _____ Serves an important role in the metabolism of nitrogen-containing compounds by animals and is the main
nitrogen-containing substance in the urine of mammals.
A. Urea   B. Bacteriophage   C. Biocatalysts   D. Exon

195. _____ The tendency of a crossbred individual to show qualities superior to those of both parents.
A. Mitosis   B. Embryology   C. Heterosis   D. Hadron

196. _____ A sub-field of ecology that deals with the dynamics of species populations and how these populations interact
with the environment.
A. Krebs Cycle   B. Conservation Biology   C. Hermaphrodite   D. Population Ecology

197. _____ Application of biological methods and systems found in nature to the study and design of engineering systems
and modern technology.
A. Monomer   B. Chemical kinetics   C. Bionics   D. Absorption

198. _____ Sperm units with egg in the open, rather than inside the body of the parents
A. External Fertilization   B. Monomer   C. Actin   D. Eukaryote

199. _____ The energy that an atomic system must acquire before a process (such as an emission or reaction) can occur.
A. Messenger RNA   B. Linked Genes   C. Activation energy   D. Urine

200. _____ A laboratory process that determines the complete DNA sequence of an organism's genome at a single time.
A. Bionics  B. Urine  C. Whole Genome Sequencing  D. Bacteria

From the words provided for each clue, provide the letter of the word which best matches the clue.

201. _____ The "control room" for the cell. the nucleus gives out all the orders.
A. Transcription  B. Cell nucleus  C. Denitrification  D. Molecular physics

202. _____ A liquid by-product of the body secreted by the kidneys through a process called urination (or micturition) and excreted through the urethra.
A. Trophic level  B. Element  C. Urine  D. Ecotype

203. _____ The organ in the lower body of a woman or female mammal where offspring are conceived and in which they gestate before birth; the womb.
A. Uterus  B. Meiosis  C. Dehydration Reaction  D. Biogeography

204. _____ The branch of science that explores the chemical processes within and related to living organisms.
A. Anatomy  B. Acoelomate  C. Biochemistry  D. Ecological Pyramid

205. _____ The modern form of the metric system and is the most widely used system of measurement.
A. Electron Carrier  B. International System  C. Mammalogy  D. Vesicle

206. _____ The branch of morphology that deals with the structure of animals
A. Anatomy  B. Deoxyribonucleic Acid  C. Biome  D. Barr body

207. _____ A large molecule, or macromolecule, composed of many repeated subunits.
A. Autoimmunity  B. Polymer  C. Binary fission  D. Cryobiology

208. _____ The scientific and objective study of non-human animal behavior rather than human behavior and usually with a focus on behavior under natural conditions.
A. Active Transport  B. Ethology  C. Barr body  D. Arachnology

209. _____ Nutrients that provide calories or energy. nutrients are substances needed for growth, metabolism, and for other body functions.
A. Mammalogy  B. Macronutrient  C. Macromolecule  D. Aerobiology

210. _____ A mammalian blastula in which some differentiation of cells has occurred.
A. Blastocyst  B. Uterus  C. Thymine  D. Endemism

211. _____ A short branched extension of a nerve cell, along which impulses received from other cells at synapses are transmitted to the cell body
A. Hormone  B. International System  C. Blastocyst  D. Dendrite

212. _____ The interaction of genes that are not alleles. The suppression of the effect of one such gene by another.
A. Macrophage  B. Anticodon  C. Eukaryote  D. Epistasis

213. _____ The study or practice of pathology with greater emphasis on the biological than on the medical aspects.
A. Pathobiology  B. Barr body  C. Natural Selection  D. Whole Genome Sequencing

214. _____ The study of the physical properties of molecules, the chemical bonds between atoms as well as the molecular dynamics.
A. Incomplete Dominance  B. Marine Biology  C. Molecular physics  D. Thymine

215. ____ An individual animal, plant, or single-celled life form.
A. Organism   B. Endocrine System   C. Expressivity   D. Active Transport

216. ____ Describes a genetically distinct geographic variety, population or race within a species, which is adapted to specific environmental conditions.
A. Ecotype   B. Endemic Species   C. Microevolution   D. Ganglion

217. ____ Threatened by factors such as habitat loss, hunting, disease and climate change, and usually have declining populations or a very limited range.
A. Electrochemical Gradient   B. Chemical kinetics   C. Endosperm   D. Endangered Species

218. ____ A chemical entity that accepts electrons transferred to it from another compound.
A. Macromolecule   B. Agrobiology   C. Electron Acceptor   D. Histology

219. ____ The study of mammals.
A. Mammalogy   B. Xanthophyll   C. Barr body   D. Deoxyribose

220. ____ Another term for adrenaline.
A. Transcription   B. Translation   C. Epinephrine   D. Endocrine System

221. ____ The reduced genetic diversity that results when a population is descended from a small number of colonizing ancestors.
A. Trophic level   B. Primase   C. Founder Effect   D. Biomass

222. ____ An undifferentiated cell of a multicellular organism that can give rise to indefinitely more cells of the same type.
A. Endangered Species   B. Stem cell   C. Active Transport   D. Mole

223. ____ Refers to the number of elements to which it can connect.
A. Valence   B. Heterosis   C. Pollination   D. Effector

224. ____ Study of living organisms.
A. Electron Acceptor   B. Biology   C. Mammalogy   D. Conservation Biology

225. ____ The highest range of electron energies in which electrons are normally present at absolute zero temperature.
A. Chromosome   B. Valence band   C. Behavioral ecology   D. Chemical bond

226. ____ A very large molecule, such as protein, commonly created by polymerization of smaller subunits (monomers).
A. Messenger RNA   B. Macromolecule   C. Deoxyribose   D. Denitrification

227. ____ The continuation of the spinal cord within the skull, forming the lowest part of the brainstem and containing control centers for the heart and lungs.
A. B cell   B. Cryobiology   C. Medulla   D. Lacteal

228. ____ The branch of biology concerned with the effects of outer space on living organisms and the search for extraterrestrial life
A. Astrobiology   B. Atom   C. Vesicle   D. Effector

229. ____ The science of drug action on biological systems.
A. Chromosome   B. Pharmacology   C. Deoxyribonucleic Acid   D. Anatomy

230. ____ A form of intermediate inheritance in which one allele for a specific trait is not completely expressed over its paired allele.
A. Human Nutrition   B. Polygene   C. Incomplete Dominance   D. Ecosystem

231. ____ A chemical substance consisting of two or more different chemically bonded chemical elements, with a fixed ratio determining the composition.
A. Interleukin   B. Autoimmunity   C. Chemical compound   D. Biophysics

232. ____ Process of reproduction involving a single parent that results in offspring that are genetically identical to the parent.
A. Exocytosis   B. Effector   C. Electrochemical Gradient   D. Asexual Reproduction

233. ____ A hierarchical series of organisms each dependent on the next as a source of food.
A. Anticodon   B. Chloride   C. Biogeography   D. Food Chain

234. ____ Refers to the provision of essential nutrients necessary to support human life and health.
A. Human Nutrition   B. Endoplasmic Reticulum   C. Ecdysone   D. Biogeography

235. ____ The ecological state of a species being unique to a defined geographic location, such as an island, nation, country or other defined zone, or habitat type.
A. Macromolecule   B. Mammalogy   C. Endemism   D. Biogeography

236. ____ A lymphatic capillary that absorbs dietary fats in the villi of the small intestine.
A. Incomplete Dominance   B. Binary fission   C. Translation   D. Lacteal

237. ____ The theory that all living things are made up of cells.
A. Myofibril   B. Cell theory   C. Epicotyl   D. Interleukin

238. ____ The complete transfer of valence electron(s) between atoms. it is a type of chemical bond that generates two oppositely charged ions.
A. Endoplasmic Reticulum   B. Pathobiology   C. Ionic Bond   D. Molecular physics

239. ____ The branch of biology that relates to the animal kingdom, including the structure, embryology, evolution, classification, habits, and distribution of all animals.
A. Endosperm   B. Zoology   C. Interleukin   D. Centroid

240. ____ A plant hormone.
A. Ganglion   B. Cell nucleus   C. External Fertilization   D. Abscisic acid

241. ____ The study of microscopic organisms, such as bacteria, viruses, archaea, fungi and protozoa.
A. Microbiology   B. Ectoderm   C. Deoxyribose   D. Cholesterol

242. ____ Rain containing acids that form in the atmosphere when industrial gas emissions (especially sulfur dioxide and nitrogen oxides) combine with water.
A. Biocatalysts   B. Valence band   C. B cell   D. Acid precipitation

243. ____ The study of the transformation of energy in living organisms.
A. Chemical kinetics   B. Genome   C. Bioenergetics   D. Biophysics

244. ____ A plant that grows harmlessly upon another plant and derives its moisture and nutrients from the air, rain, and sometimes from debris accumulating around it.
A. Environmental Biology   B. Endemism   C. Microbiology   D. Epiphyte

245. ____ the sequence of reactions by which most living cells generate energy during the process of aerobic respiration.
A. Macromolecule   B. Barr body   C. Krebs Cycle   D. Microbiology

246. ____ A membrane-bound organelle which is present in all plant and fungal cells and some protist, animal and bacterial cells.
A. Vacuole   B. Epinephrine   C. Environmental Biology   D. Invertebrate

247. ____ Work to convert light energy of the sun into sugars that can be used by cells.
A. Gular   B. Ornithology   C. Systematics   D. Chloroplast

248. ____ Refers to two solutions having the same osmotic pressure across a semipermeable membrane.
A. Transcription   B. Isotonic Solution   C. Effector   D. Electron Transport Chain

249. Plasma cells, also called plasma b cells, plasmocytes, plasmacytes, or effector b cells, are white blood cells that secrete large volumes of antibodies.
A. Biomass   B. Effector Cell   C. Natural Selection   D. Cell

250. A branch of zoology that concerns the study of birds.
A. Mass Density   B. Ornithology   C. Immune Response   D. Organ

251. Usually defined as a chemical reaction that involves the loss of a water molecule from the reacting molecule.
A. Valence electron   B. Dehydration Reaction   C. Myofibril   D. Active Transport

252. The study of the microscopic anatomy of cells and tissues of plants and animals.
A. Endoderm   B. Element   C. Zoology   D. Histology

253. The scientific study of nature and of earth's biodiversity with the aim of protecting species, their habitats, and ecosystems from excessive rates of extinction.
A. Medulla   B. Primase   C. Chemical kinetics   D. Conservation Biology

254. Single-cell microscopic organisms which lack a true nucleus. they represent one of the three domains.
A. Chemical kinetics   B. DNA Sequencing   C. Polygene   D. Bacteria

255. A unit of concentration measuring the number of moles of a solute per liter of solution.
A. Vacuole   B. DNA Sequencing   C. Endocrine System   D. Molarity

256. A chemical reaction in which the standard change in free energy is positive, and energy is absorbed
A. Centrosome   B. Mass Density   C. Microbiology   D. Endergonic Reaction

257. Organic molecules that serve as the monomers, or subunits, of nucleic acids like DNA (deoxyribonucleic acid) and RNA (ribonucleic acid).
A. Barr body   B. Epicotyl   C. Electron Donor   D. Nucleotide

258. RNA consisting of folded molecules that transport amino acids from the cytoplasm of a cell to a ribosome.
A. Founder Effect   B. Transfer RNA   C. Heterosis   D. Endosymbiotic Theory

259. Organisms that produce an egg composed of shell and membranes that creates a protected environment in which the embryo can develop out of water
A. Testosterone   B. Blastocyst   C. Amniotes   D. Organism

260. An inner layer of cells in the cortex of a root and of some stems, surrounding a vascular bundle.
A. Transcription   B. Endodermis   C. Ganglion   D. Cholesterol

261. A cluster (functional group) of nerve cell bodies in a centralized nervous system.
A. Histology   B. Species   C. Uracil   D. Ganglion

262. An interdisciplinary science that applies the approaches and methods of physics to study biological systems.
A. Ecosystem   B. Deoxyribonucleic Acid   C. Vacuole   D. Biophysics

263. A heterocyclic compound of carbon, nitrogen, oxygen, and hydrogen. it forms ions and salts known as urates and acid urates, such as ammonium acid urate.
A. Uric acid   B. Polygene   C. Chromosome   D. Gular

264. Any of the elongated contractile threads found in striated muscle cells.
A. Mass Number   B. Insulin   C. Xanthophyll   D. Myofibril

265. A threadlike strand of DNA in the cell nucleus that carries the genes in a linear order.
A. Chromosome   B. Primase   C. Urine   D. Nucleotide

266. ____ The first step of gene expression, in which a segment of DNA is copied into RNA (mRNA) by the enzyme RNA polymerase.
A. Deciduous   B. Transcription   C. Histology   D. Epiphyte

267. ____ A kind of swallowing cell, which means it functions by literally swallowing up other particles or smaller cells.
A. Uracil   B. Genetics   C. Macrophage   D. Endergonic Reaction

268. ____ The ecological region at the lowest level of a body of water such as an ocean or a lake.
A. External Fertilization   B. Aerobiology   C. Benthic zone   D. Ornithology

269. ____ Organic matter derived from living, or recently living organisms.
A. Biomass   B. Basal body   C. Lacteal   D. Autoimmunity

270. ____ Variations in a phenotype among individuals carrying a genotype.
A. Conservation Biology   B. Electric Potential   C. Expressivity   D. Biochemistry

271. ____ The site of oxidative phosphorylation in eukaryotes.
A. Nucleotide   B. Aerobiology   C. Electron Transport Chain   D. Cell

272. ____ The decoding of genetic instructions for making proteins.
A. Translation   B. Nucleotide   C. Endergonic Reaction   D. Ganglion

273. ____ A organism in which internal physiological sources of heat are of relatively small or quite negligible importance in controlling body temperature. "cold blooded".
A. Bile   B. Endoplasmic Reticulum   C. Enzyme   D. Ectotherm

274. ____ One cell dividing into two identical daughter cells.
A. Barr body   B. Thymine   C. Transcription   D. Binary fission

275. ____ A class of organic compounds containing an amino group and a carboxylic acid group
A. Amino acid   B. Valence electron   C. Polymer   D. Synthetic Biology

276. ____ The chemical name for DNA.
A. Biome   B. Xanthophyll   C. Anticodon   D. Deoxyribonucleic Acid

277. ____ The study of parasites, their hosts, and the relationship between them.
A. Thymine   B. Parasitology   C. Translation   D. Paleontology

278. ____ Variations of genomes between members of species, or between groups of species thriving in different parts of the world as a result of genetic mutation.
A. Biophysics   B. Genetic Variation   C. Membrane Potential   D. Neurotransmitter

279. ____ Stereoisomers that are non-superimposable mirror images. a molecule with 1 chiral carbon atom exists as 2 stereoisomers termed enantiomers.
A. Xanthophyll   B. Natural Selection   C. Enantiomer   D. Virology

280. ____ Biological molecules (proteins) that act as catalysts and help complex reactions occur everywhere in life.
A. Lacteal   B. Enzyme   C. Astrobiology   D. Ligament

281. ____ The ecological state of a species being unique to a defined geographic location, such as an island, nation, country or other defined zone, or habitat type.
A. Adenylate cyclase   B. Biophysics   C. Endemic Species   D. Translation

282. ____ The amount of work needed to move a unit charge from a reference point to a specific point against an electric field.
A. Krebs Cycle   B. Microbiology   C. Effector Cell   D. Electric Potential

283. ____ The region of an embryo or seedling stem above the cotyledon.
A. Epicotyl   B. Vesicle   C. Basal body   D. Centrosome

284. ____ A dark green to yellowish brown fluid, produced by the liver of most vertebrates, that aids the digestion of lipids in the small intestine.
A. Valence band   B. Bile   C. Microbiology   D. Barr body

285. ____ The study of viruses-submicroscopic, parasitic particles of genetic material contained in a protein coat and virus-like agents.
A. Dendrite   B. Thymine   C. Virology   D. Neurotransmitter

286. ____ A species of atoms having the same number of protons in their atomic nuclei.
A. Endosperm   B. Element   C. Heterosis   D. Agrobiology

287. ____ The collection of glands that produce hormones that regulate metabolism, growth and development, tissue function, sexual function, reproduction, sleep, and mood.
A. Electron Donor   B. Exon   C. Endocrine System   D. Valence

288. ____ A chemical entity that donates electrons to another compound.
A. Genetics   B. Electron Donor   C. Desmosome   D. Denitrification

289. ____ A microbially facilitated process of nitrate reduction that may ultimately produce molecular nitrogen.
A. Benthic zone   B. Denitrification   C. Ganglion   D. Anticodon

290. ____ The tendency of a crossbred individual to show qualities superior to those of both parents.
A. Bacteria   B. Heterosis   C. Biochemistry   D. Environmental Biology

291. ____ The study of the history of life on earth as reflected in the fossil record. fossils are the remains or traces of organisms.
A. Dendrite   B. Thymine   C. Enantiomer   D. Paleontology

292. ____ The vascular tissue in plants that conducts water and dissolved nutrients upward from the root and also helps to form the woody element in the stem.
A. Insulin   B. Xylem   C. Electron Shell   D. Biophysics

293. ____ An electron shell is the outside part of an atom around the atomic nucleus. it is a group of atomic orbitals with the same value of the principal quantum number n.
A. Chemical compound   B. Macrophage   C. Ornithology   D. Electron Shell

294. ____ The application of concepts and methods of biology to solve real world problems.
A. Bioengineering   B. Uric acid   C. Desmosome   D. Effector Cell

295. ____ A gene whose individual effect on a phenotype is too small to be observed, but which can act together with others to produce observable variation.
A. Mucous Membrane   B. Polygene   C. Mammalogy   D. Parallel Evolution

296. ____ Means "falling off at maturity" or "tending to fall off", and it is typically used in order to refer to trees or shrubs that lose their leaves seasonally.
A. Deciduous   B. Abscission   C. Ornithology   D. Uterus

297. ____ The total number of protons and neutrons (together known as nucleons) in an atomic nucleus
A. Microevolution   B. Systematics   C. Mass Number   D. Electron Shell

298. ____ One of the four nucleobases in the nucleic acid of RNA that are represented by the letters a, g, c and u.
A. Whole Genome Sequencing   B. Hormone   C. Uracil   D. Wood

299. _____ An organic lipid molecule that is biosynthesized by all animal cells because it is an essential structural component of all animal cell membranes.
A. Endosperm   B. Cholesterol   C. Enzyme   D. Insulin

300. _____ Helps keep blood sugar level from getting too high (hyperglycemia) or too low (hypoglycemia).
A. Testosterone   B. Electron Microscope   C. Insulin   D. Endemism

From the words provided for each clue, provide the letter of the word which best matches the clue.

1. __C__ Large superfamily of motor proteins that move along actin filaments, while hydrolyzing ATP.
   A. Reproduction   B. Chemical reaction   C. Myosin   D. Whole Genome Sequencing

2. __C__ Nutrients that provide calories or energy. nutrients are substances needed for growth, metabolism, and for other body functions.
   A. Membrane Potential   B. Psychobiology   C. Macronutrient   D. Mucous Membrane

3. __C__ The modern form of the metric system and is the most widely used system of measurement.
   A. Epidemiology   B. Meiosis   C. International System   D. Endergonic Reaction

4. __D__ The stock of different genes in an interbreeding population.
   A. Translation   B. Mole   C. Prokaryote   D. Gene Pool

5. __D__ A process in nature in which organisms possessing certain genotypic characteristics that make them better adjusted to an environment tend to survive.
   A. Agriculture   B. Valence shell   C. Bacteria   D. Natural Selection

6. __C__ The female reproductive cell (gamete) in oogamous organisms.
   A. Abscisic acid   B. Independent Assortment   C. Egg   D. Endangered Species

7. __D__ A dark green to yellowish brown fluid, produced by the liver of most vertebrates, that aids the digestion of lipids in the small intestine.
   A. Food Chain   B. Mass Density   C. Acid precipitation   D. Bile

8. __B__ Component of the blood that functions in the immune system. also known as a leukocyte.
   A. Chemical bond   B. White Blood Cell   C. Messenger RNA   D. Bioinformatics

9. __C__ The branch of biology that studies the development of gametes (sex cells), fertilization, and development of embryos and fetuses.
   A. International System   B. Stem cell   C. Embryology   D. Darwinian Fitness

10. __D__ The science of diagnosing and managing plant diseases.
    A. Stem cell   B. Biogeography   C. Neurotransmitter   D. Phytopathology

11. __C__ An epithelial tissue that secretes mucus and that lines many body cavities and tubular organs including the gut and respiratory passages.
    A. Exon   B. Lacteal   C. Mucous Membrane   D. Evolutionary Biology

12. __B__ An enzyme that synthesizes short RNA sequences called primers.
    A. Ecological Efficiency   B. Primase   C. Endergonic Reaction   D. Dendrite

13. __D__ Of or pertaining to the throat.
    A. Biodiversity   B. Cloning   C. Valence electron   D. Gular

14. __D__ The application of the principles of biology to the study of physiological, genetic, and developmental mechanisms of behavior in humans and other animals.
    A. Population Ecology   B. Fetus   C. Myosin   D. Psychobiology

15. __B__ A sub-field of ecology that deals with the dynamics of species populations and how these populations interact with the environment.
    A. Meiosis   B. Population Ecology   C. Immune Response   D. Nucleotide

16. __A__ Study of living organisms.
A. Biology   B. Ionic Bond   C. Mole   D. Biodiversity

17. __C__ The study of mammals.
A. Mass Balance   B. Evolutionary Biology   C. Mammalogy   D. Centrosome

18. __D__ A microscopic single celled organism that has no distinct nucleus
A. Uterus   B. Parasitology   C. Population Genetics   D. Prokaryote

19. __A__ Refers to genetically determined structures or attributes that have apparently lost most or all their ancestral function in a given species.
A. Vestigiality   B. Valence shell   C. Endemism   D. Organism

20. __A__ A technique used in molecular biology to amplify a single copy or a few copies of a piece of DNA across several orders of magnitude.
A. Polymerase Chain Reaction   B. Chromosome   C. Enantiomer   D. Polyploidy

21. __C__ One of the proteins into which actomyosin can be split; can exist in either a globular or a fibrous form.
A. Action potential   B. Chromosome   C. Actin   D. Gene

22. __A__ The study of plant nutrition and growth especially to increase crop yield
A. Agrobiology   B. T Cell   C. Virology   D. Electron Acceptor

23. __D__ Animals, like flatworms and jellyfish, that have no body cavity (coelom).
A. Endosperm   B. Epidemiology   C. Lacteal   D. Acoelomate

24. __C__ Any of various molecules that can accept one or two electrons from one molecule and donating them to another in the process of electron transport.
A. Isomer   B. Bionics   C. Electron Carrier   D. Cryobiology

25. __C__ Glands that secrete their products, hormones, directly into the blood rather than through a duct.
A. Membrane Potential   B. Endemism   C. Endocrine Gland   D. Ecological Niche

26. __A__ A part of an organism that is typically self-contained and has a specific vital function, such as the heart or liver in humans.
A. Organ   B. Carbonate   C. Lipoprotein   D. Darwinian Fitness

27. __B__ Stereoisomers that are non-superimposable mirror images. a molecule with 1 chiral carbon atom exists as 2 stereoisomers termed enantiomers.
A. Mucous Membrane   B. Enantiomer   C. Zoology   D. Mole

28. __D__ The study of organic particles, such as bacteria, fungal spores, very small insects, pollen grains and viruses, which are passively transported by the air.
A. Ecotype   B. Biomechanics   C. Anatomy   D. Aerobiology

29. __D__ The study of viruses-submicroscopic, parasitic particles of genetic material contained in a protein coat and virus-like agents.
A. Translation   B. Parasitology   C. Myosin   D. Virology

30. __B__ Biological molecules (proteins) that act as catalysts and help complex reactions occur everywhere in life.
A. Ethology   B. Enzyme   C. Acid precipitation   D. Electron Microscope

31. __B__ A molecule that can be bonded to other identical molecules to form a polymer.
A. Stem cell   B. Monomer   C. Hydrocarbon   D. Parasitology

32. __D__ The study of the structure and function of biological systems by means of the methods of "mechanics."
A. Messenger RNA   B. Aerobic   C. Chromosome   D. Biomechanics

33. __B__ A organism in which internal physiological sources of heat are of relatively small or quite negligible importance in controlling body temperature. "cold blooded".
A. External Fertilization   B. Ectotherm   C. Metaphase   D. Acoelomate

34. __D__ A type of microscope that uses a beam of electrons to create an image of the specimen. it is capable of much higher magnifications.
A. Valence band   B. Agriculture   C. Wood   D. Electron Microscope

35. __C__ A very large molecule, such as protein, commonly created by polymerization of smaller subunits (monomers).
A. Enzyme   B. Ecotype   C. Macromolecule   D. Independent Assortment

36. __C__ The application of computer technology to the management of biological information.
A. Absorption   B. Active Transport   C. Bioinformatics   D. Enantiomer

37. __B__ A colorless cell which circulates in the blood and body fluids and is involved in counteracting foreign substances and disease; a white (blood) cell.
A. External Fertilization   B. Leukocyte   C. Membrane Potential   D. Mucous Membrane

38. __D__ How your body recognizes and defends itself against bacteria, viruses, and substances that appear foreign and harmful.
A. Population Genetics   B. Genetics   C. Antibiotic   D. Immune Response

39. __B__ Threatened by factors such as habitat loss, hunting, disease and climate change, and usually have declining populations or a very limited range.
A. Endotherm   B. Endangered Species   C. Ethology   D. Bacteria

40. __A__ Helps keep blood sugar level from getting too high (hyperglycemia) or too low (hypoglycemia).
A. Insulin   B. Desmosome   C. Enantiomer   D. Plasmolysis

41. __C__ A class of drug used to kill bacteria.
A. Plasmolysis   B. Mass Density   C. Antibiotic   D. Enzyme

42. __D__ A hierarchical series of organisms each dependent on the next as a source of food.
A. Valence band   B. Carbonate   C. SI units   D. Food Chain

43. __B__ A group of cytokines (secreted proteins and signal molecules) that were first seen to be expressed by white blood cells (leukocytes)
A. Nucleic Acid Sequence   B. Interleukin   C. Evolutionary Biology   D. Astrobiology

44. __A__ One of the four main nucleobases found in the nucleic acids DNA and RNA, the others being adenine, cytosine, and thymine.
A. Guanine   B. Dehydration Reaction   C. Darwinian Fitness   D. Ganglion

45. __A__ A chemical synapse formed by the contact between a motor neuron and a muscle fiber.
A. Neuromuscular Junction   B. Electron Microscope   C. Anatomy   D. Zoology

46. __C__ An inner layer of cells in the cortex of a root and of some stems, surrounding a vascular bundle.
A. Deciduous   B. Biodiversity   C. Endodermis   D. Plant Nutrition

47. __C__ The study of populations of organisms, especially the regulation of population size, life history traits such as clutch size, and extinction.
A. Chloride   B. Amino acid   C. Population Biology   D. Endergonic Reaction

48. __D__ The "control room" for the cell. the nucleus gives out all the orders.
A. Aerobic   B. Ethology   C. Action potential   D. Cell nucleus

49. __A__ The study of the distribution of species and ecosystems in geographic space and through time.
A. Biogeography  B. Parallel Evolution  C. Active Transport  D. Bile

50. __D__ Sperm units with egg in the open, rather than inside the body of the parents
A. Abscisic acid  B. Ionic Bond  C. Bionics  D. External Fertilization

51. __C__ The hereditary material in humans and almost all other organisms.
A. Zygote  B. Endotherm  C. DNA  D. Cell theory

52. __B__ A gradient of electrochemical potential, usually for an ion that can move across a membrane.
A. Hydrocarbon  B. Electrochemical Gradient  C. Independent Assortment  D. Psychobiology

53. __A__ The variety of life in the world or in a habitat or ecosystem.
A. Biodiversity  B. Ecotype  C. Endemic Species  D. Mammalogy

54. __A__ The highest range of electron energies in which electrons are normally present at absolute zero temperature.
A. Valence band  B. Bile  C. Psychobiology  D. Ethology

55. __D__ Rain containing acids that form in the atmosphere when industrial gas emissions (especially sulfur dioxide and nitrogen oxides) combine with water.
A. Amino acid  B. Absorption  C. Endergonic Reaction  D. Acid precipitation

56. __A__ An undifferentiated cell of a multicellular organism that can give rise to indefinitely more cells of the same type.
A. Stem cell  B. Ecosystem  C. Endergonic Reaction  D. Amniotes

57. __D__ A measure of the tendency of an atom to attract a bonding pair of electrons. the Pauling scale is the most commonly used.
A. Population Biology  B. Chemical equilibrium  C. Physiology  D. Electronegativity

58. __D__ Any member of two classes of chemical compounds derived from carbonic acid or carbon dioxide.
A. Chemical kinetics  B. Membrane Potential  C. Symbiogenesis  D. Carbonate

59. __A__ Any of the elongated contractile threads found in striated muscle cells.
A. Myofibril  B. Endemism  C. Neuromuscular Junction  D. Mitosis

60. __D__ Also known as a macula adhaerens, is a cell structure specialized for cell to cell adhesion.
A. Chemical equilibrium  B. Actin  C. Active Transport  D. Desmosome

61. __D__ The study of parasites, their hosts, and the relationship between them.
A. Agrobiology  B. Ion  C. Biomechanics  D. Parasitology

62. __D__ The branch of biology concerned with the relations between organisms and their environment.
A. Embryo Sac  B. Organ  C. Endocrine System  D. Environmental Biology

63. __B__ Usually defined as a chemical reaction that involves the loss of a water molecule from the reacting molecule.
A. Translation  B. Dehydration Reaction  C. Deoxyribose  D. Phytopathology

64. __D__ A molecule with the same chemical formula as another molecule, but with a different chemical structure.
A. Biomechanics  B. Microevolution  C. Whole Genome Sequencing  D. Isomer

65. __C__ Giving birth to one of its kind, sexually or asexually.
A. Neurotransmitter  B. Amino acid  C. Reproduction  D. Active site

66. __B__ A lymphatic capillary that absorbs dietary fats in the villi of the small intestine.
A. Synthetic Biology  B. Lacteal  C. Molecular biology  D. DNA

67. __D__ A type of cell division that reduces the number of chromosomes in the parent cell by half and produces four gamete cells.
A. Gular   B. Organ   C. Interleukin   D. Meiosis

68. __D__ The process of reversing the charge across a cell membrane (usually a neuron), so causing an action potential.
A. Interleukin   B. Active site   C. SI units   D. Depolarization

69. __C__ The organ in the lower body of a woman or female mammal where offspring are conceived and in which they gestate before birth; the womb.
A. Nucleolus   B. White Blood Cell   C. Uterus   D. Basal body

70. __B__ A measure of the potential energy in water as well as the difference between the potential in a water sample and pure water.
A. DNA   B. Water Potential   C. Endocrine System   D. Active site

71. __D__ A cluster (functional group) of nerve cell bodies in a centralized nervous system.
A. Ectoderm   B. Epiphyte   C. Lacteal   D. Ganglion

72. __A__ An organelle formed from a centriole, and a short cylindrical array of microtubules.
A. Basal body   B. Immune Response   C. Cell theory   D. Microevolution

73. __C__ The female gametophyte of a seed plant, within which the embryo develops.
A. Polyploidy   B. Agrobiology   C. Embryo Sac   D. Membrane Potential

74. __D__ Depending on free oxygen or air.
A. Interleukin   B. Denitrification   C. Microevolution   D. Aerobic

75. __C__ The subfield of biology that studies the evolutionary processes that produced the diversity of life on earth starting from a single origin of life.
A. Parasitology   B. Cryobiology   C. Evolutionary Biology   D. Hadron

76. __D__ An application of conservation of mass to the analysis of physical systems.
A. Organism   B. Lepton   C. Mole   D. Mass Balance

77. __D__ A compound of chlorine with another element or group, especially a salt of the anion or an organic compound with chlorine bonded to an alkyl group.
A. Biology   B. Evolutionary Biology   C. T Cell   D. Chloride

78. __A__ The branch of morphology that deals with the structure of animals
A. Anatomy   B. Water Potential   C. Cryobiology   D. Ecosystem

79. __C__ An elementary, half-integer spin particle that does not undergo strong interactions.
A. Zygote   B. Mass Number   C. Lepton   D. Electron Donor

80. __B__ In organic chemistry, a hydrocarbon is an organic compound consisting entirely of hydrogen and carbon.
A. Myosin   B. Hydrocarbon   C. Prokaryote   D. Agrobiology

81. __B__ The genetic contribution of an individual to the next generation's gene pool relative to the average for the population.
A. Ecotype   B. Darwinian Fitness   C. Endemism   D. Electron

82. __C__ Means "falling off at maturity" or "tending to fall off", and it is typically used in order to refer to trees or shrubs that lose their leaves seasonally.
A. Uterus   B. Protein   C. Deciduous   D. Vestigiality

83. __B__ A microbially facilitated process of nitrate reduction that may ultimately produce molecular nitrogen.
A. Whole Genome Sequencing   B. Denitrification   C. Zygote   D. Ionic Bond

84. __B__ A chemical reaction in which the standard change in free energy is positive, and energy is absorbed
A. B cell   B. Endergonic Reaction   C. Absorption   D. Microevolution

85. __B__ One of the three primary germ layers in the very early human embryo. the other two layers are the ectoderm (outside layer) and mesoderm (middle layer).
A. Osmosis   B. Endoderm   C. Denitrification   D. Virology

86. __D__ Single-cell microscopic organisms which lack a true nucleus. they represent one of the three domains.
A. Macromolecule   B. Valence electron   C. Agrobiology   D. Bacteria

87. __A__ The inner layer of the stems of woody plants; composed of xylem.
A. Wood   B. Denitrification   C. Effector Cell   D. Aerobic

88. __D__ The branch of biology concerned with the effects of outer space on living organisms and the search for extraterrestrial life
A. Active Transport   B. Valence   C. Physiology   D. Astrobiology

89. __D__ The form of rna in which genetic information transcribed from dna as a sequence of bases is transferred to a ribosome.
A. Deciduous   B. Ecosystem   C. Biocatalysts   D. Messenger RNA

90. __D__ A form of active transport in which a cell transports molecules into the cell.
A. Dehydration Reaction   B. Genetics   C. Reproduction   D. Endocytosis

91. __C__ A tissue produced inside the seeds of most of the flowering plants around the time of fertilization.
A. Stem cell   B. Messenger RNA   C. Endosperm   D. Effector Cell

92. __C__ Virus that infects and multiplies within bacteria.
A. Darwinian Fitness   B. Parasitology   C. Bacteriophage   D. Electron Microscope

93. __A__ In cell biology, an organelle that is the main place where cell microtubules get organized. they occur only in plant and animal cells.
A. Centrosome   B. Agrobiology   C. Endosperm   D. Myosin

94. __C__ The branch of biology that studies the effects of low temperatures on living things within earth's cryosphere or in science.
A. Darwinian Fitness   B. Facultative Anaerobe   C. Cryobiology   D. Electron

95. __B__ Density is mass per volume.
A. Ecological Efficiency   B. Mass Density   C. Active site   D. Myosin

96. __D__ Catalysis in living systems. in biological processes, natural catalysts, such as protein enzymes, perform chemical transformations on organic compounds.
A. Lepton   B. Bacteriophage   C. Ganglion   D. Biocatalysts

97. __D__ A laboratory process that determines the complete DNA sequence of an organism's genome at a single time.
A. Chemical bond   B. Ectoderm   C. Active Transport   D. Whole Genome Sequencing

98. __A__ The study and analysis of the patterns, causes, and effects of health and disease conditions in defined populations.
A. Epidemiology   B. Plasmolysis   C. Whole Genome Sequencing   D. Parasitology

99. __A__ An atom or molecule with a net electric charge due to the loss or gain of one or more electrons.
A. Ion   B. Population Biology   C. Gene   D. Jejunum

100. __C__ The principle, originated by Gregor Mendel, stating that when two or more characteristics are inherited, individual hereditary factors assort independently.
A. Centrosome   B. Enantiomer   C. Independent Assortment   D. Endemic Species

From the words provided for each clue, provide the letter of the word which best matches the clue.

101. __D__ Work to convert light energy of the sun into sugars that can be used by cells.
A. Primase   B. Cloning   C. DNA   D. Chloroplast

102. __C__ The primary female sex hormone. it is responsible for the development and regulation of the female reproductive system and secondary sex characteristics.
A. Pollination   B. Jejunum   C. Estrogen   D. Herpetology

103. __B__ Any of various molecules that can accept one or two electrons from one molecule and donating them to another in the process of electron transport.
A. Barr body   B. Electron Carrier   C. Bacteriophage   D. Epinephrine

104. __B__ The act of transferring pollen grains from the male anther of a flower to the female stigma.
A. Myosin   B. Pollination   C. Macrophage   D. Internal Fertilization

105. __B__ Describes the efficiency with which energy is transferred from one trophic level to the next.
A. Herpetology   B. Ecological Efficiency   C. Chemistry   D. Epinephrine

106. __A__ The double helix is unwound and each strand acts as a template for the next strand. bases are matched to synthesize the new partner strands.
A. DNA Replication   B. Gene   C. SI units   D. Sexual Reproduction

107. __A__ A threadlike strand of DNA in the cell nucleus that carries the genes in a linear order.
A. Chromosome   B. Heterosis   C. Entomology   D. Translation

108. __C__ Also known as a macula adhaerens, is a cell structure specialized for cell to cell adhesion.
A. Pathobiology   B. Marine Biology   C. Desmosome   D. Medulla

109. __C__ A class of drug used to kill bacteria.
A. Environmental Biology   B. Molecular biology   C. Antibiotic   D. Myofibril

110. __C__ A form of terrestrial locomotion where an organism moves by means of its two rear limbs or legs.
A. Pathobiology   B. Abscisic acid   C. Bipedal   D. Plasmolysis

111. __D__ An interaction of living things and non-living things in a physical environment.
A. Uracil   B. Molecule   C. Macroevolution   D. Ecosystem

112. __B__ The study of heredity
A. Herpetology   B. Genetics   C. Mass Balance   D. DNA Sequencing

113. __D__ Known as chemical messengers, are endogenous chemicals that enable neurotransmission.
A. Metaphase   B. Marine Biology   C. Vesicle   D. Neurotransmitter

114. __B__ A biological agent that reproduces inside the cells of living hosts.
A. Interleukin   B. Virus   C. Biomechanics   D. Urine

115. __D__ The study of populations of organisms, especially the regulation of population size, life history traits such as clutch size, and extinction.
A. Biochemistry   B. Bacteria   C. Evolution   D. Population Biology

116. __A__ The study of the evolutionary basis for animal behavior due to ecological pressures.
A. Behavioral ecology   B. Habitat   C. Bile   D. Chromosome

117. __A__ The science of drug action on biological systems.
A. Pharmacology   B. Ichthyology   C. Endangered Species   D. Marine Biology

118. __D__ A group of cytokines (secreted proteins and signal molecules) that were first seen to be expressed by white blood cells (leukocytes)
A. Jejunum   B. Active Transport   C. Monomer   D. Interleukin

119. __D__ Catalysis in living systems. in biological processes, natural catalysts, such as protein enzymes, perform chemical transformations on organic compounds.
A. Chromosome   B. Cryobiology   C. Absorption spectrum   D. Biocatalysts

120. __D__ Biological molecules (proteins) that act as catalysts and help complex reactions occur everywhere in life.
A. Endocrine System   B. Wobble Base Pair   C. Abyssal zone   D. Enzyme

121. __A__ An interdisciplinary branch of biology and engineering.
A. Synthetic Biology   B. Gene Pool   C. Lipid   D. Ecological Niche

122. __B__ An application of conservation of mass to the analysis of physical systems.
A. Nucleic Acid Sequence   B. Mass Balance   C. Deoxyribonucleic Acid   D. Synthetic Biology

123. __B__ Contraction of the protoplast of a plant cell as a result of loss of water from the cell.
A. Endocrine Gland   B. Plasmolysis   C. Deoxyribonucleic Acid   D. External Fertilization

124. __B__ The total number of protons and neutrons (together known as nucleons) in an atomic nucleus
A. Endodermis   B. Mass Number   C. Desmosome   D. Valence electron

125. __D__ The smallest particle in a chemical element or compound that has the chemical properties of that element or compound.
A. Macroevolution   B. Translation   C. Antibiotic   D. Molecule

126. __A__ An undifferentiated cell of a multicellular organism that can give rise to indefinitely more cells of the same type.
A. Stem cell   B. Mammalogy   C. Astrobiology   D. Barr body

127. __D__ One of the four nucleobases in the nucleic acid of RNA that are represented by the letters a, g, c and u.
A. Mass Balance   B. Ecological Pyramid   C. Desmosome   D. Uracil

128. __C__ A unit of concentration measuring the number of moles of a solute per liter of solution.
A. Ecological Efficiency   B. Pollination   C. Molarity   D. Desmosome

129. __B__ Of or pertaining to the throat.
A. Interleukin   B. Gular   C. Chemical kinetics   D. Gene Pool

130. __C__ A gradient of electrochemical potential, usually for an ion that can move across a membrane.
A. Gular   B. Acoelomate   C. Electrochemical Gradient   D. Virus

131. __A__ A compound of chlorine with another element or group, especially a salt of the anion or an organic compound with chlorine bonded to an alkyl group.
A. Chloride   B. Action potential   C. Linked Genes   D. Deciduous

132. __B__ The scientific study of organisms in the ocean or other marine bodies of water.
A. Behavioral ecology   B. Marine Biology   C. Zygote   D. Medulla

133. __B__ Giving birth to one of its kind, sexually or asexually.
A. Messenger RNA   B. Reproduction   C. Endemic Species   D. Mass Balance

134. __D__ The collection of glands that produce hormones that regulate metabolism, growth and development, tissue function, sexual function, reproduction, sleep, and mood.
A. Molecular biology   B. Lipid   C. Gular   D. Endocrine System

135. __B__ A succession of letters that indicate the order of nucleotides within a DNA (using GACT or RNA (GACU) molecule.
A. Electronegativity   B. Nucleic Acid Sequence   C. Bacteria   D. Protein

136. __D__ The science of diagnosing and managing plant diseases.
A. Gene Pool   B. Phloem   C. Bioengineering   D. Phytopathology

137. __A__ Organisms that produce an egg composed of shell and membranes that creates a protected environment in which the embryo can develop out of water
A. Amniotes   B. Absorption spectrum   C. Ecdysone   D. Bioengineering

138. __C__ A measure of the potential energy in water as well as the difference between the potential in a water sample and pure water.
A. Primase   B. T Cell   C. Water Potential   D. Integrative Biology

139. __C__ A fluid or air-filled cavity or sac.
A. Cloning   B. Lipid   C. Vesicle   D. Hermaphrodite

140. __A__ One of the four main nucleobases found in the nucleic acids DNA and RNA, the others being adenine, cytosine, and thymine.
A. Guanine   B. SI units   C. Amniotes   D. Electric Potential

141. __A__ The study or practice of pathology with greater emphasis on the biological than on the medical aspects.
A. Pathobiology   B. Active Transport   C. B cell   D. Chromosome

142. __B__ The si unit of measurement used to measure the number of things, usually atoms or molecules.
A. Medulla   B. Mole   C. Xanthophyll   D. Osmosis

143. __A__ Large biomolecules, or macromolecules, consisting of one or more long chains of amino acid residues.
A. Protein   B. Herpetology   C. Population Biology   D. Macronutrient

144. __D__ The branch of biology that studies the development of gametes (sex cells), fertilization, and development of embryos and fetuses.
A. Pollination   B. Prokaryote   C. DNA   D. Embryology

145. __D__ A type of cell division that reduces the number of chromosomes in the parent cell by half and produces four gamete cells.
A. T Cell   B. Neurotransmitter   C. Electron Acceptor   D. Meiosis

146. __A__ A type of microscope that uses a beam of electrons to create an image of the specimen. it is capable of much higher magnifications.
A. Electron Microscope   B. Zygote   C. Biology   D. Immune Response

147. __D__ Threatened by factors such as habitat loss, hunting, disease and climate change, and usually have declining populations or a very limited range.
A. Artificial Selection   B. Predation   C. Cryobiology   D. Endangered Species

148. __D__ One of the three primary germ layers in the very early human embryo. the other two layers are the ectoderm (outside layer) and mesoderm (middle layer).
A. Prokaryote   B. Reproduction   C. Epinephrine   D. Endoderm

149. B  The midsection of the small intestine of many higher vertebrates like mammals, birds, reptiles. it is present between the duodenum and the ileum.
A. Monomer   B. Jejunum   C. Psychobiology   D. Translation

150. A  The collective term for all possible frequencies of electromagnetic radiation.
A. Electromagnetic Spectrum   B. Hermaphrodite   C. Mole   D. Chemical bond

151. B  The application of the principles of biology to the study of physiological, genetic, and developmental mechanisms of behavior in humans and other animals.
A. Linked Genes   B. Psychobiology   C. Entomology   D. Physiology

152. A  Plasma cells, also called plasma b cells, plasmocytes, plasmacytes, or effector b cells, are white blood cells that secrete large volumes of antibodies.
A. Effector Cell   B. DNA Replication   C. Desmosome   D. Predation

153. A  Conducted or conducting outwards or away from something (for nerves, the central nervous system; for blood vessels, the organ supplied).
A. Efferent   B. Arachnology   C. Evolution   D. Neuromuscular Junction

154. B  An electrically excitable cell that processes and transmits information through electrical and chemical signals.
A. Transfer RNA   B. Neuron   C. Uracil   D. Vacuole

155. B  The study of the structure and function of biological systems by means of the methods of "mechanics."
A. Prokaryote   B. Biomechanics   C. Astrobiology   D. Herpetology

156. B  A organism in which internal physiological sources of heat are of relatively small or quite negligible importance in controlling body temperature. "cold blooded".
A. Ecosystem   B. Ectotherm   C. Chemistry   D. Embryo Sac

157. D  When two genes are close together on the same chromosome, they do not assort independently.
A. Hermaphrodite   B. Bioengineering   C. Darwinian Fitness   D. Linked Genes

158. A  The branch of science that explores the chemical processes within and related to living organisms.
A. Biochemistry   B. Metaphase   C. Cell   D. Electron Carrier

159. D  The study of the history of life on earth as reflected in the fossil record. fossils are the remains or traces of organisms.
A. Ecdysone   B. Messenger RNA   C. Chemistry   D. Paleontology

160. A  A microscopic single celled organism that has no distinct nucleus
A. Prokaryote   B. T Cell   C. Chromosome   D. Barr body

161. B  An electron that is associated with an atom, and that can participate in the formation of a chemical bond.
A. Ecosystem   B. Valence electron   C. DNA   D. Hermaphrodite

162. A  Any of the elongated contractile threads found in striated muscle cells.
A. Myofibril   B. Paleontology   C. Human Nutrition   D. SI units

163. B  The scientific study of nature and of earth's biodiversity with the aim of protecting species, their habitats, and ecosystems from excessive rates of extinction.
A. Testosterone   B. Conservation Biology   C. Electromagnetic Spectrum   D. Eukaryote

164. D  The interaction of genes that are not alleles. The suppression of the effect of one such gene by another.
A. Gene Pool   B. Efferent   C. Chromosome   D. Epistasis

165. D  A molecule that can be bonded to other identical molecules to form a polymer.
A. Antibiotic   B. Mole   C. Molecule   D. Monomer

166. C  Scientific study of spiders, scorpions, pseudo-scorpions, and harvestmen.
A. Valence bond theory   B. Xanthophyll   C. Arachnology   D. Artificial Selection

167. A  Depending on free oxygen or air.
A. Aerobic   B. Bacteriophage   C. Messenger RNA   D. Asexual Reproduction

168. C  The study and discussion of chemical reactions with respect to reaction rates.
A. Osmosis   B. SI units   C. Chemical kinetics   D. Electron Microscope

169. D  Any organism whose cells contain a nucleus and other organelles enclosed within membranes.
A. Virology   B. Gular   C. Electron   D. Eukaryote

170. C  One of the proteins into which actomyosin can be split; can exist in either a globular or a fibrous form.
A. Water Potential   B. Benthic zone   C. Actin   D. Phenotype

171. C  Means "falling off at maturity" or "tending to fall off", and it is typically used in order to refer to trees or shrubs that lose their leaves seasonally.
A. Valence band   B. Deoxyribonucleic Acid   C. Deciduous   D. Bacteria

172. C  A pairing between two nucleotides in RNA molecules that does not follow Watson crick base pair rules
A. Bipedal   B. Herpetology   C. Wobble Base Pair   D. Plasmolysis

173. B  In organic chemistry, a hydrocarbon is an organic compound consisting entirely of hydrogen and carbon.
A. Chloroplast   B. Hydrocarbon   C. Metaphase   D. Cloning

174. D  The amount of work needed to move a unit charge from a reference point to a specific point against an electric field.
A. Integrative Biology   B. Mass Number   C. Chemical kinetics   D. Electric Potential

175. C  Type of reproduction in which cells from two parents unite to form the first cell of a new organism.
A. Ichthyology   B. Metaphase   C. Sexual Reproduction   D. Pharmacology

176. D  Hadronic subatomic particles composed of one quark and one antiquark, bound together by the strong interaction.
A. Genetic Code   B. Histology   C. Cholesterol   D. Meson

177. C  Organism with both male and female reproductive organs.
A. Genetics   B. Cell   C. Hermaphrodite   D. Electron Donor

178. B  The branch of biology dealing with the functions and activities of living organisms and their parts, including all physical and chemical processes.
A. Biomechanics   B. Physiology   C. Prokaryote   D. Hermaphrodite

179. A  An inner layer of cells in the cortex of a root and of some stems, surrounding a vascular bundle.
A. Endodermis   B. Messenger RNA   C. Uracil   D. Electron Acceptor

180. A  Known as fish science, is the branch of biology devoted to the study of fish.
A. Ichthyology   B. Zygote   C. Dalton   D. Electron

181. D  Study of living organisms.
A. Chemical compound   B. Arachnology   C. Denaturation   D. Biology

182. D  The nucleotide triplets of DNA and RNA molecules that carry genetic information in living cells.
A. Adenine   B. Biochemistry   C. Antibiotic   D. Genetic Code

183. __C__ An animal that is dependent on or capable of the internal generation of heat; a warm
A. Molecule   B. Desmosome   C. Endotherm   D. Chloride

184. __D__ Any part of a gene that will become a part of the final mature RNA produced by that gene after introns have
been removed by RNA splicing.
A. Amniotes   B. Antibiotic   C. Mass Balance   D. Exon

185. __A__ One of the two purine nucleobases (the other being guanine) used in forming nucleotides of the nucleic acids.
A. Adenine   B. Heterosis   C. Molecule   D. Macronutrient

186. __A__ The intersection of the three medians of the triangle (each median connecting a vertex with the midpoint of the
opposite side).
A. Centroid   B. Darwinian Fitness   C. Epistasis   D. Biocatalysts

187. __B__ The highest range of electron energies in which electrons are normally present at absolute zero temperature.
A. Action potential   B. Valence band   C. Efferent   D. Interleukin

188. __C__ The vascular tissue in plants that conducts sugars and other metabolic products downward from the leaves.
A. Mitosis   B. Molecular biology   C. Phloem   D. Biomechanics

189. __A__ The branch of zoology concerned with reptiles and amphibians.
A. Herpetology   B. Neuron   C. Bacteria   D. Incomplete Dominance

190. __C__ A place for animals, people and plants and non-living things
A. Physiology   B. Wobble Base Pair   C. Habitat   D. Amniotes

191. __C__ An organic compound with four rings arranged in a specific configuration. examples include the dietary lipid
cholesterol and the sex hormones.
A. Chemical bond   B. Integrative Biology   C. Steroid   D. Antibiotic

192. __B__ The hereditary material in humans and almost all other organisms.
A. Chemistry   B. DNA   C. Prokaryote   D. Linked Genes

193. __C__ A subatomic particle with a negative elementary electric charge.
A. Ichthyology   B. T Cell   C. Electron   D. Embryology

194. __A__ Serves an important role in the metabolism of nitrogen-containing compounds by animals and is the main
nitrogen-containing substance in the urine of mammals.
A. Urea   B. Bacteriophage   C. Biocatalysts   D. Exon

195. __C__ The tendency of a crossbred individual to show qualities superior to those of both parents.
A. Mitosis   B. Embryology   C. Heterosis   D. Hadron

196. __D__ A sub-field of ecology that deals with the dynamics of species populations and how these populations interact
with the environment.
A. Krebs Cycle   B. Conservation Biology   C. Hermaphrodite   D. Population Ecology

197. __C__ Application of biological methods and systems found in nature to the study and design of engineering systems
and modern technology.
A. Monomer   B. Chemical kinetics   C. Bionics   D. Absorption

198. __A__ Sperm units with egg in the open, rather than inside the body of the parents
A. External Fertilization   B. Monomer   C. Actin   D. Eukaryote

199. __C__ The energy that an atomic system must acquire before a process (such as an emission or reaction) can occur.
A. Messenger RNA   B. Linked Genes   C. Activation energy   D. Urine

200. __C__ A laboratory process that determines the complete DNA sequence of an organism's genome at a single time.
A. Bionics  B. Urine  C. Whole Genome Sequencing  D. Bacteria

From the words provided for each clue, provide the letter of the word which best matches the clue.

201. __B__ The "control room" for the cell. the nucleus gives out all the orders.
A. Transcription  B. Cell nucleus  C. Denitrification  D. Molecular physics

202. __C__ A liquid by-product of the body secreted by the kidneys through a process called urination (or micturition) and excreted through the urethra.
A. Trophic level  B. Element  C. Urine  D. Ecotype

203. __A__ The organ in the lower body of a woman or female mammal where offspring are conceived and in which they gestate before birth; the womb.
A. Uterus  B. Meiosis  C. Dehydration Reaction  D. Biogeography

204. __C__ The branch of science that explores the chemical processes within and related to living organisms.
A. Anatomy  B. Acoelomate  C. Biochemistry  D. Ecological Pyramid

205. __B__ The modern form of the metric system and is the most widely used system of measurement.
A. Electron Carrier  B. International System  C. Mammalogy  D. Vesicle

206. __A__ The branch of morphology that deals with the structure of animals
A. Anatomy  B. Deoxyribonucleic Acid  C. Biome  D. Barr body

207. __B__ A large molecule, or macromolecule, composed of many repeated subunits.
A. Autoimmunity  B. Polymer  C. Binary fission  D. Cryobiology

208. __B__ The scientific and objective study of non-human animal behavior rather than human behavior and usually with a focus on behavior under natural conditions.
A. Active Transport  B. Ethology  C. Barr body  D. Arachnology

209. __B__ Nutrients that provide calories or energy. nutrients are substances needed for growth, metabolism, and for other body functions.
A. Mammalogy  B. Macronutrient  C. Macromolecule  D. Aerobiology

210. __A__ A mammalian blastula in which some differentiation of cells has occurred.
A. Blastocyst  B. Uterus  C. Thymine  D. Endemism

211. __D__ A short branched extension of a nerve cell, along which impulses received from other cells at synapses are transmitted to the cell body
A. Hormone  B. International System  C. Blastocyst  D. Dendrite

212. __D__ The interaction of genes that are not alleles. The suppression of the effect of one such gene by another.
A. Macrophage  B. Anticodon  C. Eukaryote  D. Epistasis

213. __A__ The study or practice of pathology with greater emphasis on the biological than on the medical aspects.
A. Pathobiology  B. Barr body  C. Natural Selection  D. Whole Genome Sequencing

214. __C__ The study of the physical properties of molecules, the chemical bonds between atoms as well as the molecular dynamics.
A. Incomplete Dominance  B. Marine Biology  C. Molecular physics  D. Thymine

215. A  An individual animal, plant, or single-celled life form.
A. Organism   B. Endocrine System   C. Expressivity   D. Active Transport

216. A  Describes a genetically distinct geographic variety, population or race within a species, which is adapted to specific environmental conditions.
A. Ecotype   B. Endemic Species   C. Microevolution   D. Ganglion

217. D  Threatened by factors such as habitat loss, hunting, disease and climate change, and usually have declining populations or a very limited range.
A. Electrochemical Gradient   B. Chemical kinetics   C. Endosperm   D. Endangered Species

218. C  A chemical entity that accepts electrons transferred to it from another compound.
A. Macromolecule   B. Agrobiology   C. Electron Acceptor   D. Histology

219. A  The study of mammals.
A. Mammalogy   B. Xanthophyll   C. Barr body   D. Deoxyribose

220. C  Another term for adrenaline.
A. Transcription   B. Translation   C. Epinephrine   D. Endocrine System

221. C  The reduced genetic diversity that results when a population is descended from a small number of colonizing ancestors.
A. Trophic level   B. Primase   C. Founder Effect   D. Biomass

222. B  An undifferentiated cell of a multicellular organism that can give rise to indefinitely more cells of the same type.
A. Endangered Species   B. Stem cell   C. Active Transport   D. Mole

223. A  Refers to the number of elements to which it can connect.
A. Valence   B. Heterosis   C. Pollination   D. Effector

224. B  Study of living organisms.
A. Electron Acceptor   B. Biology   C. Mammalogy   D. Conservation Biology

225. B  The highest range of electron energies in which electrons are normally present at absolute zero temperature.
A. Chromosome   B. Valence band   C. Behavioral ecology   D. Chemical bond

226. B  A very large molecule, such as protein, commonly created by polymerization of smaller subunits (monomers).
A. Messenger RNA   B. Macromolecule   C. Deoxyribose   D. Denitrification

227. C  The continuation of the spinal cord within the skull, forming the lowest part of the brainstem and containing control centers for the heart and lungs.
A. B cell   B. Cryobiology   C. Medulla   D. Lacteal

228. A  The branch of biology concerned with the effects of outer space on living organisms and the search for extraterrestrial life
A. Astrobiology   B. Atom   C. Vesicle   D. Effector

229. B  The science of drug action on biological systems.
A. Chromosome   B. Pharmacology   C. Deoxyribonucleic Acid   D. Anatomy

230. C  A form of intermediate inheritance in which one allele for a specific trait is not completely expressed over its paired allele.
A. Human Nutrition   B. Polygene   C. Incomplete Dominance   D. Ecosystem

231. C  A chemical substance consisting of two or more different chemically bonded chemical elements, with a fixed ratio determining the composition.
A. Interleukin   B. Autoimmunity   C. Chemical compound   D. Biophysics

232. __D__ Process of reproduction involving a single parent that results in offspring that are genetically identical to the parent.
A. Exocytosis   B. Effector   C. Electrochemical Gradient   D. Asexual Reproduction

233. __D__ A hierarchical series of organisms each dependent on the next as a source of food.
A. Anticodon   B. Chloride   C. Biogeography   D. Food Chain

234. __A__ Refers to the provision of essential nutrients necessary to support human life and health.
A. Human Nutrition   B. Endoplasmic Reticulum   C. Ecdysone   D. Biogeography

235. __C__ The ecological state of a species being unique to a defined geographic location, such as an island, nation, country or other defined zone, or habitat type.
A. Macromolecule   B. Mammalogy   C. Endemism   D. Biogeography

236. __D__ A lymphatic capillary that absorbs dietary fats in the villi of the small intestine.
A. Incomplete Dominance   B. Binary fission   C. Translation   D. Lacteal

237. __B__ The theory that all living things are made up of cells.
A. Myofibril   B. Cell theory   C. Epicotyl   D. Interleukin

238. __C__ The complete transfer of valence electron(s) between atoms. it is a type of chemical bond that generates two oppositely charged ions.
A. Endoplasmic Reticulum   B. Pathobiology   C. Ionic Bond   D. Molecular physics

239. __B__ The branch of biology that relates to the animal kingdom, including the structure, embryology, evolution, classification, habits, and distribution of all animals.
A. Endosperm   B. Zoology   C. Interleukin   D. Centroid

240. __D__ A plant hormone.
A. Ganglion   B. Cell nucleus   C. External Fertilization   D. Abscisic acid

241. __A__ The study of microscopic organisms, such as bacteria, viruses, archaea, fungi and protozoa.
A. Microbiology   B. Ectoderm   C. Deoxyribose   D. Cholesterol

242. __D__ Rain containing acids that form in the atmosphere when industrial gas emissions (especially sulfur dioxide and nitrogen oxides) combine with water.
A. Biocatalysts   B. Valence band   C. B cell   D. Acid precipitation

243. __C__ The study of the transformation of energy in living organisms.
A. Chemical kinetics   B. Genome   C. Bioenergetics   D. Biophysics

244. __D__ A plant that grows harmlessly upon another plant and derives its moisture and nutrients from the air, rain, and sometimes from debris accumulating around it.
A. Environmental Biology   B. Endemism   C. Microbiology   D. Epiphyte

245. __C__ the sequence of reactions by which most living cells generate energy during the process of aerobic respiration.
A. Macromolecule   B. Barr body   C. Krebs Cycle   D. Microbiology

246. __A__ A membrane-bound organelle which is present in all plant and fungal cells and some protist, animal and bacterial cells.
A. Vacuole   B. Epinephrine   C. Environmental Biology   D. Invertebrate

247. __D__ Work to convert light energy of the sun into sugars that can be used by cells.
A. Gular   B. Ornithology   C. Systematics   D. Chloroplast

248. __B__ Refers to two solutions having the same osmotic pressure across a semipermeable membrane.
A. Transcription   B. Isotonic Solution   C. Effector   D. Electron Transport Chain

249. __B__ Plasma cells, also called plasma b cells, plasmocytes, plasmacytes, or effector b cells, are white blood cells that secrete large volumes of antibodies.
A. Biomass  B. Effector Cell  C. Natural Selection  D. Cell

250. __B__ A branch of zoology that concerns the study of birds.
A. Mass Density  B. Ornithology  C. Immune Response  D. Organ

251. __B__ Usually defined as a chemical reaction that involves the loss of a water molecule from the reacting molecule.
A. Valence electron  B. Dehydration Reaction  C. Myofibril  D. Active Transport

252. __D__ The study of the microscopic anatomy of cells and tissues of plants and animals.
A. Endoderm  B. Element  C. Zoology  D. Histology

253. __D__ The scientific study of nature and of earth's biodiversity with the aim of protecting species, their habitats, and ecosystems from excessive rates of extinction.
A. Medulla  B. Primase  C. Chemical kinetics  D. Conservation Biology

254. __D__ Single-cell microscopic organisms which lack a true nucleus. they represent one of the three domains.
A. Chemical kinetics  B. DNA Sequencing  C. Polygene  D. Bacteria

255. __D__ A unit of concentration measuring the number of moles of a solute per liter of solution.
A. Vacuole  B. DNA Sequencing  C. Endocrine System  D. Molarity

256. __D__ A chemical reaction in which the standard change in free energy is positive, and energy is absorbed
A. Centrosome  B. Mass Density  C. Microbiology  D. Endergonic Reaction

257. __D__ Organic molecules that serve as the monomers, or subunits, of nucleic acids like DNA (deoxyribonucleic acid) and RNA (ribonucleic acid).
A. Barr body  B. Epicotyl  C. Electron Donor  D. Nucleotide

258. __B__ RNA consisting of folded molecules that transport amino acids from the cytoplasm of a cell to a ribosome.
A. Founder Effect  B. Transfer RNA  C. Heterosis  D. Endosymbiotic Theory

259. __C__ Organisms that produce an egg composed of shell and membranes that creates a protected environment in which the embryo can develop out of water
A. Testosterone  B. Blastocyst  C. Amniotes  D. Organism

260. __B__ An inner layer of cells in the cortex of a root and of some stems, surrounding a vascular bundle.
A. Transcription  B. Endodermis  C. Ganglion  D. Cholesterol

261. __D__ A cluster (functional group) of nerve cell bodies in a centralized nervous system.
A. Histology  B. Species  C. Uracil  D. Ganglion

262. __D__ An interdisciplinary science that applies the approaches and methods of physics to study biological systems.
A. Ecosystem  B. Deoxyribonucleic Acid  C. Vacuole  D. Biophysics

263. __A__ A heterocyclic compound of carbon, nitrogen, oxygen, and hydrogen. it forms ions and salts known as urates and acid urates, such as ammonium acid urate.
A. Uric acid  B. Polygene  C. Chromosome  D. Gular

264. __D__ Any of the elongated contractile threads found in striated muscle cells.
A. Mass Number  B. Insulin  C. Xanthophyll  D. Myofibril

265. __A__ A threadlike strand of DNA in the cell nucleus that carries the genes in a linear order.
A. Chromosome  B. Primase  C. Urine  D. Nucleotide

266. B The first step of gene expression, in which a segment of DNA is copied into RNA (mRNA) by the enzyme RNA polymerase.
A. Deciduous   B. Transcription   C. Histology   D. Epiphyte

267. C A kind of swallowing cell, which means it functions by literally swallowing up other particles or smaller cells.
A. Uracil   B. Genetics   C. Macrophage   D. Endergonic Reaction

268. C The ecological region at the lowest level of a body of water such as an ocean or a lake.
A. External Fertilization   B. Aerobiology   C. Benthic zone   D. Ornithology

269. A Organic matter derived from living, or recently living organisms.
A. Biomass   B. Basal body   C. Lacteal   D. Autoimmunity

270. C Variations in a phenotype among individuals carrying a genotype.
A. Conservation Biology   B. Electric Potential   C. Expressivity   D. Biochemistry

271. C The site of oxidative phosphorylation in eukaryotes.
A. Nucleotide   B. Aerobiology   C. Electron Transport Chain   D. Cell

272. A The decoding of genetic instructions for making proteins.
A. Translation   B. Nucleotide   C. Endergonic Reaction   D. Ganglion

273. D A organism in which internal physiological sources of heat are of relatively small or quite negligible importance in controlling body temperature. "cold blooded".
A. Bile   B. Endoplasmic Reticulum   C. Enzyme   D. Ectotherm

274. D One cell dividing into two identical daughter cells.
A. Barr body   B. Thymine   C. Transcription   D. Binary fission

275. A A class of organic compounds containing an amino group and a carboxylic acid group
A. Amino acid   B. Valence electron   C. Polymer   D. Synthetic Biology

276. D The chemical name for DNA.
A. Biome   B. Xanthophyll   C. Anticodon   D. Deoxyribonucleic Acid

277. B The study of parasites, their hosts, and the relationship between them.
A. Thymine   B. Parasitology   C. Translation   D. Paleontology

278. B Variations of genomes between members of species, or between groups of species thriving in different parts of the world as a result of genetic mutation.
A. Biophysics   B. Genetic Variation   C. Membrane Potential   D. Neurotransmitter

279. C Stereoisomers that are non-superimposable mirror images. a molecule with 1 chiral carbon atom exists as 2 stereoisomers termed enantiomers.
A. Xanthophyll   B. Natural Selection   C. Enantiomer   D. Virology

280. B Biological molecules (proteins) that act as catalysts and help complex reactions occur everywhere in life.
A. Lacteal   B. Enzyme   C. Astrobiology   D. Ligament

281. C The ecological state of a species being unique to a defined geographic location, such as an island, nation, country or other defined zone, or habitat type.
A. Adenylate cyclase   B. Biophysics   C. Endemic Species   D. Translation

282. D The amount of work needed to move a unit charge from a reference point to a specific point against an electric field.
A. Krebs Cycle   B. Microbiology   C. Effector Cell   D. Electric Potential

283. **A**    The region of an embryo or seedling stem above the cotyledon.
A. Epicotyl   B. Vesicle   C. Basal body   D. Centrosome

284. **B**    A dark green to yellowish brown fluid, produced by the liver of most vertebrates, that aids the digestion of lipids in the small intestine.
A. Valence band   B. Bile   C. Microbiology   D. Barr body

285. **C**    The study of viruses-submicroscopic, parasitic particles of genetic material contained in a protein coat and virus-like agents.
A. Dendrite   B. Thymine   C. Virology   D. Neurotransmitter

286. **B**    A species of atoms having the same number of protons in their atomic nuclei.
A. Endosperm   B. Element   C. Heterosis   D. Agrobiology

287. **C**    The collection of glands that produce hormones that regulate metabolism, growth and development, tissue function, sexual function, reproduction, sleep, and mood.
A. Electron Donor   B. Exon   C. Endocrine System   D. Valence

288. **B**    A chemical entity that donates electrons to another compound.
A. Genetics   B. Electron Donor   C. Desmosome   D. Denitrification

289. **B**    A microbially facilitated process of nitrate reduction that may ultimately produce molecular nitrogen.
A. Benthic zone   B. Denitrification   C. Ganglion   D. Anticodon

290. **B**    The tendency of a crossbred individual to show qualities superior to those of both parents.
A. Bacteria   B. Heterosis   C. Biochemistry   D. Environmental Biology

291. **D**    The study of the history of life on earth as reflected in the fossil record. fossils are the remains or traces of organisms.
A. Dendrite   B. Thymine   C. Enantiomer   D. Paleontology

292. **B**    The vascular tissue in plants that conducts water and dissolved nutrients upward from the root and also helps to form the woody element in the stem.
A. Insulin   B. Xylem   C. Electron Shell   D. Biophysics

293. **D**    An electron shell is the outside part of an atom around the atomic nucleus. it is a group of atomic orbitals with the same value of the principal quantum number n.
A. Chemical compound   B. Macrophage   C. Ornithology   D. Electron Shell

294. **A**    The application of concepts and methods of biology to solve real world problems.
A. Bioengineering   B. Uric acid   C. Desmosome   D. Effector Cell

295. **B**    A gene whose individual effect on a phenotype is too small to be observed, but which can act together with others to produce observable variation.
A. Mucous Membrane   B. Polygene   C. Mammalogy   D. Parallel Evolution

296. **A**    Means "falling off at maturity" or "tending to fall off", and it is typically used in order to refer to trees or shrubs that lose their leaves seasonally.
A. Deciduous   B. Abscission   C. Ornithology   D. Uterus

297. **C**    The total number of protons and neutrons (together known as nucleons) in an atomic nucleus
A. Microevolution   B. Systematics   C. Mass Number   D. Electron Shell

298. **C**    One of the four nucleobases in the nucleic acid of RNA that are represented by the letters a, g, c and u.
A. Whole Genome Sequencing   B. Hormone   C. Uracil   D. Wood

299. __B__ An organic lipid molecule that is biosynthesized by all animal cells because it is an essential structural component of all animal cell membranes.
A. Endosperm   B. Cholesterol   C. Enzyme   D. Insulin

300. __C__ Helps keep blood sugar level from getting too high (hyperglycemia) or too low (hypoglycemia).
A. Testosterone   B. Electron Microscope   C. Insulin   D. Endemism

## Matching

Provide the word that best matches each clue.

1. _____  Sperm units with egg in the open, rather than inside the body of the parents

2. _____  The structural and functional unit of all organisms.

3. _____  A cluster (functional group) of nerve cell bodies in a centralized nervous system.

4. _____  A branch of science concerning biological activity at the molecular level.

5. _____  A chemical entity that donates electrons to another compound.

6. _____  The total number of protons and neutrons (together known as nucleons) in an atomic nucleus

7. _____  Study of living organisms.

8. _____  Cytosine, guanine, adenine (which can be found in DNA and RNA), thymine (found only in DNA), and uracil (found only in RNA).

9. _____  A branch of medicine that deals with the prevention, diagnosis and treatment of cancer.

10. _____  Any organism whose cells contain a nucleus and other organelles enclosed within membranes.

11. _____  An electron that is associated with an atom, and that can participate in the formation of a chemical bond.

12. _____  Evolution on a scale of separated gene pools. studies focus on change that occurs at or above the level of species, in contrast with microevolution.

13. _____  The study of genetic variation within populations and involves the examination and modeling of changes in the frequencies of genes and alleles.

14. _____  An organ or cell that acts in response to a stimulus.

15. _____  The branch of biology that studies the development of gametes (sex cells), fertilization, and development of embryos and fetuses.

16. _____  Any of the elongated contractile threads found in striated muscle cells.

17. _____ A steroidal prohormone of the major insect molting hormone is secreted from the prothoracic glands.

18. _____ The study of populations of organisms, especially the regulation of population size, life history traits such as clutch size, and extinction.

19. _____ the sequence of reactions by which most living cells generate energy during the process of aerobic respiration.

20. _____ A gene is a locus (or region) of DNA that encodes a functional RNA or protein product and is the molecular unit of heredity.

21. _____ A chemical synapse formed by the contact between a motor neuron and a muscle fiber.

22. _____ A nucleotide derived from adenosine that occurs in muscle tissue; the major source of energy for cellular reactions.

23. _____ The inner layer of the stems of woody plants; composed of xylem.

24. _____ Any of various molecules that can accept one or two electrons from one molecule and donating them to another in the process of electron transport.

25. _____ A biological agent that reproduces inside the cells of living hosts.

A. Electron Carrier                B. Effector                          C. Ecdysone
D. Biology                         E. Neuromuscular Junction            F. Wood
G. Nucleobase                      H. Embryology                        I. Gene
J. Adenosine Triphosphate          K. Eukaryote                         L. Macroevolution
M. Myofibril                       N. Population Biology                O. Molecular biology
P. Cell                            Q. Electron Donor                    R. Ganglion
S. Valence electron                T. Krebs Cycle                       U. External Fertilization
V. Population Genetics             W. Mass Number                       X. Oncology
Y. Virus

Provide the word that best matches each clue.

26. _____ A diploid cell resulting from the fusion of two haploid gametes; a fertilized ovum.

27. _____ A branch of medicine that deals with the prevention, diagnosis and treatment of cancer.

28. _____ The study of the evolutionary basis for animal behavior due to ecological pressures.

29. _____ A chemical entity that accepts electrons transferred to it from another compound.

30. _____ Glands that secrete their products, hormones, directly into the blood rather than through a duct.

31. _____ Known as fish science, is the branch of biology devoted to the study of fish.

32. _____ The branch of biology dealing with the functions and activities of living organisms and their parts, including all physical and chemical processes.

33. _____ In cell biology, an organelle that is the main place where cell microtubules get organized. they occur only in plant and animal cells.

34. _____ The study of organic particles, such as bacteria, fungal spores, very small insects, pollen grains and viruses, which are passively transported by the air.

35. _____ A place for animals, people and plants and non-living things

36. _____ The continuation of the spinal cord within the skull, forming the lowest part of the brainstem and containing control centers for the heart and lungs.

37. _____ An enzyme that catalyzes the formation of cyclic amp from ATP.

38. _____ A gene is a locus (or region) of DNA that encodes a functional RNA or protein product and is the molecular unit of heredity.

39. _____ The ecological state of a species being unique to a defined geographic location, such as an island, nation, country or other defined zone, or habitat type.

40. _____ A branch of physical science that studies the composition, structure, properties and change of matter.

41. _____ Application of biological methods and systems found in nature to the study and design of engineering systems and modern technology.

42. _____ A biological agent that reproduces inside the cells of living hosts.

43. _____ Density is mass per volume.

44. _____ An application of conservation of mass to the analysis of physical systems.

45. _____ Large biomolecules, or macromolecules, consisting of one or more long chains of amino acid residues.

46. _____ A kind of swallowing cell, which means it functions by literally swallowing up other particles or smaller cells.

47. _____ The vascular tissue in plants that conducts sugars and other metabolic products downward from the leaves.

48. _____ The branch of biology concerned with the effects of outer space on living organisms and the search for extraterrestrial life

49. _____ A medical specialty that is concerned with the diagnosis of disease based on the laboratory analysis of bodily fluids such as blood and urine.

50. _____ The smallest particle in a chemical element or compound that has the chemical properties of that element or compound.

A. Mass Density        B. Adenylate cyclase      C. Endocrine Gland
D. Aerobiology         E. Mass Balance           F. Pathology
G. Zygote              H. Gene                   I. Astrobiology
J. Centrosome          K. Oncology               L. Virus
M. Physiology          N. Bionics                O. Medulla
P. Habitat             Q. Macrophage             R. Chemistry
S. Molecule            T. Endemic Species        U. Ichthyology
V. Electron Acceptor   W. Protein                X. Behavioral ecology
Y. Phloem

## Provide the word that best matches each clue.

51. _____ A gene whose individual effect on a phenotype is too small to be observed, but which can act together with others to produce observable variation.

52. _____ A process in which proteins or nucleic acids lose the quaternary structure, tertiary structure and secondary structure which is present in their native state.

53. _____ A subatomic particle with a negative elementary electric charge.

54. _____ The reduced genetic diversity that results when a population is descended from a small number of colonizing ancestors.

55. _____ Propagate (an organism or cell) to make an identical copy of.

56. _____ The study and analysis of the patterns, causes, and effects of health and disease conditions in defined populations.

57. _____ A plant hormone.

58. _____ Catalysis in living systems. in biological processes, natural catalysts, such as protein enzymes, perform chemical transformations on organic compounds.

59. _____  The state in which both reactants and products are present in concentrations which have no further tendency to change with time.

60. _____  Of or pertaining to the throat.

61. _____  The process in which a eukaryotic cell nucleus splits in two, followed by division of the parent cell into two daughter cells.

62. _____  An atom or molecule with a net electric charge due to the loss or gain of one or more electrons.

63. _____  The chemical name for DNA.

64. _____  Organism which can produce energy through aerobic respiration and then switching to anaerobic respiration depending on the amounts of oxygen.

65. _____  The process of reversing the charge across a cell membrane (usually a neuron), so causing an action potential.

66. _____  The smallest particle in a chemical element or compound that has the chemical properties of that element or compound.

67. _____  The form of rna in which genetic information transcribed from dna as a sequence of bases is transferred to a ribosome.

68. _____  The part of an enzyme or antibody where the chemical reaction occurs

69. _____  A microscopic single celled organism that has no distinct nucleus

70. _____  One of the three primary germ layers in the very early human embryo. the other two layers are the ectoderm (outside layer) and mesoderm (middle layer).

71. _____  The genetic contribution of an individual to the next generation's gene pool relative to the average for the population.

72. _____  The study of cells of the nervous system and the organization of these cells into functional circuits that process information and mediate behavior.

73. _____  A chemical substance produced in the body that controls and regulates the activity of certain cells or organs.

74. _____  Process of reproduction involving a single parent that results in offspring that are genetically identical to the parent.

75. _____  The ecological state of a species being unique to a defined geographic location, such as an island, nation, country or other defined zone, or habitat type.

A. Facultative Anaerobe
B. Chemical equilibrium
C. Deoxyribonucleic Acid
D. Denaturation
E. Electron
F. Founder Effect
G. Hormone
H. Endemism
I. Depolarization
J. Mitosis
K. Cloning
L. Endoderm
M. Ion
N. Neurobiology
O. Molecule
P. Messenger RNA
Q. Abscisic acid
R. Polygene
S. Gular
T. Prokaryote
U. Active site
V. Biocatalysts
W. Asexual Reproduction
X. Darwinian Fitness
Y. Epidemiology

Provide the word that best matches each clue.

76. _____  Hadronic subatomic particles composed of one quark and one antiquark, bound together by the strong interaction.

77. _____  A nucleotide derived from adenosine that occurs in muscle tissue; the major source of energy for cellular reactions.

78. _____  Large biomolecules, or macromolecules, consisting of one or more long chains of amino acid residues.

79. _____  The lowest theoretically attainable temperature (at which the kinetic energy of atoms and molecules is minimal)

80. _____  The process of determining the precise order of nucleotides within a DNA molecule.

81. _____  An evolutionary theory that explains the origin of eukaryotic cells from prokaryotes.

82. _____  The smallest component of an element having the chemical properties of the element

83. _____  Evolution on a scale of separated gene pools. studies focus on change that occurs at or above the level of species, in contrast with microevolution.

84. _____  The inactive x chromosome in a female somatic cell, rendered inactive in a process called lyonization

85. _____  The application of engineering principles and design concepts to medicine and biology for healthcare purposes (e.g. diagnostic or therapeutic).

86. _____ The genetic contribution of an individual to the next generation's gene pool relative to the average for the population.

87. _____ The tendency of a crossbred individual to show qualities superior to those of both parents.

88. _____ One cell dividing into two identical daughter cells.

89. _____ A plant that grows harmlessly upon another plant and derives its moisture and nutrients from the air, rain, and sometimes from debris accumulating around it.

90. _____ Known as fish science, is the branch of biology devoted to the study of fish.

91. _____ Application of biological methods and systems found in nature to the study and design of engineering systems and modern technology.

92. _____ Of or pertaining to the throat.

93. _____ Organic matter derived from living, or recently living organisms.

94. _____ The spontaneous net movement of solvent molecules through a semi-permeable membrane into a region of higher solute concentration.

95. _____ The organ in the lower body of a woman or female mammal where offspring are conceived and in which they gestate before birth; the womb.

96. _____ A succession of letters that indicate the order of nucleotides within a DNA (using GACT or RNA (GACU) molecule.

97. _____ Helps keep blood sugar level from getting too high (hyperglycemia) or too low (hypoglycemia).

98. _____ One of the proteins into which actomyosin can be split; can exist in either a globular or a fibrous form.

99. _____ A kind of swallowing cell, which means it functions by literally swallowing up other particles or smaller cells.

100. _____ The application of the principles of biology to the study of physiological, genetic, and developmental mechanisms of behavior in humans and other animals.

A. Bionics

D. Meson

B. Endosymbiotic Theory

E. Adenosine Triphosphate

C. Insulin

F. Biomedical engineering

G. Macrophage   H. Nucleic Acid Sequence   I. Heterosis
J. Absolute Zero   K. Barr body   L. Osmosis
M. Macroevolution   N. Gular   O. Binary fission
P. DNA Sequencing   Q. Psychobiology   R. Protein
S. Biomass   T. Ichthyology   U. Actin
V. Uterus   W. Atom   X. Darwinian Fitness
Y. Epiphyte

## Provide the word that best matches each clue.

101. _____ A place for animals, people and plants and non-living things

102. _____ A nucleotide derived from adenosine that occurs in muscle tissue; the major source of energy for cellular reactions.

103. _____ A sequence of three nucleotides forming a unit of genetic code in a transfer RNA molecule, corresponding to a complementary codon in messenger RNA.

104. _____ Serves an important role in the metabolism of nitrogen-containing compounds by animals and is the main nitrogen-containing substance in the urine of mammals.

105. _____ A form of intermediate inheritance in which one allele for a specific trait is not completely expressed over its paired allele.

106. _____ The hereditary material in humans and almost all other organisms.

107. _____ A technique used in molecular biology to amplify a single copy or a few copies of a piece of DNA across several orders of magnitude.

108. _____ A cluster (functional group) of nerve cell bodies in a centralized nervous system.

109. _____ A chemical reaction in which the standard change in free energy is positive, and energy is absorbed

110. _____ The act of transferring pollen grains from the male anther of a flower to the female stigma.

111. _____ Propagate (an organism or cell) to make an identical copy of.

112. _____ Organisms that produce an egg composed of shell and membranes that creates a protected environment in which the embryo can develop out of water

113. _____ A harmless pill, medicine, or procedure prescribed more for the psychological benefit to the patient than for any physiological effect.

114. _____ The ecological state of a species being unique to a defined geographic location, such as an island, nation, country or other defined zone, or habitat type.

115. _____ The study of organic particles, such as bacteria, fungal spores, very small insects, pollen grains and viruses, which are passively transported by the air.

116. _____ The study of mammals.

117. _____ The study and analysis of the patterns, causes, and effects of health and disease conditions in defined populations.

118. _____ One of the proteins into which actomyosin can be split; can exist in either a globular or a fibrous form.

119. _____ Refers to the provision of essential nutrients necessary to support human life and health.

120. _____ A colorless cell which circulates in the blood and body fluids and is involved in counteracting foreign substances and disease; a white (blood) cell.

121. _____ The application of the principles of biology to the study of physiological, genetic, and developmental mechanisms of behavior in humans and other animals.

122. _____ The term used to describe what happens to an ecological community over time.

123. _____ The intersection of the three medians of the triangle (each median connecting a vertex with the midpoint of the opposite side).

124. _____ A plant that grows harmlessly upon another plant and derives its moisture and nutrients from the air, rain, and sometimes from debris accumulating around it.

125. _____ The process of determining the precise order of nucleotides within a DNA molecule.

| | | |
|---|---|---|
| A. Human Nutrition | B. Incomplete Dominance | C. Urea |
| D. Adenosine Triphosphate | E. Anticodon | F. Amniotes |
| G. Cloning | H. Ecological Succession | I. Aerobiology |
| J. Endemism | K. Mammalogy | L. Centroid |

M. Epiphyte        N. Habitat        O. Endergonic Reaction
P. DNA        Q. Polymerase Chain Reaction        R. Ganglion
S. Pollination        T. Placebo        U. Epidemiology
V. Actin        W. Leukocyte        X. DNA Sequencing
Y. Psychobiology

## Provide the word that best matches each clue.

126. _____  The application of engineering principles and design concepts to medicine and biology for healthcare purposes (e.g. diagnostic or therapeutic).

127. _____  Any organism whose cells contain a nucleus and other organelles enclosed within membranes.

128. _____  One cell dividing into two identical daughter cells.

129. _____  The study of genetic variation within populations and involves the examination and modeling of changes in the frequencies of genes and alleles.

130. _____  The site of oxidative phosphorylation in eukaryotes.

131. _____  The stock of different genes in an interbreeding population.

132. _____  A type of cell division that reduces the number of chromosomes in the parent cell by half and produces four gamete cells.

133. _____  The spontaneous net movement of solvent molecules through a semi-permeable membrane into a region of higher solute concentration.

134. _____  A microbially facilitated process of nitrate reduction that may ultimately produce molecular nitrogen.

135. _____  The yellow internal part of a bird's egg, which is surrounded by the white, is rich in protein and fat, and nourishes the developing embryo.

136. _____  When a nerve or muscle cell is at "rest", its membrane potential is called the resting membrane potential.

137. _____  A technique used in molecular biology to amplify a single copy or a few copies of a piece of DNA across several orders of magnitude.

138. _____  The variety of life in the world or in a habitat or ecosystem.

139. _____ A fluid or air-filled cavity or sac.

140. _____ A species of atoms having the same number of protons in their atomic nuclei.

141. _____ A steroidal prohormone of the major insect molting hormone is secreted from the prothoracic glands.

142. _____ Organic molecules that serve as the monomers, or subunits, of nucleic acids like DNA (deoxyribonucleic acid) and RNA (ribonucleic acid).

143. _____ A subatomic particle with a negative elementary electric charge.

144. _____ A gene whose individual effect on a phenotype is too small to be observed, but which can act together with others to produce observable variation.

145. _____ A diploid cell resulting from the fusion of two haploid gametes; a fertilized ovum.

146. _____ Helps keep blood sugar level from getting too high (hyperglycemia) or too low (hypoglycemia).

147. _____ A distinct juvenile form many animals undergo before metamorphosis into adults. animals with indirect development such as insects, amphibians, or cnidarians.

148. _____ A network of membranous tubules within the cytoplasm of a eukaryotic cell, continuous with the nuclear membrane.

149. _____ A threadlike strand of DNA in the cell nucleus that carries the genes in a linear order.

150. _____ A chemical reaction in which the standard change in free energy is positive, and energy is absorbed

| | | |
|---|---|---|
| A. Endergonic Reaction | B. Denitrification | C. Zygote |
| D. Electron | E. Electron Transport Chain | F. Polymerase Chain Reaction |
| G. Membrane Potential | H. Meiosis | I. Eukaryote |
| J. Chromosome | K. Nucleotide | L. Insulin |
| M. Osmosis | N. Yolk | O. Larva |
| P. Gene Pool | Q. Ecdysone | R. Population Genetics |
| S. Polygene | T. Vesicle | U. Element |
| V. Biomedical engineering | W. Endoplasmic Reticulum | X. Biodiversity |
| Y. Binary fission | | |

Provide the word that best matches each clue.

151. _____  An undifferentiated cell of a multicellular organism that can give rise to indefinitely more cells of the same type.

152. _____  A pairing between two nucleotides in RNA molecules that does not follow Watson crick base pair rules

153. _____  Shedding of flowers and leaves and fruit following formation of scar tissue in a plant.

154. _____  Means "falling off at maturity" or "tending to fall off", and it is typically used in order to refer to trees or shrubs that lose their leaves seasonally.

155. _____  Type of reproduction in which cells from two parents unite to form the first cell of a new organism.

156. _____  The study and analysis of the patterns, causes, and effects of health and disease conditions in defined populations.

157. _____  The local voltage change across the cell wall as a nerve impulse is transmitted.

158. _____  The reduced genetic diversity that results when a population is descended from a small number of colonizing ancestors.

159. _____  An epithelial tissue that secretes mucus and that lines many body cavities and tubular organs including the gut and respiratory passages.

160. _____  A hierarchical series of organisms each dependent on the next as a source of food.

161. _____  A large molecule, or macromolecule, composed of many repeated subunits.

162. _____  The vascular tissue in plants that conducts water and dissolved nutrients upward from the root and also helps to form the woody element in the stem.

163. _____  The science of diagnosing and managing plant diseases.

164. _____  The si unit of measurement used to measure the number of things, usually atoms or molecules.

165. _____  A medical specialty that is concerned with the diagnosis of disease based on the laboratory analysis of bodily fluids such as blood and urine.

166. _____ An interdisciplinary science that applies the approaches and methods of physics to study biological systems.

167. _____ The vascular tissue in plants that conducts sugars and other metabolic products downward from the leaves.

168. _____ The branch of biology that studies the development of gametes (sex cells), fertilization, and development of embryos and fetuses.

169. _____ A part of an organism that is typically self-contained and has a specific vital function, such as the heart or liver in humans.

170. _____ A dark green to yellowish brown fluid, produced by the liver of most vertebrates, that aids the digestion of lipids in the small intestine.

171. _____ An enzyme that synthesizes short RNA sequences called primers.

172. _____ Large superfamily of motor proteins that move along actin filaments, while hydrolyzing ATP.

173. _____ In cell biology, an organelle that is the main place where cell microtubules get organized. they occur only in plant and animal cells.

174. _____ A label frequently used to describe various forms of cross-disciplinary and multitaxon research.

175. _____ The variety of life in the world or in a habitat or ecosystem.

A. Mucous Membrane
B. Stem cell
C. Phloem
D. Founder Effect
E. Primase
F. Action potential
G. Xylem
H. Food Chain
I. Abscission
J. Sexual Reproduction
K. Organ
L. Biophysics
M. Embryology
N. Centrosome
O. Epidemiology
P. Deciduous
Q. Myosin
R. Mole
S. Biodiversity
T. Bile
U. Wobble Base Pair
V. Pathology
W. Integrative Biology
X. Polymer
Y. Phytopathology

Provide the word that best matches each clue.

176. _____ A sub-field of ecology that deals with the dynamics of species populations and how these populations interact with the environment.

177. _____ A gradient of electrochemical potential, usually for an ion that can move across a membrane.

178. _____ A chemical reaction in which the standard change in free energy is positive, and energy is absorbed

179. _____ A plant hormone.

180. _____ The study of heredity

181. _____ Any of various molecules that can accept one or two electrons from one molecule and donating them to another in the process of electron transport.

182. _____ A type of cell division that reduces the number of chromosomes in the parent cell by half and produces four gamete cells.

183. _____ The study and analysis of the patterns, causes, and effects of health and disease conditions in defined populations.

184. _____ One of the proteins into which actomyosin can be split; can exist in either a globular or a fibrous form.

185. _____ A nucleotide derived from adenosine that occurs in muscle tissue; the major source of energy for cellular reactions.

186. _____ Contraction of the protoplast of a plant cell as a result of loss of water from the cell.

187. _____ An organic compound with four rings arranged in a specific configuration. examples include the dietary lipid cholesterol and the sex hormones.

188. _____ A branch of medicine that deals with the prevention, diagnosis and treatment of cancer.

189. _____ The variety of life in the world or in a habitat or ecosystem.

190. _____ Evolution on a scale of separated gene pools. studies focus on change that occurs at or above the level of species, in contrast with microevolution.

191. _____ The outermost layer of cells or tissue of an embryo in early development, or the parts derived from this, which include the epidermis, nerve tissue, and nephridia.

192. _____ Any part of a gene that will become a part of the final mature RNA produced by that gene after introns have been removed by RNA splicing.

193. _____ A tissue produced inside the seeds of most of the flowering plants around the time of fertilization.

194. _____ The study of mammals.

195. _____ The application of concepts and methods of biology to solve real world problems.

196. _____ A medical specialty that is concerned with the diagnosis of disease based on the laboratory analysis of bodily fluids such as blood and urine.

197. _____ Density is mass per volume.

198. _____ Variations in a phenotype among individuals carrying a genotype.

199. _____ An organelle formed from a centriole, and a short cylindrical array of microtubules.

200. _____ The study of the physical properties of molecules, the chemical bonds between atoms as well as the molecular dynamics.

| | | |
|---|---|---|
| A. Ectoderm | B. Plasmolysis | C. Basal body |
| D. Abscisic acid | E. Oncology | F. Actin |
| G. Steroid | H. Mass Density | I. Exon |
| J. Biodiversity | K. Endergonic Reaction | L. Expressivity |
| M. Adenosine Triphosphate | N. Endosperm | O. Bioengineering |
| P. Electrochemical Gradient | Q. Population Ecology | R. Mammalogy |
| S. Macroevolution | T. Meiosis | U. Molecular physics |
| V. Genetics | W. Pathology | X. Epidemiology |
| Y. Electron Carrier | | |

Provide the word that best matches each clue.

201. _____ A hierarchical series of organisms each dependent on the next as a source of food.

202. _____ The science of diagnosing and managing plant diseases.

203. _____ A chemical entity that donates electrons to another compound.

204. _____ The part of an enzyme or antibody where the chemical reaction occurs

205. _____ Depending on free oxygen or air.

206. _____ A measure of the potential energy in water as well as the difference between the potential in a water sample and pure water.

207. _____  Organism which can produce energy through aerobic respiration and then switching to anaerobic respiration depending on the amounts of oxygen.

208. _____  Biological molecules (proteins) that act as catalysts and help complex reactions occur everywhere in life.

209. _____  A small dense spherical structure in the nucleus of a cell during interphase.

210. _____  A steroidal prohormone of the major insect molting hormone is secreted from the prothoracic glands.

211. _____  A medical specialty that is concerned with the diagnosis of disease based on the laboratory analysis of bodily fluids such as blood and urine.

212. _____  A species of atoms having the same number of protons in their atomic nuclei.

213. _____  The double helix is unwound and each strand acts as a template for the next strand. bases are matched to synthesize the new partner strands.

214. _____  A subatomic particle with a negative elementary electric charge.

215. _____  The scientific study of organisms in the ocean or other marine bodies of water.

216. _____  Of or pertaining to the throat.

217. _____  Scientific study of spiders, scorpions, pseudo-scorpions, and harvestmen.

218. _____  Catalysis in living systems. in biological processes, natural catalysts, such as protein enzymes, perform chemical transformations on organic compounds.

219. _____  A microbially facilitated process of nitrate reduction that may ultimately produce molecular nitrogen.

220. _____  An evolutionary theory that explains the origin of eukaryotic cells from prokaryotes.

221. _____  An electrically excitable cell that processes and transmits information through electrical and chemical signals.

222. _____  The female reproductive cell (gamete) in oogamous organisms.

223. _____ Plasma cells, also called plasma b cells, plasmocytes, plasmacytes, or effector b cells, are white blood cells that secrete large volumes of antibodies.

224. _____ Component of the blood that functions in the immune system. also known as a leukocyte.

225. _____ The application of computer technology to the management of biological information.

| | | |
|---|---|---|
| A. White Blood Cell | B. Egg | C. Facultative Anaerobe |
| D. Ecdysone | E. Endosymbiotic Theory | F. Marine Biology |
| G. Active site | H. Effector Cell | I. Water Potential |
| J. Bioinformatics | K. Aerobic | L. Nucleolus |
| M. Element | N. Electron | O. Electron Donor |
| P. Phytopathology | Q. DNA Replication | R. Enzyme |
| S. Arachnology | T. Gular | U. Neuron |
| V. Pathology | W. Food Chain | X. Denitrification |
| Y. Biocatalysts | | |

Provide the word that best matches each clue.

226. _____ A chemical synapse formed by the contact between a motor neuron and a muscle fiber.

227. _____ The primary female sex hormone. it is responsible for the development and regulation of the female reproductive system and secondary sex characteristics.

228. _____ A medical specialty that is concerned with the diagnosis of disease based on the laboratory analysis of bodily fluids such as blood and urine.

229. _____ The outermost layer of cells or tissue of an embryo in early development, or the parts derived from this, which include the epidermis, nerve tissue, and nephridia.

230. _____ The branch of biology dealing with the functions and activities of living organisms and their parts, including all physical and chemical processes.

231. _____ Density is mass per volume.

232. _____ The study of the history of life on earth as reflected in the fossil record. fossils are the remains or traces of organisms.

233. _____ Shedding of flowers and leaves and fruit following formation of scar tissue in a plant.

234. _____ Organism which can produce energy through aerobic respiration and then switching to anaerobic respiration depending on the amounts of oxygen.

235. _____ Another term for adrenaline.

236. _____ An evolutionary theory that explains the origin of eukaryotic cells from prokaryotes.

237. _____ An interdisciplinary branch of biology and engineering.

238. _____ The study and discussion of chemical reactions with respect to reaction rates.

239. _____ An electron shell is the outside part of an atom around the atomic nucleus. it is a group of atomic orbitals with the same value of the principal quantum number n.

240. _____ Often defined as the largest group of organisms in which two individuals can reproduce fertile offspring, typically using sexual reproduction.

241. _____ Sperm units with egg in the open, rather than inside the body of the parents

242. _____ Component of the blood that functions in the immune system. also known as a leukocyte.

243. _____ Propagate (an organism or cell) to make an identical copy of.

244. _____ Virus that infects and multiplies within bacteria.

245. _____ Containing more than two homologous sets of chromosomes.

246. _____ The study of the structure and function of biological systems by means of the methods of "mechanics."

247. _____ The si unit of measurement used to measure the number of things, usually atoms or molecules.

248. _____ A gene is a locus (or region) of DNA that encodes a functional RNA or protein product and is the molecular unit of heredity.

249. _____ Stereoisomers that are non-superimposable mirror images. a molecule with 1 chiral carbon atom exists as 2 stereoisomers termed enantiomers.

250. _____  A small dense spherical structure in the nucleus of a cell during interphase.

A. External Fertilization
D. Epinephrine
G. Abscission
J. Synthetic Biology
M. Bacteriophage
P. Pathology
S. Facultative Anaerobe
V. Nucleolus
Y. Species

B. Mass Density
E. Paleontology
H. Electron Shell
K. Enantiomer
N. Mole
Q. Physiology
T. Cloning
W. Polyploidy

C. Neuromuscular Junction
F. White Blood Cell
I. Ectoderm
L. Chemical kinetics
O. Estrogen
R. Gene
U. Biomechanics
X. Symbiogenesis

Provide the word that best matches each clue.

251. _____  A form of intermediate inheritance in which one allele for a specific trait is not completely expressed over its paired allele.

252. _____  A gene is a locus (or region) of DNA that encodes a functional RNA or protein product and is the molecular unit of heredity.

253. _____  The study of insects.

254. _____  A measure of the tendency of an atom to attract a bonding pair of electrons. the Pauling scale is the most commonly used.

255. _____  The study of heredity

256. _____  A branch of science concerning biological activity at the molecular level.

257. _____  The deep sea (2000 meters or more) where there is no light.

258. _____  A group of animals that have no backbone, unlike animals such as reptiles, amphibians, fish, birds and mammals who all have a backbone.

259. _____  The scientific study of nature and of earth's biodiversity with the aim of protecting species, their habitats, and ecosystems from excessive rates of extinction.

260. _____  The study of plant nutrition and growth especially to increase crop yield

261. _____  The intersection of the three medians of the triangle (each median connecting a vertex with the midpoint of the opposite side).

262. _____ Scientific study of spiders, scorpions, pseudo-scorpions, and harvestmen.

263. _____ The total number of protons and neutrons (together known as nucleons) in an atomic nucleus

264. _____ The variety of life in the world or in a habitat or ecosystem.

265. _____ RNA consisting of folded molecules that transport amino acids from the cytoplasm of a cell to a ribosome.

266. _____ Containing more than two homologous sets of chromosomes.

267. _____ A group of cytokines (secreted proteins and signal molecules) that were first seen to be expressed by white blood cells (leukocytes)

268. _____ A threadlike strand of DNA in the cell nucleus that carries the genes in a linear order.

269. _____ A type of cell division that reduces the number of chromosomes in the parent cell by half and produces four gamete cells.

270. _____ Component of the blood that functions in the immune system. also known as a leukocyte.

271. _____ The amount of work needed to move a unit charge from a reference point to a specific point against an electric field.

272. _____ Stereoisomers that are non-superimposable mirror images. a molecule with 1 chiral carbon atom exists as 2 stereoisomers termed enantiomers.

273. _____ The structural and functional unit of all organisms.

274. _____ A lymphocyte of a type produced or processed by the thymus gland and actively participating in the immune response.

275. _____ A complex organic substance present in living cells, especially DNA or RNA, whose molecules consist of many nucleotides linked in a long chain.

A. T Cell
D. Conservation Biology
G. Entomology
J. Gene
M. Transfer RNA
P. White Blood Cell
S. Molecular biology
V. Mass Number

B. Arachnology
E. Enantiomer
H. Nucleic Acid
K. Centroid
N. Polyploidy
Q. Invertebrate
T. Agrobiology
W. Electric Potential

C. Meiosis
F. Cell
I. Genetics
L. Incomplete Dominance
O. Interleukin
R. Chromosome
U. Abyssal zone
X. Biodiversity

Y. Electronegativity

## Provide the word that best matches each clue.

276. _____ The study and analysis of the patterns, causes, and effects of health and disease conditions in defined populations.

277. _____ A straightforward extension of Lewis structures. states that electrons in a covalent bond reside in a region that is the overlap of individual atomic orbitals.

278. _____ An organic lipid molecule that is biosynthesized by all animal cells because it is an essential structural component of all animal cell membranes.

279. _____ The branch of biology that studies the effects of low temperatures on living things within earth's cryosphere or in science.

280. _____ The site of oxidative phosphorylation in eukaryotes.

281. _____ Serves an important role in the metabolism of nitrogen-containing compounds by animals and is the main nitrogen-containing substance in the urine of mammals.

282. _____ Transport of a substance (as a protein or drug) across a cell membrane against the concentration gradient; requires an expenditure of energy

283. _____ Density is mass per volume.

284. _____ A very large molecule, such as protein, commonly created by polymerization of smaller subunits (monomers).

285. _____ A process in which proteins or nucleic acids lose the quaternary structure, tertiary structure and secondary structure which is present in their native state.

286. _____ The part of an enzyme or antibody where the chemical reaction occurs

287. _____ Depending on free oxygen or air.

288. _____ The study of plant nutrition and growth especially to increase crop yield

289. _____ The highest range of electron energies in which electrons are normally present at absolute zero temperature.

290. _____ A gene is a locus (or region) of DNA that encodes a functional RNA or protein product and is the molecular unit of heredity.

291. _____ The scientific study of nature and of earth's biodiversity with the aim of protecting species, their habitats, and ecosystems from excessive rates of extinction.

292. _____ The "control room" for the cell. the nucleus gives out all the orders.

293. _____ A form of active transport in which a cell transports molecules into the cell.

294. _____ An enzyme that synthesizes short RNA sequences called primers.

295. _____ Containing more than two homologous sets of chromosomes.

296. _____ A dark green to yellowish brown fluid, produced by the liver of most vertebrates, that aids the digestion of lipids in the small intestine.

297. _____ Study of living organisms.

298. _____ Biological molecules (proteins) that act as catalysts and help complex reactions occur everywhere in life.

299. _____ A branch of medicine that deals with the prevention, diagnosis and treatment of cancer.

300. _____ The study of organic particles, such as bacteria, fungal spores, very small insects, pollen grains and viruses, which are passively transported by the air.

A. Primase
D. Biology
G. Conservation Biology
J. Enzyme
M. Macromolecule
P. Urea
S. Gene
V. Valence band
Y. Cell nucleus

B. Active site
E. Cryobiology
H. Cholesterol
K. Epidemiology
N. Oncology
Q. Mass Density
T. Aerobiology
W. Aerobic

C. Electron Transport Chain
F. Valence bond theory
I. Agrobiology
L. Bile
O. Polyploidy
R. Endocytosis
U. Denaturation
X. Active Transport

Provide the word that best matches each clue.

1. EXTERNAL FERTILIZATION — Sperm units with egg in the open, rather than inside the body of the parents

2. CELL — The structural and functional unit of all organisms.

3. GANGLION — A cluster (functional group) of nerve cell bodies in a centralized nervous system.

4. MOLECULAR BIOLOGY — A branch of science concerning biological activity at the molecular level.

5. ELECTRON DONOR — A chemical entity that donates electrons to another compound.

6. MASS NUMBER — The total number of protons and neutrons (together known as nucleons) in an atomic nucleus

7. BIOLOGY — Study of living organisms.

8. NUCLEOBASE — Cytosine, guanine, adenine (which can be found in DNA and RNA), thymine (found only in DNA), and uracil (found only in RNA).

9. ONCOLOGY — A branch of medicine that deals with the prevention, diagnosis and treatment of cancer.

10. EUKARYOTE — Any organism whose cells contain a nucleus and other organelles enclosed within membranes.

11. VALENCE ELECTRON — An electron that is associated with an atom, and that can participate in the formation of a chemical bond.

12. MACROEVOLUTION — Evolution on a scale of separated gene pools. studies focus on change that occurs at or above the level of species, in contrast with microevolution.

13. POPULATION GENETICS — The study of genetic variation within populations and involves the examination and modeling of changes in the frequencies of genes and alleles.

14. EFFECTOR — An organ or cell that acts in response to a stimulus.

15. EMBRYOLOGY — The branch of biology that studies the development of gametes (sex cells), fertilization, and development of embryos and fetuses.

16. MYOFIBRIL — Any of the elongated contractile threads found in striated muscle cells.

17. ECDYSONE _____ A steroidal prohormone of the major insect molting hormone is secreted from the prothoracic glands.

18. POPULATION BIOLOGY _____ The study of populations of organisms, especially the regulation of population size, life history traits such as clutch size, and extinction.

19. KREBS CYCLE _____ the sequence of reactions by which most living cells generate energy during the process of aerobic respiration.

20. GENE _____ A gene is a locus (or region) of DNA that encodes a functional RNA or protein product and is the molecular unit of heredity.

21. NEUROMUSCULAR JUNCTION _____ A chemical synapse formed by the contact between a motor neuron and a muscle fiber.

22. ADENOSINE TRIPHOSPHATE _____ A nucleotide derived from adenosine that occurs in muscle tissue; the major source of energy for cellular reactions.

23. WOOD _____ The inner layer of the stems of woody plants; composed of xylem.

24. ELECTRON CARRIER _____ Any of various molecules that can accept one or two electrons from one molecule and donating them to another in the process of electron transport.

25. VIRUS _____ A biological agent that reproduces inside the cells of living hosts.

A. Electron Carrier | B. Effector | C. Ecdysone
D. Biology | E. Neuromuscular Junction | F. Wood
G. Nucleobase | H. Embryology | I. Gene
J. Adenosine Triphosphate | K. Eukaryote | L. Macroevolution
M. Myofibril | N. Population Biology | O. Molecular biology
P. Cell | Q. Electron Donor | R. Ganglion
S. Valence electron | T. Krebs Cycle | U. External Fertilization
V. Population Genetics | W. Mass Number | X. Oncology
Y. Virus

Provide the word that best matches each clue.

26. ZYGOTE _____ A diploid cell resulting from the fusion of two haploid gametes; a fertilized ovum.

27. ONCOLOGY _____ A branch of medicine that deals with the prevention, diagnosis and treatment of cancer.

28. BEHAVIORAL ECOLOGY _____ The study of the evolutionary basis for animal behavior due to ecological pressures.

29. ELECTRON ACCEPTOR — A chemical entity that accepts electrons transferred to it from another compound.

30. ENDOCRINE GLAND — Glands that secrete their products, hormones, directly into the blood rather than through a duct.

31. ICHTHYOLOGY — Known as fish science, is the branch of biology devoted to the study of fish.

32. PHYSIOLOGY — The branch of biology dealing with the functions and activities of living organisms and their parts, including all physical and chemical processes.

33. CENTROSOME — In cell biology, an organelle that is the main place where cell microtubules get organized. they occur only in plant and animal cells.

34. AEROBIOLOGY — The study of organic particles, such as bacteria, fungal spores, very small insects, pollen grains and viruses, which are passively transported by the air.

35. HABITAT — A place for animals, people and plants and non-living things

36. MEDULLA — The continuation of the spinal cord within the skull, forming the lowest part of the brainstem and containing control centers for the heart and lungs.

37. ADENYLATE CYCLASE — An enzyme that catalyzes the formation of cyclic amp from ATP.

38. GENE — A gene is a locus (or region) of DNA that encodes a functional RNA or protein product and is the molecular unit of heredity.

39. ENDEMIC SPECIES — The ecological state of a species being unique to a defined geographic location, such as an island, nation, country or other defined zone, or habitat type.

40. CHEMISTRY — A branch of physical science that studies the composition, structure, properties and change of matter.

41. BIONICS — Application of biological methods and systems found in nature to the study and design of engineering systems and modern technology.

42. VIRUS — A biological agent that reproduces inside the cells of living hosts.

43. MASS DENSITY — Density is mass per volume.

44. MASS BALANCE — An application of conservation of mass to the analysis of physical systems.

45. PROTEIN — Large biomolecules, or macromolecules, consisting of one or more long chains of amino acid residues.

46. MACROPHAGE — A kind of swallowing cell, which means it functions by literally swallowing up other particles or smaller cells.

47. PHLOEM _____ The vascular tissue in plants that conducts sugars and other metabolic products downward from the leaves.

48. ASTROBIOLOGY _____ The branch of biology concerned with the effects of outer space on living organisms and the search for extraterrestrial life

49. PATHOLOGY _____ A medical specialty that is concerned with the diagnosis of disease based on the laboratory analysis of bodily fluids such as blood and urine.

50. MOLECULE _____ The smallest particle in a chemical element or compound that has the chemical properties of that element or compound.

| | | |
|---|---|---|
| A. Mass Density | B. Adenylate cyclase | C. Endocrine Gland |
| D. Aerobiology | E. Mass Balance | F. Pathology |
| G. Zygote | H. Gene | I. Astrobiology |
| J. Centrosome | K. Oncology | L. Virus |
| M. Physiology | N. Bionics | O. Medulla |
| P. Habitat | Q. Macrophage | R. Chemistry |
| S. Molecule | T. Endemic Species | U. Ichthyology |
| V. Electron Acceptor | W. Protein | X. Behavioral ecology |
| Y. Phloem | | |

Provide the word that best matches each clue.

51. POLYGENE _____ A gene whose individual effect on a phenotype is too small to be observed, but which can act together with others to produce observable variation.

52. DENATURATION _____ A process in which proteins or nucleic acids lose the quaternary structure, tertiary structure and secondary structure which is present in their native state.

53. ELECTRON _____ A subatomic particle with a negative elementary electric charge.

54. FOUNDER EFFECT _____ The reduced genetic diversity that results when a population is descended from a small number of colonizing ancestors.

55. CLONING _____ Propagate (an organism or cell) to make an identical copy of.

56. EPIDEMIOLOGY _____ The study and analysis of the patterns, causes, and effects of health and disease conditions in defined populations.

57. ABSCISIC ACID _____ A plant hormone.

58. BIOCATALYSTS _____ Catalysis in living systems. in biological processes, natural catalysts, such as protein enzymes, perform chemical transformations on organic compounds.

59. CHEMICAL EQUILIBRIUM — The state in which both reactants and products are present in concentrations which have no further tendency to change with time.

60. GULAR — Of or pertaining to the throat.

61. MITOSIS — The process in which a eukaryotic cell nucleus splits in two, followed by division of the parent cell into two daughter cells.

62. ION — An atom or molecule with a net electric charge due to the loss or gain of one or more electrons.

63. DEOXYRIBONUCLEIC ACID — The chemical name for DNA.

64. FACULTATIVE ANAEROBE — Organism which can produce energy through aerobic respiration and then switching to anaerobic respiration depending on the amounts of oxygen.

65. DEPOLARIZATION — The process of reversing the charge across a cell membrane (usually a neuron), so causing an action potential.

66. MOLECULE — The smallest particle in a chemical element or compound that has the chemical properties of that element or compound.

67. MESSENGER RNA — The form of rna in which genetic information transcribed from dna as a sequence of bases is transferred to a ribosome.

68. ACTIVE SITE — The part of an enzyme or antibody where the chemical reaction occurs

69. PROKARYOTE — A microscopic single celled organism that has no distinct nucleus

70. ENDODERM — One of the three primary germ layers in the very early human embryo. the other two layers are the ectoderm (outside layer) and mesoderm (middle layer).

71. DARWINIAN FITNESS — The genetic contribution of an individual to the next generation's gene pool relative to the average for the population.

72. NEUROBIOLOGY — The study of cells of the nervous system and the organization of these cells into functional circuits that process information and mediate behavior.

73. HORMONE — A chemical substance produced in the body that controls and regulates the activity of certain cells or organs.

74. ASEXUAL REPRODUCTION — Process of reproduction involving a single parent that results in offspring that are genetically identical to the parent.

75. ENDEMISM _____ The ecological state of a species being unique to a defined geographic location, such as an island, nation, country or other defined zone, or habitat type.

| | | |
|---|---|---|
| A. Facultative Anaerobe | B. Chemical equilibrium | C. Deoxyribonucleic Acid |
| D. Denaturation | E. Electron | F. Founder Effect |
| G. Hormone | H. Endemism | I. Depolarization |
| J. Mitosis | K. Cloning | L. Endoderm |
| M. Ion | N. Neurobiology | O. Molecule |
| P. Messenger RNA | Q. Abscisic acid | R. Polygene |
| S. Gular | T. Prokaryote | U. Active site |
| V. Biocatalysts | W. Asexual Reproduction | X. Darwinian Fitness |
| Y. Epidemiology | | |

Provide the word that best matches each clue.

76. MESON _____ Hadronic subatomic particles composed of one quark and one antiquark, bound together by the strong interaction.

77. ADENOSINE TRIPHOSPHATE _____ A nucleotide derived from adenosine that occurs in muscle tissue; the major source of energy for cellular reactions.

78. PROTEIN _____ Large biomolecules, or macromolecules, consisting of one or more long chains of amino acid residues.

79. ABSOLUTE ZERO _____ The lowest theoretically attainable temperature (at which the kinetic energy of atoms and molecules is minimal)

80. DNA SEQUENCING _____ The process of determining the precise order of nucleotides within a DNA molecule.

81. ENDOSYMBIOTIC THEORY _____ An evolutionary theory that explains the origin of eukaryotic cells from prokaryotes.

82. ATOM _____ The smallest component of an element having the chemical properties of the element

83. MACROEVOLUTION _____ Evolution on a scale of separated gene pools. studies focus on change that occurs at or above the level of species, in contrast with microevolution.

84. BARR BODY _____ The inactive x chromosome in a female somatic cell, rendered inactive in a process called lyonization

85. BIOMEDICAL ENGINEERING _____ The application of engineering principles and design concepts to medicine and biology for healthcare purposes (e.g. diagnostic or therapeutic).

86. DARWINIAN FITNESS — The genetic contribution of an individual to the next generation's gene pool relative to the average for the population.

87. HETEROSIS — The tendency of a crossbred individual to show qualities superior to those of both parents.

88. BINARY FISSION — One cell dividing into two identical daughter cells.

89. EPIPHYTE — A plant that grows harmlessly upon another plant and derives its moisture and nutrients from the air, rain, and sometimes from debris accumulating around it.

90. ICHTHYOLOGY — Known as fish science, is the branch of biology devoted to the study of fish.

91. BIONICS — Application of biological methods and systems found in nature to the study and design of engineering systems and modern technology.

92. GULAR — Of or pertaining to the throat.

93. BIOMASS — Organic matter derived from living, or recently living organisms.

94. OSMOSIS — The spontaneous net movement of solvent molecules through a semi-permeable membrane into a region of higher solute concentration.

95. UTERUS — The organ in the lower body of a woman or female mammal where offspring are conceived and in which they gestate before birth; the womb.

96. NUCLEIC ACID SEQUENCE — A succession of letters that indicate the order of nucleotides within a DNA (using GACT or RNA (GACU) molecule.

97. INSULIN — Helps keep blood sugar level from getting too high (hyperglycemia) or too low (hypoglycemia).

98. ACTIN — One of the proteins into which actomyosin can be split; can exist in either a globular or a fibrous form.

99. MACROPHAGE — A kind of swallowing cell, which means it functions by literally swallowing up other particles or smaller cells.

100. PSYCHOBIOLOGY — The application of the principles of biology to the study of physiological, genetic, and developmental mechanisms of behavior in humans and other animals.

A. Bionics  
D. Meson

B. Endosymbiotic Theory  
E. Adenosine Triphosphate

C. Insulin  
F. Biomedical engineering

G. Macrophage  H. Nucleic Acid Sequence  I. Heterosis
J. Absolute Zero  K. Barr body  L. Osmosis
M. Macroevolution  N. Gular  O. Binary fission
P. DNA Sequencing  Q. Psychobiology  R. Protein
S. Biomass  T. Ichthyology  U. Actin
V. Uterus  W. Atom  X. Darwinian Fitness
Y. Epiphyte

Provide the word that best matches each clue.

101. HABITAT _____ A place for animals, people and plants and non-living things

102. ADENOSINE TRIPHOSPHATE _____ A nucleotide derived from adenosine that occurs in muscle tissue; the major source of energy for cellular reactions.

103. ANTICODON _____ A sequence of three nucleotides forming a unit of genetic code in a transfer RNA molecule, corresponding to a complementary codon in messenger RNA.

104. UREA _____ Serves an important role in the metabolism of nitrogen-containing compounds by animals and is the main nitrogen-containing substance in the urine of mammals.

105. INCOMPLETE DOMINANCE _____ A form of intermediate inheritance in which one allele for a specific trait is not completely expressed over its paired allele.

106. DNA _____ The hereditary material in humans and almost all other organisms.

107. POLYMERASE CHAIN REACTION _____ A technique used in molecular biology to amplify a single copy or a few copies of a piece of DNA across several orders of magnitude.

108. GANGLION _____ A cluster (functional group) of nerve cell bodies in a centralized nervous system.

109. ENDERGONIC REACTION _____ A chemical reaction in which the standard change in free energy is positive, and energy is absorbed

110. POLLINATION _____ The act of transferring pollen grains from the male anther of a flower to the female stigma.

111. CLONING _____ Propagate (an organism or cell) to make an identical copy of.

112. AMNIOTES _____ Organisms that produce an egg composed of shell and membranes that creates a protected environment in which the embryo can develop out of water

113. PLACEBO _____ A harmless pill, medicine, or procedure prescribed more for the psychological benefit to the patient than for any physiological effect.

114. ENDEMISM _____ The ecological state of a species being unique to a defined geographic location, such as an island, nation, country or other defined zone, or habitat type.

115. AEROBIOLOGY _____ The study of organic particles, such as bacteria, fungal spores, very small insects, pollen grains and viruses, which are passively transported by the air.

116. MAMMALOGY _____ The study of mammals.

117. EPIDEMIOLOGY _____ The study and analysis of the patterns, causes, and effects of health and disease conditions in defined populations.

118. ACTIN _____ One of the proteins into which actomyosin can be split; can exist in either a globular or a fibrous form.

119. HUMAN NUTRITION _____ Refers to the provision of essential nutrients necessary to support human life and health.

120. LEUKOCYTE _____ A colorless cell which circulates in the blood and body fluids and is involved in counteracting foreign substances and disease; a white (blood) cell.

121. PSYCHOBIOLOGY _____ The application of the principles of biology to the study of physiological, genetic, and developmental mechanisms of behavior in humans and other animals.

122. ECOLOGICAL SUCCESSION _____ The term used to describe what happens to an ecological community over time.

123. CENTROID _____ The intersection of the three medians of the triangle (each median connecting a vertex with the midpoint of the opposite side).

124. EPIPHYTE _____ A plant that grows harmlessly upon another plant and derives its moisture and nutrients from the air, rain, and sometimes from debris accumulating around it.

125. DNA SEQUENCING _____ The process of determining the precise order of nucleotides within a DNA molecule.

A. Human Nutrition
B. Incomplete Dominance
C. Urea
D. Adenosine Triphosphate
E. Anticodon
F. Amniotes
G. Cloning
H. Ecological Succession
I. Aerobiology
J. Endemism
K. Mammalogy
L. Centroid

M. Epiphyte             N. Habitat                      O. Endergonic Reaction
P. DNA                  Q. Polymerase Chain Reaction    R. Ganglion
S. Pollination          T. Placebo                      U. Epidemiology
V. Actin                W. Leukocyte                    X. DNA Sequencing
Y. Psychobiology

Provide the word that best matches each clue.

126. BIOMEDICAL ENGINEERING     The application of engineering principles and design concepts to medicine and biology for healthcare purposes (e.g. diagnostic or therapeutic).

127. EUKARYOTE     Any organism whose cells contain a nucleus and other organelles enclosed within membranes.

128. BINARY FISSION     One cell dividing into two identical daughter cells.

129. POPULATION GENETICS     The study of genetic variation within populations and involves the examination and modeling of changes in the frequencies of genes and alleles.

130. ELECTRON TRANSPORT CHAIN     The site of oxidative phosphorylation in eukaryotes.

131. GENE POOL     The stock of different genes in an interbreeding population.

132. MEIOSIS     A type of cell division that reduces the number of chromosomes in the parent cell by half and produces four gamete cells.

133. OSMOSIS     The spontaneous net movement of solvent molecules through a semi-permeable membrane into a region of higher solute concentration.

134. DENITRIFICATION     A microbially facilitated process of nitrate reduction that may ultimately produce molecular nitrogen.

135. YOLK     The yellow internal part of a bird's egg, which is surrounded by the white, is rich in protein and fat, and nourishes the developing embryo.

136. MEMBRANE POTENTIAL     When a nerve or muscle cell is at "rest", its membrane potential is called the resting membrane potential.

137. POLYMERASE CHAIN REACTION     A technique used in molecular biology to amplify a single copy or a few copies of a piece of DNA across several orders of magnitude.

138. BIODIVERSITY     The variety of life in the world or in a habitat or ecosystem.

139. VESICLE _____ A fluid or air-filled cavity or sac.

140. ELEMENT _____ A species of atoms having the same number of protons in their atomic nuclei.

141. ECDYSONE _____ A steroidal prohormone of the major insect molting hormone is secreted from the prothoracic glands.

142. NUCLEOTIDE _____ Organic molecules that serve as the monomers, or subunits, of nucleic acids like DNA (deoxyribonucleic acid) and RNA (ribonucleic acid).

143. ELECTRON _____ A subatomic particle with a negative elementary electric charge.

144. POLYGENE _____ A gene whose individual effect on a phenotype is too small to be observed, but which can act together with others to produce observable variation.

145. ZYGOTE _____ A diploid cell resulting from the fusion of two haploid gametes; a fertilized ovum.

146. INSULIN _____ Helps keep blood sugar level from getting too high (hyperglycemia) or too low (hypoglycemia).

147. LARVA _____ A distinct juvenile form many animals undergo before metamorphosis into adults. animals with indirect development such as insects, amphibians, or cnidarians.

148. ENDOPLASMIC RETICULUM _____ A network of membranous tubules within the cytoplasm of a eukaryotic cell, continuous with the nuclear membrane.

149. CHROMOSOME _____ A threadlike strand of DNA in the cell nucleus that carries the genes in a linear order.

150. ENDERGONIC REACTION _____ A chemical reaction in which the standard change in free energy is positive, and energy is absorbed

A. Endergonic Reaction
B. Denitrification
C. Zygote
D. Electron
E. Electron Transport Chain
F. Polymerase Chain Reaction
G. Membrane Potential
H. Meiosis
I. Eukaryote
J. Chromosome
K. Nucleotide
L. Insulin
M. Osmosis
N. Yolk
O. Larva
P. Gene Pool
Q. Ecdysone
R. Population Genetics
S. Polygene
T. Vesicle
U. Element
V. Biomedical engineering
W. Endoplasmic Reticulum
X. Biodiversity
Y. Binary fission

Provide the word that best matches each clue.

151. STEM CELL — An undifferentiated cell of a multicellular organism that can give rise to indefinitely more cells of the same type.

152. WOBBLE BASE PAIR — A pairing between two nucleotides in RNA molecules that does not follow Watson crick base pair rules

153. ABSCISSION — Shedding of flowers and leaves and fruit following formation of scar tissue in a plant.

154. DECIDUOUS — Means "falling off at maturity" or "tending to fall off", and it is typically used in order to refer to trees or shrubs that lose their leaves seasonally.

155. SEXUAL REPRODUCTION — Type of reproduction in which cells from two parents unite to form the first cell of a new organism.

156. EPIDEMIOLOGY — The study and analysis of the patterns, causes, and effects of health and disease conditions in defined populations.

157. ACTION POTENTIAL — The local voltage change across the cell wall as a nerve impulse is transmitted.

158. FOUNDER EFFECT — The reduced genetic diversity that results when a population is descended from a small number of colonizing ancestors.

159. MUCOUS MEMBRANE — An epithelial tissue that secretes mucus and that lines many body cavities and tubular organs including the gut and respiratory passages.

160. FOOD CHAIN — A hierarchical series of organisms each dependent on the next as a source of food.

161. POLYMER — A large molecule, or macromolecule, composed of many repeated subunits.

162. XYLEM — The vascular tissue in plants that conducts water and dissolved nutrients upward from the root and also helps to form the woody element in the stem.

163. PHYTOPATHOLOGY — The science of diagnosing and managing plant diseases.

164. MOLE — The si unit of measurement used to measure the number of things, usually atoms or molecules.

165. PATHOLOGY — A medical specialty that is concerned with the diagnosis of disease based on the laboratory analysis of bodily fluids such as blood and urine.

166. BIOPHYSICS — An interdisciplinary science that applies the approaches and methods of physics to study biological systems.

167. PHLOEM — The vascular tissue in plants that conducts sugars and other metabolic products downward from the leaves.

168. EMBRYOLOGY — The branch of biology that studies the development of gametes (sex cells), fertilization, and development of embryos and fetuses.

169. ORGAN — A part of an organism that is typically self-contained and has a specific vital function, such as the heart or liver in humans.

170. BILE — A dark green to yellowish brown fluid, produced by the liver of most vertebrates, that aids the digestion of lipids in the small intestine.

171. PRIMASE — An enzyme that synthesizes short RNA sequences called primers.

172. MYOSIN — Large superfamily of motor proteins that move along actin filaments, while hydrolyzing ATP.

173. CENTROSOME — In cell biology, an organelle that is the main place where cell microtubules get organized. they occur only in plant and animal cells.

174. INTEGRATIVE BIOLOGY — A label frequently used to describe various forms of cross-disciplinary and multitaxon research.

175. BIODIVERSITY — The variety of life in the world or in a habitat or ecosystem.

A. Mucous Membrane
B. Stem cell
C. Phloem
D. Founder Effect
E. Primase
F. Action potential
G. Xylem
H. Food Chain
I. Abscission
J. Sexual Reproduction
K. Organ
L. Biophysics
M. Embryology
N. Centrosome
O. Epidemiology
P. Deciduous
Q. Myosin
R. Mole
S. Biodiversity
T. Bile
U. Wobble Base Pair
V. Pathology
W. Integrative Biology
X. Polymer
Y. Phytopathology

Provide the word that best matches each clue.

176. POPULATION ECOLOGY — A sub-field of ecology that deals with the dynamics of species populations and how these populations interact with the environment.

177. ELECTROCHEMICAL GRADIENT — A gradient of electrochemical potential, usually for an ion that can move across a membrane.

178. ENDERGONIC REACTION — A chemical reaction in which the standard change in free energy is positive, and energy is absorbed

179. ABSCISIC ACID — A plant hormone.

180. GENETICS — The study of heredity

181. ELECTRON CARRIER — Any of various molecules that can accept one or two electrons from one molecule and donating them to another in the process of electron transport.

182. MEIOSIS — A type of cell division that reduces the number of chromosomes in the parent cell by half and produces four gamete cells.

183. EPIDEMIOLOGY — The study and analysis of the patterns, causes, and effects of health and disease conditions in defined populations.

184. ACTIN — One of the proteins into which actomyosin can be split; can exist in either a globular or a fibrous form.

185. ADENOSINE TRIPHOSPHATE — A nucleotide derived from adenosine that occurs in muscle tissue; the major source of energy for cellular reactions.

186. PLASMOLYSIS — Contraction of the protoplast of a plant cell as a result of loss of water from the cell.

187. STEROID — An organic compound with four rings arranged in a specific configuration. examples include the dietary lipid cholesterol and the sex hormones.

188. ONCOLOGY — A branch of medicine that deals with the prevention, diagnosis and treatment of cancer.

189. BIODIVERSITY — The variety of life in the world or in a habitat or ecosystem.

190. MACROEVOLUTION — Evolution on a scale of separated gene pools. studies focus on change that occurs at or above the level of species, in contrast with microevolution.

191. ECTODERM — The outermost layer of cells or tissue of an embryo in early development, or the parts derived from this, which include the epidermis, nerve tissue, and nephridia.

192. EXON — Any part of a gene that will become a part of the final mature RNA produced by that gene after introns have been removed by RNA splicing.

193. ENDOSPERM — A tissue produced inside the seeds of most of the flowering plants around the time of fertilization.

194. MAMMALOGY — The study of mammals.

195. BIOENGINEERING — The application of concepts and methods of biology to solve real world problems.

196. PATHOLOGY — A medical specialty that is concerned with the diagnosis of disease based on the laboratory analysis of bodily fluids such as blood and urine.

197. MASS DENSITY — Density is mass per volume.

198. EXPRESSIVITY — Variations in a phenotype among individuals carrying a genotype.

199. BASAL BODY — An organelle formed from a centriole, and a short cylindrical array of microtubules.

200. MOLECULAR PHYSICS — The study of the physical properties of molecules, the chemical bonds between atoms as well as the molecular dynamics.

A. Ectoderm
B. Plasmolysis
C. Basal body
D. Abscisic acid
E. Oncology
F. Actin
G. Steroid
H. Mass Density
I. Exon
J. Biodiversity
K. Endergonic Reaction
L. Expressivity
M. Adenosine Triphosphate
N. Endosperm
O. Bioengineering
P. Electrochemical Gradient
Q. Population Ecology
R. Mammalogy
S. Macroevolution
T. Meiosis
U. Molecular physics
V. Genetics
W. Pathology
X. Epidemiology
Y. Electron Carrier

Provide the word that best matches each clue.

201. FOOD CHAIN — A hierarchical series of organisms each dependent on the next as a source of food.

202. PHYTOPATHOLOGY — The science of diagnosing and managing plant diseases.

203. ELECTRON DONOR — A chemical entity that donates electrons to another compound.

204. ACTIVE SITE — The part of an enzyme or antibody where the chemical reaction occurs

205. AEROBIC — Depending on free oxygen or air.

206. WATER POTENTIAL — A measure of the potential energy in water as well as the difference between the potential in a water sample and pure water.

207. FACULTATIVE ANAEROBE — Organism which can produce energy through aerobic respiration and then switching to anaerobic respiration depending on the amounts of oxygen.

208. ENZYME — Biological molecules (proteins) that act as catalysts and help complex reactions occur everywhere in life.

209. NUCLEOLUS — A small dense spherical structure in the nucleus of a cell during interphase.

210. ECDYSONE — A steroidal prohormone of the major insect molting hormone is secreted from the prothoracic glands.

211. PATHOLOGY — A medical specialty that is concerned with the diagnosis of disease based on the laboratory analysis of bodily fluids such as blood and urine.

212. ELEMENT — A species of atoms having the same number of protons in their atomic nuclei.

213. DNA REPLICATION — The double helix is unwound and each strand acts as a template for the next strand. bases are matched to synthesize the new partner strands.

214. ELECTRON — A subatomic particle with a negative elementary electric charge.

215. MARINE BIOLOGY — The scientific study of organisms in the ocean or other marine bodies of water.

216. GULAR — Of or pertaining to the throat.

217. ARACHNOLOGY — Scientific study of spiders, scorpions, pseudo-scorpions, and harvestmen.

218. BIOCATALYSTS — Catalysis in living systems. in biological processes, natural catalysts, such as protein enzymes, perform chemical transformations on organic compounds.

219. DENITRIFICATION — A microbially facilitated process of nitrate reduction that may ultimately produce molecular nitrogen.

220. ENDOSYMBIOTIC THEORY — An evolutionary theory that explains the origin of eukaryotic cells from prokaryotes.

221. NEURON — An electrically excitable cell that processes and transmits information through electrical and chemical signals.

222. EGG — The female reproductive cell (gamete) in oogamous organisms.

223. EFFECTOR CELL

Plasma cells, also called plasma b cells, plasmocytes, plasmacytes, or effector b cells, are white blood cells that secrete large volumes of antibodies.

224. WHITE BLOOD CELL

Component of the blood that functions in the immune system. also known as a leukocyte.

225. BIOINFORMATICS

The application of computer technology to the management of biological information.

A. White Blood Cell
D. Ecdysone
G. Active site
J. Bioinformatics
M. Element
P. Phytopathology
S. Arachnology
V. Pathology
Y. Biocatalysts

B. Egg
E. Endosymbiotic Theory
H. Effector Cell
K. Aerobic
N. Electron
Q. DNA Replication
T. Gular
W. Food Chain

C. Facultative Anaerobe
F. Marine Biology
I. Water Potential
L. Nucleolus
O. Electron Donor
R. Enzyme
U. Neuron
X. Denitrification

Provide the word that best matches each clue.

226. NEUROMUSCULAR JUNCTION

A chemical synapse formed by the contact between a motor neuron and a muscle fiber.

227. ESTROGEN

The primary female sex hormone. it is responsible for the development and regulation of the female reproductive system and secondary sex characteristics.

228. PATHOLOGY

A medical specialty that is concerned with the diagnosis of disease based on the laboratory analysis of bodily fluids such as blood and urine.

229. ECTODERM

The outermost layer of cells or tissue of an embryo in early development, or the parts derived from this, which include the epidermis, nerve tissue, and nephridia.

230. PHYSIOLOGY

The branch of biology dealing with the functions and activities of living organisms and their parts, including all physical and chemical processes.

231. MASS DENSITY

Density is mass per volume.

232. PALEONTOLOGY

The study of the history of life on earth as reflected in the fossil record. fossils are the remains or traces of organisms.

233. ABSCISSION

Shedding of flowers and leaves and fruit following formation of scar tissue in a plant.

234. FACULTATIVE ANAEROBE — Organism which can produce energy through aerobic respiration and then switching to anaerobic respiration depending on the amounts of oxygen.

235. EPINEPHRINE — Another term for adrenaline.

236. SYMBIOGENESIS — An evolutionary theory that explains the origin of eukaryotic cells from prokaryotes.

237. SYNTHETIC BIOLOGY — An interdisciplinary branch of biology and engineering.

238. CHEMICAL KINETICS — The study and discussion of chemical reactions with respect to reaction rates.

239. ELECTRON SHELL — An electron shell is the outside part of an atom around the atomic nucleus. it is a group of atomic orbitals with the same value of the principal quantum number n.

240. SPECIES — Often defined as the largest group of organisms in which two individuals can reproduce fertile offspring, typically using sexual reproduction.

241. EXTERNAL FERTILIZATION — Sperm units with egg in the open, rather than inside the body of the parents

242. WHITE BLOOD CELL — Component of the blood that functions in the immune system. also known as a leukocyte.

243. CLONING — Propagate (an organism or cell) to make an identical copy of.

244. BACTERIOPHAGE — Virus that infects and multiplies within bacteria.

245. POLYPLOIDY — Containing more than two homologous sets of chromosomes.

246. BIOMECHANICS — The study of the structure and function of biological systems by means of the methods of "mechanics."

247. MOLE — The si unit of measurement used to measure the number of things, usually atoms or molecules.

248. GENE — A gene is a locus (or region) of DNA that encodes a functional RNA or protein product and is the molecular unit of heredity.

249. ENANTIOMER — Stereoisomers that are non-superimposable mirror images. a molecule with 1 chiral carbon atom exists as 2 stereoisomers termed enantiomers.

250. NUCLEOLUS _____ A small dense spherical structure in the nucleus of a cell during interphase.

A. External Fertilization
B. Mass Density
C. Neuromuscular Junction
D. Epinephrine
E. Paleontology
F. White Blood Cell
G. Abscission
H. Electron Shell
I. Ectoderm
J. Synthetic Biology
K. Enantiomer
L. Chemical kinetics
M. Bacteriophage
N. Mole
O. Estrogen
P. Pathology
Q. Physiology
R. Gene
S. Facultative Anaerobe
T. Cloning
U. Biomechanics
V. Nucleolus
W. Polyploidy
X. Symbiogenesis
Y. Species

Provide the word that best matches each clue.

251. INCOMPLETE DOMINANCE _____ A form of intermediate inheritance in which one allele for a specific trait is not completely expressed over its paired allele.

252. GENE _____ A gene is a locus (or region) of DNA that encodes a functional RNA or protein product and is the molecular unit of heredity.

253. ENTOMOLOGY _____ The study of insects.

254. ELECTRONEGATIVITY _____ A measure of the tendency of an atom to attract a bonding pair of electrons. the Pauling scale is the most commonly used.

255. GENETICS _____ The study of heredity

256. MOLECULAR BIOLOGY _____ A branch of science concerning biological activity at the molecular level.

257. ABYSSAL ZONE _____ The deep sea (2000 meters or more) where there is no light.

258. INVERTEBRATE _____ A group of animals that have no backbone, unlike animals such as reptiles, amphibians, fish, birds and mammals who all have a backbone.

259. CONSERVATION BIOLOGY _____ The scientific study of nature and of earth's biodiversity with the aim of protecting species, their habitats, and ecosystems from excessive rates of extinction.

260. AGROBIOLOGY _____ The study of plant nutrition and growth especially to increase crop yield

261. CENTROID _____ The intersection of the three medians of the triangle (each median connecting a vertex with the midpoint of the opposite side).

262. ARACHNOLOGY _____ Scientific study of spiders, scorpions, pseudo-scorpions, and harvestmen.

263. MASS NUMBER _____ The total number of protons and neutrons (together known as nucleons) in an atomic nucleus

264. BIODIVERSITY _____ The variety of life in the world or in a habitat or ecosystem.

265. TRANSFER RNA _____ RNA consisting of folded molecules that transport amino acids from the cytoplasm of a cell to a ribosome.

266. POLYPLOIDY _____ Containing more than two homologous sets of chromosomes.

267. INTERLEUKIN _____ A group of cytokines (secreted proteins and signal molecules) that were first seen to be expressed by white blood cells (leukocytes)

268. CHROMOSOME _____ A threadlike strand of DNA in the cell nucleus that carries the genes in a linear order.

269. MEIOSIS _____ A type of cell division that reduces the number of chromosomes in the parent cell by half and produces four gamete cells.

270. WHITE BLOOD CELL _____ Component of the blood that functions in the immune system. also known as a leukocyte.

271. ELECTRIC POTENTIAL _____ The amount of work needed to move a unit charge from a reference point to a specific point against an electric field.

272. ENANTIOMER _____ Stereoisomers that are non-superimposable mirror images. a molecule with 1 chiral carbon atom exists as 2 stereoisomers termed enantiomers.

273. CELL _____ The structural and functional unit of all organisms.

274. T CELL _____ A lymphocyte of a type produced or processed by the thymus gland and actively participating in the immune response.

275. NUCLEIC ACID _____ A complex organic substance present in living cells, especially DNA or RNA, whose molecules consist of many nucleotides linked in a long chain.

A. T Cell
D. Conservation Biology
G. Entomology
J. Gene
M. Transfer RNA
P. White Blood Cell
S. Molecular biology
V. Mass Number

B. Arachnology
E. Enantiomer
H. Nucleic Acid
K. Centroid
N. Polyploidy
Q. Invertebrate
T. Agrobiology
W. Electric Potential

C. Meiosis
F. Cell
I. Genetics
L. Incomplete Dominance
O. Interleukin
R. Chromosome
U. Abyssal zone
X. Biodiversity

Provide the word that best matches each clue.

276. EPIDEMIOLOGY

The study and analysis of the patterns, causes, and effects of health and disease conditions in defined populations.

277. VALENCE BOND THEORY

A straightforward extension of Lewis structures. states that electrons in a covalent bond reside in a region that is the overlap of individual atomic orbitals.

278. CHOLESTEROL

An organic lipid molecule that is biosynthesized by all animal cells because it is an essential structural component of all animal cell membranes.

279. CRYOBIOLOGY

The branch of biology that studies the effects of low temperatures on living things within earth's cryosphere or in science.

280. ELECTRON TRANSPORT CHAIN

The site of oxidative phosphorylation in eukaryotes.

281. UREA

Serves an important role in the metabolism of nitrogen-containing compounds by animals and is the main nitrogen-containing substance in the urine of mammals.

282. ACTIVE TRANSPORT

Transport of a substance (as a protein or drug) across a cell membrane against the concentration gradient; requires an expenditure of energy

283. MASS DENSITY

Density is mass per volume.

284. MACROMOLECULE

A very large molecule, such as protein, commonly created by polymerization of smaller subunits (monomers).

285. DENATURATION

A process in which proteins or nucleic acids lose the quaternary structure, tertiary structure and secondary structure which is present in their native state.

286. ACTIVE SITE

The part of an enzyme or antibody where the chemical reaction occurs

287. AEROBIC

Depending on free oxygen or air.

288. AGROBIOLOGY

The study of plant nutrition and growth especially to increase crop yield

289. VALENCE BAND

The highest range of electron energies in which electrons are normally present at absolute zero temperature.

290. GENE _____ A gene is a locus (or region) of DNA that encodes a functional RNA or protein product and is the molecular unit of heredity.

291. CONSERVATION BIOLOGY _____ The scientific study of nature and of earth's biodiversity with the aim of protecting species, their habitats, and ecosystems from excessive rates of extinction.

292. CELL NUCLEUS _____ The "control room" for the cell. the nucleus gives out all the orders.

293. ENDOCYTOSIS _____ A form of active transport in which a cell transports molecules into the cell.

294. PRIMASE _____ An enzyme that synthesizes short RNA sequences called primers.

295. POLYPLOIDY _____ Containing more than two homologous sets of chromosomes.

296. BILE _____ A dark green to yellowish brown fluid, produced by the liver of most vertebrates, that aids the digestion of lipids in the small intestine.

297. BIOLOGY _____ Study of living organisms.

298. ENZYME _____ Biological molecules (proteins) that act as catalysts and help complex reactions occur everywhere in life.

299. ONCOLOGY _____ A branch of medicine that deals with the prevention, diagnosis and treatment of cancer.

300. AEROBIOLOGY _____ The study of organic particles, such as bacteria, fungal spores, very small insects, pollen grains and viruses, which are passively transported by the air.

A. Primase
D. Biology
G. Conservation Biology
J. Enzyme
M. Macromolecule
P. Urea
S. Gene
V. Valence band
Y. Cell nucleus

B. Active site
E. Cryobiology
H. Cholesterol
K. Epidemiology
N. Oncology
Q. Mass Density
T. Aerobiology
W. Aerobic

C. Electron Transport Chain
F. Valence bond theory
I. Agrobiology
L. Bile
O. Polyploidy
R. Endocytosis
U. Denaturation
X. Active Transport

## Word Search

1. Find the hidden words. The words have been placed horizontally, vertically, or diagonally. When you locate a word, draw an ellipse around it.

| | | | | | | | | | | | | | | | | | | | | | | |
|---|---|---|---|---|---|---|---|---|---|---|---|---|---|---|---|---|---|---|---|---|---|---|
| P | O | L | Y | M | E | R | A | S | E | C | H | A | I | N | R | E | A | C | T | I | O | N |
| O | P | H | G | J | E | U | C | H | L | O | R | O | P | L | A | S | T | N | F | M | J | W |
| S | B | Y | U | R | K | E | L | E | C | T | R | O | N | A | C | C | E | P | T | O | R | R |
| J | L | A | A | I | K | L | U | K | N | V | P | Y | A | M | N | I | O | T | E | S | W | O |
| C | C | X | N | M | K | I | H | R | E | G | P | E | G | O | R | C | E | A | G | J | O | Q |
| P | P | N | I | U | Q | H | D | E | U | D | N | O | O | V | Q | Q | J | G | B | Z | F | Q |
| P | K | D | N | C | F | F | M | B | R | Q | C | L | O | N | I | N | G | H | O | H | T | P |
| G | J | F | E | Z | M | O | C | S | O | V | D | E | D | T | A | P | K | Y | T | A | T | X |
| B | A | S | Y | G | L | N | I | C | N | P | E | Q | W | W | U | Z | I | L | A | K | R | W |
| B | A | S | A | L | B | O | D | Y | S | W | K | N | L | G | K | B | Q | V | N | N | Q | N |
| J | R | O | N | L | Z | N | Y | C | G | N | R | N | I | H | Y | B | G | Y | Y | N | J | W |
| F | F | Q | F | N | A | B | M | L | S | T | R | Z | I | M | C | K | V | A | L | E | X | L |
| I | S | Z | C | Y | L | A | J | E | W | Z | A | G | R | I | C | U | L | T | U | R | E | H |
| R | E | M | E | L | E | C | T | R | I | C | P | O | T | E | N | T | I | A | L | Y | H | X |
| Z | B | I | O | E | N | G | I | N | E | E | R | I | N | G | L | M | O | T | A | N | Z | U |
| W | Q | L | G | E | N | E | X | C | E | U | R | I | N | E | Y | T | W | X | F | L | B | Q |

1. An electrically excitable cell that processes and transmits information through electrical and chemical signals.
2. One of the four main nucleobases found in the nucleic acids DNA and RNA, the others being adenine, cytosine, and thymine.
3. The practice of cultivating land, growing food, and raising stock.
4. A liquid by-product of the body secreted by the kidneys through a process called urination (or micturition) and excreted through the urethra.
5. The study of plants.
6. A chemical entity that accepts electrons transferred to it from another compound.
7. A gene is a locus (or region) of DNA that encodes a functional RNA or protein product and is the molecular unit of heredity.
8. The amount of work needed to move a unit charge from a reference point to a specific point against an electric field.
9. The application of concepts and methods of biology to solve real world problems.
10. Organisms that produce an egg composed of shell and membranes that creates a protected environment in which the embryo can develop out of water
11. A technique used in molecular biology to amplify a single copy or a few copies of a piece of DNA across several orders of magnitude.
12. Propagate (an organism or cell) to make an identical copy of.
13. the sequence of reactions by which most living cells generate energy during the process of aerobic respiration.
14. An organelle formed from a centriole, and a short cylindrical array of microtubules.
15. Work to convert light energy of the sun into sugars that can be used by cells.

A. Botany
D. Amniotes
G. Guanine
J. Neuron
M. Agriculture
B. Polymerase Chain Reaction
E. Basal body
H. Urine
K. Electric Potential
N. Krebs Cycle
C. Gene
F. Electron Acceptor
I. Bioengineering
L. Chloroplast
O. Cloning

2. Find the hidden words. The words have been placed horizontally, vertically, or diagonally. When you locate a word, draw an ellipse around it.

| V | I | R | O | L | O | G | Y | M | B | I | X | R | S | R | I | Q | L | N | D | L | T | L |
|---|---|---|---|---|---|---|---|---|---|---|---|---|---|---|---|---|---|---|---|---|---|---|
| E | W | P | S | M | D | E | P | J | L | X | Y | X | C | S | K | M | E | S | O | N | Q | B |
| N | B | M | Y | V | A | F | W | J | A | U | H | M | F | E | Y | U | Q | L | N | X | H | E |
| D | T | H | W | A | C | L | Y | T | S | Q | Z | Y | A | K | L | R | N | X | K | R | S | A |
| O | J | R | W | S | J | F | Y | E | T | G | Q | E | N | J | W | I | E | B | U | Y | U | C |
| D | X | P | E | H | N | F | U | M | O | C | D | E | P | I | S | T | A | S | I | S | N | T |
| E | D | D | Y | N | E | I | N | G | C | O | V | B | L | E | R | X | M | U | N | H | Z | I |
| R | V | L | R | N | C | N | M | D | Y | M | W | V | U | N | O | E | B | E | K | A | L | V |
| M | G | E | N | E | T | I | C | S | S | B | D | D | B | H | U | B | I | H | S | B | W | E |
| I | D | B | H | D | G | E | N | E | T | I | C | C | O | D | E | B | L | F | M | I | C | S |
| S | N | G | K | P | Q | K | R | J | M | E | D | U | L | L | A | T | E | B | N | T | X | I |
| A | M | M | A | S | K | W | U | E | W | M | V | U | P | A | K | P | R | S | I | A | C | T |
| B | Q | E | B | M | M | S | J | X | B | Z | U | V | W | Q | P | G | K | Q | I | T | R | E |
| Y | R | U | P | U | B | K | N | A | T | U | R | A | L | S | E | L | E | C | T | I | O | N |
| G | T | B | I | F | U | Y | A | C | C | L | I | M | A | T | I | Z | A | T | I | O | N | V |
| I | Z | G | Y | D | K | G | E | L | E | C | T | R | O | N | C | A | R | R | I | E | R | U |

1. An inner layer of cells in the cortex of a root and of some stems, surrounding a vascular bundle.
2. A dark green to yellowish brown fluid, produced by the liver of most vertebrates, that aids the digestion of lipids in the small intestine.
3. The continuation of the spinal cord within the skull, forming the lowest part of the brainstem and containing control centers for the heart and lungs.
4. A mammalian blastula in which some differentiation of cells has occurred.
5. Adaptation to a new climate (a new temperature or altitude or environment).
6. A place for animals, people and plants and non-living things
7. The nucleotide triplets of DNA and RNA molecules that carry genetic information in living cells.
8. The interaction of genes that are not alleles. The suppression of the effect of one such gene by another.

9. The study of viruses-submicroscopic, parasitic particles of genetic material contained in a protein coat and virus-like agents.
10. A process in nature in which organisms possessing certain genotypic characteristics that make them better adjusted to an environment tend to survive.
11. The study of heredity
12. Hadronic subatomic particles composed of one quark and one antiquark, bound together by the strong interaction.
13. A motor protein in cells which converts the chemical energy contained in ATP into the mechanical energy of movement
14. Any of various molecules that can accept one or two electrons from one molecule and donating them to another in the process of electron transport.
15. The part of an enzyme or antibody where the chemical reaction occurs

A. Medulla
E. Bile
I. Active site
M. Habitat

B. Virology
F. Genetics
J. Electron Carrier
N. Natural Selection

C. Meson
G. Dynein
K. Epistasis
O. Acclimatization

D. Endodermis
H. Blastocyst
L. Genetic Code

3. Find the hidden words. The words have been placed horizontally, vertically, or diagonally. When you locate a word, draw an ellipse around it.

| M | A | Z | T | J | V | E | P | I | N | E | P | H | R | I | N | E | I | H | B | Z | K | D |
|---|---|---|---|---|---|---|---|---|---|---|---|---|---|---|---|---|---|---|---|---|---|---|
| Z | J | M | R | K | I | D | E | A | R | P | A | X | V | G | H | D | S | F | H | S | W | H |
| O | V | D | A | R | W | I | N | I | A | N | F | I | T | N | E | S | S | H | A | K | L | T |
| G | F | K | V | W | Y | N | P | N | E | N | D | O | C | R | I | N | E | G | L | A | N | D |
| U | G | C | U | V | L | Y | W | E | C | T | O | T | H | E | R | M | N | O | B | D | J | T |
| D | K | C | C | M | X | W | D | H | T | M | Y | O | S | I | N | S | G | K | J | Q | B | Z |
| I | U | O | E | A | L | V | E | S | T | I | G | I | A | L | I | T | Y | A | Q | C | L | C |
| W | L | M | V | S | K | P | W | L | H | H | E | T | E | R | O | S | I | S | K | T | V | P |
| T | K | M | N | S | J | N | K | C | I | U | O | F | G | P | F | I | C | U | A | Q | V | Z |
| S | U | X | I | D | B | I | O | D | I | V | E | R | S | I | T | Y | Q | N | Y | J | Q | F |
| N | E | V | T | E | Y | M | H | P | A | A | O | Q | Y | P | D | A | R | C | E | Q | T | E |
| U | T | S | R | N | Q | A | W | G | E | N | E | P | O | O | L | X | E | Z | D | J | S | B |
| T | L | K | P | S | N | K | P | A | B | S | O | L | U | T | E | Z | E | R | O | V | K | B |
| W | H | F | Q | I | W | S | Y | N | T | H | E | T | I | C | B | I | O | L | O | G | Y | V |
| E | A | L | I | T | K | B | B | A | R | R | B | O | D | Y | A | N | A | T | O | M | Y | B |
| G | W | G | S | Y | D | W | P | N | O | X | A | B | S | O | R | P | T | I | O | N | B | G |

1. Large superfamily of motor proteins that move along actin filaments, while hydrolyzing ATP.
2. An interdisciplinary branch of biology and engineering.
3. The stock of different genes in an interbreeding population.
4. Density is mass per volume.
5. Refers to genetically determined structures or attributes that have apparently lost most or all their ancestral function in a given species.
6. The inactive x chromosome in a female somatic cell, rendered inactive in a process called lyonization
7. A process in which one substance permeates another; a fluid permeates or is dissolved by a liquid or solid.
8. The tendency of a crossbred individual to show qualities superior to those of both parents.
9. A organism in which internal physiological sources of heat are of relatively small or quite negligible importance in controlling body temperature. "cold blooded".
10. The lowest theoretically attainable temperature (at which the kinetic energy of atoms and molecules is minimal)
11. Another term for adrenaline.
12. The variety of life in the world or in a habitat or ecosystem.
13. The genetic contribution of an individual to the next generation's gene pool relative to the average for the population.
14. Glands that secrete their products, hormones, directly into the blood rather than through a duct.
15. The branch of morphology that deals with the structure of animals

A. Barr body
E. Vestigiality
I. Absolute Zero
M. Mass Density
B. Myosin
F. Biodiversity
J. Endocrine Gland
N. Synthetic Biology
C. Anatomy
G. Gene Pool
K. Absorption
O. Ectotherm
D. Heterosis
H. Epinephrine
L. Darwinian Fitness

4. Find the hidden words. The words have been placed horizontally, vertically, or diagonally. When you locate a word, draw an ellipse around it.

| G | S | O | D | I | P | Z | J | Q | V | J | V | G | B | I | U | M | O | L | E | D | X | K |
|---|---|---|---|---|---|---|---|---|---|---|---|---|---|---|---|---|---|---|---|---|---|---|
| R | S | J | D | T | G | S | M | Y | U | O | I | K | D | J | Q | D | P | W | D | S | L | S |
| L | L | M | E | V | O | L | U | T | I | O | N | A | R | Y | B | I | O | L | O | G | Y | K |
| M | C | N | V | K | M | A | S | S | N | U | M | B | E | R | Q | M | K | O | W | O | V | W |
| Q | D | A | O | P | C | N | Z | S | W | K | F | E | G | U | R | F | A | Y | S | G | V | G |
| J | B | L | Z | R | E | R | X | S | V | T | O | U | Z | N | C | E | N | T | R | O | I | D |
| P | I | L | D | O | I | E | L | E | C | T | R | I | C | P | O | T | E | N | T | I | A | L |
| Y | O | N | S | K | P | R | I | Q | D | W | U | F | N | X | V | P | B | K | T | P | O | X |
| V | M | B | Z | A | C | H | E | M | I | S | T | R | Y | A | R | F | E | T | U | S | M | Q |
| K | A | G | H | R | S | W | A | T | E | R | P | O | T | E | N | T | I | A | L | B | O | U |
| X | S | P | U | Y | T | S | D | Q | S | C | I | A | U | C | N | I | W | S | E | Y | L | C |
| W | S | W | O | O | E | L | C | M | T | P | H | A | B | I | T | A | T | A | R | G | A | X |
| P | T | K | Q | T | R | H | B | W | X | T | A | M | G | X | B | Y | L | S | U | Y | R | F |
| H | E | E | X | E | O | I | E | A | G | R | I | C | U | L | T | U | R | E | S | G | I | K |
| A | R | L | C | D | I | F | J | C | R | O | R | H | B | I | V | K | I | N | A | N | T | H |
| X | F | T | A | P | D | K | O | N | I | D | I | Q | E | C | D | Y | S | O | N | E | Y | N |

1. A branch of physical science that studies the composition, structure, properties and change of matter.
2. A human embryo after eight weeks of development.
3. A microscopic single celled organism that has no distinct nucleus
4. The amount of work needed to move a unit charge from a reference point to a specific point against an electric field.
5. The total number of protons and neutrons (together known as nucleons) in an atomic nucleus
6. A place for animals, people and plants and non-living things
7. A measure of the potential energy in water as well as the difference between the potential in a water sample and pure water.
8. The intersection of the three medians of the triangle (each median connecting a vertex with the midpoint of the opposite side).

9. An organic compound with four rings arranged in a specific configuration. examples include the dietary lipid cholesterol and the sex hormones.
10. Organic matter derived from living, or recently living organisms.
11. The practice of cultivating land, growing food, and raising stock.
12. The si unit of measurement used to measure the number of things, usually atoms or molecules.
13. A steroidal prohormone of the major insect molting hormone is secreted from the prothoracic glands.
14. A unit of concentration measuring the number of moles of a solute per liter of solution.
15. The subfield of biology that studies the evolutionary processes that produced the diversity of life on earth starting from a single origin of life.

A. Molarity
E. Mass Number
I. Centroid
M. Habitat

B. Steroid
F. Mole
J. Electric Potential
N. Prokaryote

C. Fetus
G. Evolutionary Biology
K. Agriculture
O. Ecdysone

D. Biomass
H. Chemistry
L. Water Potential

5. Find the hidden words. The words have been placed horizontally, vertically, or diagonally. When you locate a word, draw an ellipse around it.

| R | F | Q | H | U | M | A | N | N | U | T | R | I | T | I | O | N | Z | L | G | G | P | F |
| S | J | G | V | R | U | J | N | A | T | U | R | A | L | S | E | L | E | C | T | I | O | N |
| L | H | N | B | M | J | E | W | D | P | A | X | U | C | A | H | A | D | R | O | N | E | W |
| G | G | P | D | I | H | F | Y | I | J | U | P | H | G | U | I | P | F | Y | R | H | N | O |
| E | J | C | G | E | R | H | B | T | V | W | F | I | E | T | V | C | L | D | R | R | D | B |
| I | N | E | M | Z | D | G | W | C | V | G | Y | Q | N | O | J | P | P | T | P | D | E | B |
| Z | L | M | A | G | L | C | L | D | M | U | E | W | E | I | M | O | G | I | H | B | M | L |
| U | A | W | D | C | X | U | F | F | N | X | G | V | T | M | S | F | J | H | E | A | I | E |
| D | F | F | I | G | M | O | L | E | C | U | L | E | I | M | T | K | N | A | N | R | C | B |
| U | C | Y | Z | U | K | J | B | U | P | X | A | X | C | U | N | R | V | B | O | R | S | A |
| X | G | E | N | O | M | E | F | F | H | T | O | V | C | N | O | I | I | B | T | B | P | S |
| Z | N | G | L | Q | C | L | E | P | T | O | N | D | O | I | S | H | G | S | Y | O | E | E |
| M | W | U | X | P | L | H | G | S | O | N | F | V | D | T | E | I | S | B | P | D | C | P |
| N | C | K | L | B | I | C | G | I | M | J | V | K | E | Y | Z | N | U | E | E | Y | I | A |
| S | I | N | V | Z | K | H | C | Q | M | G | A | N | G | L | I | O | N | M | I | L | E | I |
| H | H | J | E | C | O | L | O | G | I | C | A | L | N | I | C | H | E | B | E | E | S | R |

1. A process in nature in which organisms possessing certain genotypic characteristics that make them better adjusted to an environment tend to survive.
2. The inactive x chromosome in a female somatic cell, rendered inactive in a process called lyonization
3. The haploid set of chromosomes in a gamete or microorganism, or in each cell of a multicellular organism.
4. The system of immune responses of an organism against its own healthy cells and tissues.
5. The nucleotide triplets of DNA and RNA molecules that carry genetic information in living cells.
6. A pairing between two nucleotides in RNA molecules that does not follow Watson crick base pair rules
7. Refers to the provision of essential nutrients necessary to support human life and health.
8. A cluster (functional group) of nerve cell bodies in a centralized nervous system.
9. The ecological state of a species being unique to a defined geographic location, such as an island, nation, country or other defined zone, or habitat type.
10. An elementary, half-integer spin particle that does not undergo strong interactions.
11. The role and position a species has in its environment; how it meets its needs for food and shelter, how it survives, and how it reproduces.
12. The smallest particle in a chemical element or compound that has the chemical properties of that element or compound.
13. Any particle that is made from quarks, antiquarks and gluons.
14. The set of observable characteristics of an individual resulting from the interaction of its genotype with the environment.

A. Genetic Code
B. Lepton
C. Genome
D. Ganglion
E. Ecological Niche
F. Natural Selection
G. Wobble Base Pair
H. Molecule
I. Hadron
J. Phenotype
K. Autoimmunity
L. Endemic Species
M. Barr body
N. Human Nutrition

6. Find the hidden words. The words have been placed horizontally, vertically, or diagonally. When you locate a word, draw an ellipse around it.

| W | H | K | O | S | Q | H | Z | X | K | H | O | Z | K | Q | L | Z | F | F | O | S | C | J |
|---|---|---|---|---|---|---|---|---|---|---|---|---|---|---|---|---|---|---|---|---|---|---|
| L | V | P | O | R | G | A | N | I | S | M | H | Y | X | E | C | M | I | V | J | Y | X | H |
| P | L | A | S | M | O | L | Y | S | I | S | A | T | V | F | S | L | J | R | J | X | N | X |
| V | V | H | D | W | E | P | L | T | X | Z | B | T | C | R | J | U | V | Y | Y | T | P | L |
| S | D | G | K | A | P | W | H | T | R | C | I | X | C | B | B | I | U | I | M | F | Y | F |
| A | I | A | S | N | I | I | Q | O | T | K | T | J | E | J | U | N | U | M | E | X | L | F |
| C | S | B | T | W | N | S | D | Z | F | W | A | V | A | Q | H | L | B | Q | M | N | R | O |
| G | S | U | F | R | E | N | O | R | F | Y | T | H | E | T | E | R | O | S | I | S | R | O |
| T | E | P | Z | Q | P | M | O | L | E | C | U | L | A | R | P | H | Y | S | I | C | S | D |
| S | P | P | N | U | H | F | U | L | E | C | H | E | M | I | C | A | L | B | O | N | D | C |
| S | W | E | S | T | R | O | G | E | N | A | F | M | D | Y | Q | G | F | K | X | W | B | H |
| J | E | M | U | H | I | C | H | E | M | I | C | A | L | C | O | M | P | O | U | N | D | A |
| E | C | V | B | I | N | U | I | A | W | H | E | R | P | E | T | O | L | O | G | Y | A | I |
| W | A | X | I | A | E | Y | Q | O | M | C | H | E | M | I | S | T | R | Y | S | V | T | N |
| C | B | I | O | M | E | D | I | C | A | L | E | N | G | I | N | E | E | R | I | N | G | Y |
| K | O | T | W | N | G | J | I | K | N | H | C | X | V | R | K | D | C | B | P | K | E | M |

1. A place for animals, people and plants and non-living things
2. A branch of physical science that studies the composition, structure, properties and change of matter.
3. An individual animal, plant, or single-celled life form.
4. A hierarchical series of organisms each dependent on the next as a source of food.
5. The primary female sex hormone. it is responsible for the development and regulation of the female reproductive system and secondary sex characteristics.
6. Another term for adrenaline.
7. The study of the physical properties of molecules, the chemical bonds between atoms as well as the molecular dynamics.
8. A chemical substance consisting of two or more different chemically bonded chemical elements, with a fixed ratio determining the composition.
9. The midsection of the small intestine of many higher vertebrates like mammals, birds, reptiles. it is present between the duodenum and the ileum.
10. Contraction of the protoplast of a plant cell as a result of loss of water from the cell.
11. The application of engineering principles and design concepts to medicine and biology for healthcare purposes (e.g. diagnostic or therapeutic).
12. The branch of zoology concerned with reptiles and amphibians.
13. A lasting attraction between atoms that enables the formation of chemical compounds.
14. The tendency of a crossbred individual to show qualities superior to those of both parents.

A. Plasmolysis
D. Chemistry
G. Estrogen
J. Organism
M. Herpetology
B. Chemical compound
E. Habitat
H. Epinephrine
K. Biomedical engineering
N. Jejunum
C. Food Chain
F. Heterosis
I. Molecular physics
L. Chemical bond

7. Find the hidden words. The words have been placed horizontally, vertically, or diagonally. When you locate a word, draw an ellipse around it.

| O | V | C | B | E | H | A | V | I | O | R | A | L | E | C | O | L | O | G | Y | S | P | A |
|---|---|---|---|---|---|---|---|---|---|---|---|---|---|---|---|---|---|---|---|---|---|---|
| P | I | N | C | O | M | P | L | E | T | E | D | O | M | I | N | A | N | C | E | C | L | L |
| O | Z | X | Q | U | B | M | N | Q | R | O | P | K | B | Y | B | V | X | I | B | O | T | S |
| L | M | N | F | I | B | F | B | K | N | T | H | I | B | V | C | A | E | C | X | I | R | O |
| L | N | L | Y | O | W | P | C | M | W | B | W | S | Y | N | S | T | M | H | J | L | S | W |
| I | U | L | D | N | C | Y | G | G | I | G | V | B | Q | Z | T | X | E | T | G | O | R | P |
| N | C | Z | S | E | I | Q | B | J | V | J | C | P | Q | T | E | M | F | H | L | I | A | P |
| A | L | I | U | G | B | A | A | N | T | I | C | O | D | O | N | G | S | Y | F | P | N | M |
| T | E | Y | R | V | T | D | A | B | S | O | L | U | T | E | Z | E | R | O | H | U | L | W |
| I | I | X | M | A | C | R | O | E | V | O | L | U | T | I | O | N | L | L | Z | D | F | K |
| O | C | X | V | G | S | T | Y | O | B | H | F | M | D | I | K | I | D | O | F | V | Q | R |
| N | A | Y | X | L | J | P | L | A | S | M | O | L | Y | S | I | S | Y | G | Q | W | D | S |
| X | C | U | D | V | P | I | X | Z | X | U | N | K | P | O | O | Q | D | Y | L | A | O | T |
| B | I | O | L | O | G | Y | G | D | M | O | L | I | O | N | I | C | B | O | N | D | Z | J |
| W | D | R | E | P | R | O | D | U | C | T | I | O | N | T | C | B | K | J | K | K | J | I |
| N | E | U | R | O | M | U | S | C | U | L | A | R | J | U | N | C | T | I | O | N | T | C |

1. The study of the evolutionary basis for animal behavior due to ecological pressures.
2. The lowest theoretically attainable temperature (at which the kinetic energy of atoms and molecules is minimal)
3. Known as fish science, is the branch of biology devoted to the study of fish.
4. A complex organic substance present in living cells, especially DNA or RNA, whose molecules consist of many nucleotides linked in a long chain.
5. Study of living organisms.
6. Evolution on a scale of separated gene pools. studies focus on change that occurs at or above the level of species, in contrast with microevolution.
7. A sequence of three nucleotides forming a unit of genetic code in a transfer RNA molecule, corresponding to a complementary codon in messenger RNA.
8. An atom or molecule with a net electric charge due to the loss or gain of one or more electrons.
9. Contraction of the protoplast of a plant cell as a result of loss of water from the cell.
10. The act of transferring pollen grains from the male anther of a flower to the female stigma.
11. The complete transfer of valence electron(s) between atoms. it is a type of chemical bond that generates two oppositely charged ions.
12. Giving birth to one of its kind, sexually or asexually.
13. A form of intermediate inheritance in which one allele for a specific trait is not completely expressed over its paired allele.
14. A chemical synapse formed by the contact between a motor neuron and a muscle fiber.

A. Ionic Bond
B. Plasmolysis
C. Absolute Zero
D. Nucleic Acid
E. Behavioral ecology
F. Ion
G. Ichthyology
H. Pollination
I. Neuromuscular Junction
J. Incomplete Dominance
K. Biology
L. Anticodon
M. Macroevolution
N. Reproduction

8. Find the hidden words. The words have been placed horizontally, vertically, or diagonally. When you locate a word, draw an ellipse around it.

| | | | | | | | | | | | | | | | | | | | | | | |
|---|---|---|---|---|---|---|---|---|---|---|---|---|---|---|---|---|---|---|---|---|---|---|
| F | Q | S | S | G | N | C | M | J | U | S | Z | W | O | Q | P | F | F | H | W | C | Q | U |
| U | A | G | R | O | B | I | O | L | O | G | Y | K | W | K | Y | H | H | E | T | H | N | P |
| X | X | D | H | R | Q | V | D | A | G | X | O | E | Y | Z | M | H | I | P | I | E | O | S |
| F | G | K | W | H | V | W | O | V | E | F | A | F | C | Z | L | J | X | P | J | M | E | Y |
| T | V | K | X | F | F | X | L | M | B | A | S | A | L | B | O | D | Y | A | I | I | Z | C |
| C | O | K | Y | S | Q | S | K | J | U | Z | P | F | B | R | N | Z | W | Z | N | C | A | H |
| E | M | Y | O | F | I | B | R | I | L | X | K | Z | Z | K | J | W | N | Q | S | A | B | O |
| L | Y | V | E | S | I | C | L | E | E | M | B | R | Y | O | L | O | G | Y | U | L | L | B |
| L | B | U | F | Q | P | H | J | I | D | E | S | M | O | S | O | M | E | S | L | R | Y | I |
| C | H | E | M | I | C | A | L | E | Q | U | I | L | I | B | R | I | U | M | I | E | N | O |
| U | K | P | P | I | F | S | G | A | L | M | C | P | P | L | N | I | U | F | N | A | T | L |
| U | R | I | N | E | M | A | C | R | O | N | U | T | R | I | E | N | T | I | W | C | O | O |
| N | K | W | A | X | R | N | R | H | Y | W | E | O | V | T | N | H | Y | U | X | T | A | G |
| P | S | P | B | E | T | A | O | N | E | F | Y | W | B | F | M | E | U | P | N | I | U | Y |
| E | D | T | K | O | R | N | I | T | H | O | L | O | G | Y | X | S | P | G | X | O | V | N |
| Z | V | A | L | E | N | C | E | B | O | N | D | T | H | E | O | R | Y | N | Y | N | S | G |

1. A lymphocyte of a type produced or processed by the thymus gland and actively participating in the immune response.
2. A branch of zoology that concerns the study of birds.
3. Usually characterized by a chemical change, and they yield one or more products, which usually have properties different from the reactants
4. Nutrients that provide calories or energy. nutrients are substances needed for growth, metabolism, and for other body functions.
5. The application of the principles of biology to the study of physiological, genetic, and developmental mechanisms of behavior in humans and other animals.
6. A liquid by-product of the body secreted by the kidneys through a process called urination (or micturition) and excreted through the urethra.
7. Any of the elongated contractile threads found in striated muscle cells.
8. An organelle formed from a centriole, and a short cylindrical array of microtubules.
9. The study of plant nutrition and growth especially to increase crop yield
10. A fluid or air-filled cavity or sac.
11. The state in which both reactants and products are present in concentrations which have no further tendency to change with time.
12. Helps keep blood sugar level from getting too high (hyperglycemia) or too low (hypoglycemia).
13. Also known as a macula adhaerens, is a cell structure specialized for cell to cell adhesion.
14. The branch of biology that studies the development of gametes (sex cells), fertilization, and development of embryos and fetuses.
15. A straightforward extension of Lewis structures. states that electrons in a covalent bond reside in a region that is the overlap of individual atomic orbitals.

A. Urine
D. Agrobiology
G. Psychobiology
J. Desmosome
M. Myofibril

B. Ornithology
E. Macronutrient
H. Embryology
K. Vesicle
N. Insulin

C. Chemical reaction
F. Chemical equilibrium
I. Basal body
L. T Cell
O. Valence bond theory

9. Find the hidden words. The words have been placed horizontally, vertically, or diagonally. When you locate a word, draw an ellipse around it.

| T | W | U | N | C | T | J | R | F | U | S | P | F | B | B | I | T | J | S | J | P | V | O |
|---|---|---|---|---|---|---|---|---|---|---|---|---|---|---|---|---|---|---|---|---|---|---|
| A | K | G | M | Y | Y | I | U | A | X | M | O | I | E | I | B | T | F | F | F | H | V | U |
| Z | Y | G | O | T | E | O | F | G | P | P | N | Z | V | P | T | O | U | O | F | O | V | J |
| H | P | U | K | J | L | U | U | D | R | T | D | S | Q | E | M | E | J | A | T | R | L | F |
| A | X | I | L | I | Y | G | J | R | Z | D | I | R | L | D | Q | K | V | M | J | M | U | K |
| C | C | Y | W | K | H | E | G | K | K | O | L | K | E | A | H | S | M | Z | A | O | M | N |
| R | L | L | R | Q | V | B | E | W | T | O | N | K | R | L | U | X | Y | L | A | N | B | T |
| Y | Z | Z | H | L | E | N | D | A | N | G | E | R | E | D | S | P | E | C | I | E | S | R |
| O | G | E | N | E | T | I | C | C | O | D | E | Y | M | E | U | R | I | C | A | C | I | D |
| B | X | A | S | E | X | U | A | L | R | E | P | R | O | D | U | C | T | I | O | N | X | W |
| I | L | W | G | Z | R | G | G | O | O | F | Z | J | Q | W | A | B | T | K | J | U | B | Y |
| O | Y | S | N | M | E | G | Y | N | D | N | A | S | E | Q | U | E | N | C | I | N | G | W |
| L | O | A | Z | V | S | B | N | I | K | V | F | S | E | M | W | T | Q | I | K | K | Q | F |
| O | C | U | D | W | X | N | E | N | V | A | L | E | N | C | E | B | A | N | D | T | N | M |
| G | A | H | R | Q | Z | K | U | G | D | E | P | O | L | A | R | I | Z | A | T | I | O | N |
| Y | E | I | N | T | E | R | N | A | L | F | E | R | T | I | L | I | Z | A | T | I | O | N |

1. A heterocyclic compound of carbon, nitrogen, oxygen, and hydrogen. it forms ions and salts known as urates and acid urates, such as ammonium acid urate.
2. The highest range of electron energies in which electrons are normally present at absolute zero temperature.
3. Threatened by factors such as habitat loss, hunting, disease and climate change, and usually have declining populations or a very limited range.
4. A form of terrestrial locomotion where an organism moves by means of its two rear limbs or legs.
5. The process of determining the precise order of nucleotides within a DNA molecule.
6. Propagate (an organism or cell) to make an identical copy of.
7. A diploid cell resulting from the fusion of two haploid gametes; a fertilized ovum.
8. Process of reproduction involving a single parent that results in offspring that are genetically identical to the parent.
9. A chemical substance produced in the body that controls and regulates the activity of certain cells or organs.
10. The branch of biology that studies the effects of low temperatures on living things within earth's cryosphere or in science.
11. Fertilization that takes place inside the egg-producing individual.
12. The nucleotide triplets of DNA and RNA molecules that carry genetic information in living cells.
13. The process of reversing the charge across a cell membrane (usually a neuron), so causing an action potential.

A. DNA Sequencing
B. Genetic Code
C. Cryobiology
D. Hormone
E. Endangered Species
F. Asexual Reproduction
G. Depolarization
H. Internal Fertilization
I. Uric acid
J. Valence band
K. Zygote
L. Cloning
M. Bipedal

10. Find the hidden words. The words have been placed horizontally, vertically, or diagonally. When you locate a word, draw an ellipse around it.

| H | X | L | L | Y | Z | E | D | Y | F | H | A | J | X | L | M | N | D | F | H | W | S | L |
|---|---|---|---|---|---|---|---|---|---|---|---|---|---|---|---|---|---|---|---|---|---|---|
| M | E | S | S | E | N | G | E | R | R | N | A | E | M | B | R | Y | O | L | O | G | Y | N |
| Y | X | E | N | V | I | R | O | N | M | E | N | T | A | L | B | I | O | L | O | G | Y | O |
| A | F | V | V | E | U | D | W | K | O | T | C | M | K | D | V | R | C | Z | Z | V | V | |
| L | D | R | E | C | O | M | Y | N | A | K | D | Y | D | K | M | W | O | T | P | C | Z | J |
| E | L | E | C | T | R | O | M | A | G | N | E | T | I | C | S | P | E | C | T | R | U | M |
| B | I | O | M | E | D | I | C | A | L | E | N | G | I | N | E | E | R | I | N | G | C | V |
| E | C | O | L | O | G | I | C | A | L | E | F | F | I | C | I | E | N | C | Y | L | O | P |
| V | W | V | Y | P | F | K | J | R | D | Z | R | O | J | M | B | T | S | I | L | A | K | E |
| A | G | K | F | F | T | M | T | P | J | Q | A | W | C | S | C | V | X | N | U | S | J | X |
| L | X | F | F | P | Y | Q | K | M | A | O | F | R | O | N | J | Z | R | W | X | N | Q | A |
| E | N | M | K | I | Q | W | E | N | Z | Y | M | E | K | X | F | R | U | J | N | A | A | D |
| N | O | D | E | W | Q | M | R | K | D | P | M | X | W | X | U | F | E | T | U | S | V | G |
| C | W | R | S | E | P | Z | O | C | C | I | N | W | F | O | R | G | A | N | I | S | M | Z |
| E | J | Z | N | O | R | G | A | N | I | U | C | R | Y | O | B | I | O | L | O | G | Y | J |
| T | J | B | E | C | O | S | Y | S | T | E | M | V | A | E | U | K | A | R | Y | O | T | E |

1. An interaction of living things and non-living things in a physical environment.
2. Biological molecules (proteins) that act as catalysts and help complex reactions occur everywhere in life.
3. The branch of biology that studies the development of gametes (sex cells), fertilization, and development of embryos and fetuses.
4. Describes the efficiency with which energy is transferred from one trophic level to the next.
5. Refers to the number of elements to which it can connect.
6. The collective term for all possible frequencies of electromagnetic radiation.
7. The application of engineering principles and design concepts to medicine and biology for healthcare purposes (e.g. diagnostic or therapeutic).
8. The branch of biology concerned with the relations between organisms and their environment.
9. The form of rna in which genetic information transcribed from dna as a sequence of bases is transferred to a ribosome.
10. Any organism whose cells contain a nucleus and other organelles enclosed within membranes.
11. An individual animal, plant, or single-celled life form.
12. A human embryo after eight weeks of development.
13. The branch of biology that studies the effects of low temperatures on living things within earth's cryosphere or in science.
14. A part of an organism that is typically self-contained and has a specific vital function, such as the heart or liver in humans.

A. Ecosystem
D. Valence
G. Electromagnetic Spectrum
J. Fetus
M. Organism
B. Biomedical engineering
E. Cryobiology
H. Embryology
K. Enzyme
N. Eukaryote
C. Ecological Efficiency
F. Messenger RNA
I. Environmental Biology
L. Organ

11. Find the hidden words. The words have been placed horizontally, vertically, or diagonally. When you locate a word, draw an ellipse around it.

| F | S | M | E | I | O | S | I | S | B | K | M | A | H | W | Z | C | Q | I | H | Y | Z | D |
|---|---|---|---|---|---|---|---|---|---|---|---|---|---|---|---|---|---|---|---|---|---|---|
| Q | I | U | E | V | O | L | U | T | I | O | N | A | R | Y | B | I | O | L | O | G | Y | T |
| O | U | E | N | D | O | P | L | A | S | M | I | C | R | E | T | I | C | U | L | U | M | R |
| D | N | G | D | N | X | P | C | Y | J | P | A | M | N | N | P | X | R | E | J | X | D | A |
| P | I | E | B | A | Q | X | C | J | B | S | O | J | L | Q | T | Y | E | V | X | R | M | N |
| H | T | N | M | I | O | R | S | W | M | P | D | S | I | K | T | P | P | G | M | F | N | S |
| C | S | E | M | P | U | G | B | F | U | G | J | T | P | O | R | R | R | F | S | B | L | L |
| V | E | L | E | M | E | N | T | A | J | I | U | K | O | N | D | F | O | I | I | U | T | A |
| L | E | P | T | O | N | K | E | G | T | I | U | F | P | W | E | M | D | G | G | I | W | T |
| M | M | T | A | L | A | E | C | B | N | U | Q | E | R | D | S | U | U | S | F | H | A | I |
| S | H | I | S | T | O | L | O | G | Y | X | A | M | O | Z | M | M | C | U | J | W | A | O |
| V | A | L | E | N | C | E | T | V | O | F | O | S | T | N | O | V | T | I | R | N | U | N |
| H | D | T | G | Q | P | P | Y | F | A | M | R | F | E | F | S | N | I | K | W | A | N | G |
| F | C | E | E | G | Z | O | P | B | M | Q | Y | K | I | N | O | T | O | F | L | U | H | G |
| J | X | F | E | W | N | E | E | I | Z | B | H | Q | N | V | M | U | N | K | H | S | D | Z |
| N | G | B | N | D | O | B | C | D | L | A | C | Q | P | U | E | E | J | A | X | H | Q | B |

1. A biochemical assembly that contains both proteins and lipids, bound to the proteins, which allow fats to move through the water inside and outside cells.
2. A species of atoms having the same number of protons in their atomic nuclei.
3. Describes a genetically distinct geographic variety, population or race within a species, which is adapted to specific environmental conditions.
4. A system of physical units-based on the meter, kilogram, second, ampere, kelvin, candela, and mole, together with a set of prefixes.
5. The decoding of genetic instructions for making proteins.
6. Also known as a macula adhaerens, is a cell structure specialized for cell to cell adhesion.
7. A network of membranous tubules within the cytoplasm of a eukaryotic cell, continuous with the nuclear membrane.

8. Giving birth to one of its kind, sexually or asexually.
9. A type of cell division that reduces the number of chromosomes in the parent cell by half and produces four gamete cells.
10. The study of the microscopic anatomy of cells and tissues of plants and animals.
11. Refers to the number of elements to which it can connect.
12. The subfield of biology that studies the evolutionary processes that produced the diversity of life on earth starting from a single origin of life.
13. A gene is a locus (or region) of DNA that encodes a functional RNA or protein product and is the molecular unit of heredity.
14. An elementary, half-integer spin particle that does not undergo strong interactions.

A. Element
D. Evolutionary Biology
G. Gene
J. Valence
M. Lepton

B. Histology
E. Meiosis
H. Translation
K. Reproduction
N. Endoplasmic Reticulum

C. Ecotype
F. Desmosome
I. SI units
L. Lipoprotein

12. Find the hidden words. The words have been placed horizontally, vertically, or diagonally. When you locate a word, draw an ellipse around it.

| Q | I | N | D | E | P | E | N | D | E | N | T | A | S | S | O | R | T | M | E | N | T | D |
|---|---|---|---|---|---|---|---|---|---|---|---|---|---|---|---|---|---|---|---|---|---|---|
| P | A | F | Z | D | P | D | M | N | I | V | T | Z | H | J | C | P | V | K | A | X | Z | E |
| P | H | U | M | A | N | N | U | T | R | I | T | I | O | N | Y | Q | A | A | B | Q | A | N |
| S | H | U | W | I | L | Q | M | N | X | P | X | N | Z | Z | M | U | G | V | V | U | W | I |
| Y | A | Y | H | L | G | A | T | Q | C | O | Z | C | P | Y | D | F | R | S | M | M | I | T |
| C | I | V | W | E | A | X | W | B | X | M | E | U | H | F | G | U | O | Z | J | M | K | R |
| H | B | K | X | W | K | J | P | V | P | W | U | U | L | I | J | M | B | M | B | E | T | I |
| O | H | O | J | O | R | G | A | N | I | S | M | Z | O | V | D | X | I | U | T | V | E | F |
| B | D | W | F | B | L | Y | K | Z | L | V | K | C | E | H | E | D | O | R | W | L | S | I |
| I | T | T | V | P | F | W | S | K | C | S | N | O | M | W | Z | K | L | S | X | O | G | C |
| O | X | B | A | C | T | E | R | I | A | O | B | B | T | Y | W | L | O | B | V | R | L | A |
| L | A | D | E | N | Y | L | A | T | E | C | Y | C | L | A | S | E | G | B | J | B | B | T |
| O | D | E | P | O | L | A | R | I | Z | A | T | I | O | N | L | I | Y | G | Z | F | S | I |
| G | N | I | G | X | E | L | E | C | T | R | O | N | S | H | E | L | L | G | O | C | W | O |
| Y | M | F | B | I | O | G | E | O | G | R | A | P | H | Y | C | P | N | D | S | R | B | N |
| R | J | C | H | L | O | R | O | P | L | A | S | T | D | E | C | I | D | U | O | U | S | K |

1. The study of plant nutrition and growth especially to increase crop yield
2. The vascular tissue in plants that conducts sugars and other metabolic products downward from the leaves.
3. An electron shell is the outside part of an atom around the atomic nucleus. it is a group of atomic orbitals with the same value of the principal quantum number n.
4. Means "falling off at maturity" or "tending to fall off", and it is typically used in order to refer to trees or shrubs that lose their leaves seasonally.
5. The study of the distribution of species and ecosystems in geographic space and through time.
6. Refers to the provision of essential nutrients necessary to support human life and health.
7. A microbially facilitated process of nitrate reduction that may ultimately produce molecular nitrogen.
8. The principle, originated by Gregor Mendel, stating that when two or more characteristics are inherited, individual hereditary factors assort independently.
9. Single-cell microscopic organisms which lack a true nucleus. they represent one of the three domains.
10. An individual animal, plant, or single-celled life form.
11. The application of the principles of biology to the study of physiological, genetic, and developmental mechanisms of behavior in humans and other animals.
12. An enzyme that catalyzes the formation of cyclic amp from ATP.
13. Work to convert light energy of the sun into sugars that can be used by cells.
14. The process of reversing the charge across a cell membrane (usually a neuron), so causing an action potential.

A. Deciduous
D. Organism
G. Chloroplast
J. Depolarization
M. Phloem
B. Human Nutrition
E. Agrobiology
H. Bacteria
K. Independent Assortment
N. Psychobiology
C. Biogeography
F. Electron Shell
I. Adenylate cyclase
L. Denitrification

13. Find the hidden words. The words have been placed horizontally, vertically, or diagonally. When you locate a word, draw an ellipse around it.

| | | | | | | | | | | | | | | | | | | | | | | |
|---|---|---|---|---|---|---|---|---|---|---|---|---|---|---|---|---|---|---|---|---|---|---|
| E | U | X | S | Y | S | T | E | M | A | T | I | C | S | B | G | I | H | L | V | T | Z | F |
| Z | P | H | A | R | M | A | C | O | L | O | G | Y | G | L | B | Q | R | O | P | I | L | Y |
| A | Z | J | O | L | B | E | X | C | P | M | A | B | N | A | Y | Q | H | Y | F | J | I | E |
| S | X | N | P | A | I | V | U | I | P | N | Q | W | K | S | H | A | P | D | U | N | R | D |
| B | J | J | F | R | O | E | H | Z | E | E | L | E | C | T | R | O | N | D | O | N | O | R |
| A | L | I | L | V | E | S | I | B | I | L | E | A | S | O | I | G | A | H | G | C | M | U |
| R | U | V | I | A | N | I | O | Y | Q | P | U | T | M | C | I | M | M | K | O | G | Y | U |
| R | M | Q | N | K | G | C | I | A | E | E | X | O | N | Y | E | G | T | I | B | I | T | X |
| B | H | B | V | G | I | L | Q | J | K | Z | Z | M | Z | S | W | I | U | A | C | M | U | L |
| O | Y | J | L | V | N | E | E | K | B | C | K | N | T | T | Z | L | E | Q | Q | Y | W | Z |
| D | F | Z | D | S | E | X | U | A | L | R | E | P | R | O | D | U | C | T | I | O | N | A |
| Y | J | B | E | I | E | P | T | E | D | G | O | P | J | K | M | M | X | L | F | O | Z | W |
| F | Z | N | S | R | R | D | B | F | M | P | M | U | E | P | I | S | T | A | S | I | S | J |
| B | T | Z | C | L | I | I | G | J | M | L | W | A | B | S | O | R | P | T | I | O | N | U |
| G | E | L | Z | O | N | I | N | V | E | R | T | E | B | R | A | T | E | Z | L | E | E | E |
| B | R | P | Y | Q | G | C | C | H | E | M | I | C | A | L | R | E | A | C | T | I | O | N |

1. The smallest component of an element having the chemical properties of the element
2. The interaction of genes that are not alleles. The suppression of the effect of one such gene by another.
3. The application of concepts and methods of biology to solve real world problems.
4. A mammalian blastula in which some differentiation of cells has occurred.
5. The science of drug action on biological systems.
6. Type of reproduction in which cells from two parents unite to form the first cell of a new organism.
7. A dark green to yellowish brown fluid, produced by the liver of most vertebrates, that aids the digestion of lipids in the small intestine.
8. The inactive x chromosome in a female somatic cell, rendered inactive in a process called lyonization
9. A distinct juvenile form many animals undergo before metamorphosis into adults. animals with indirect development such as insects, amphibians, or cnidarians.
10. A chemical entity that donates electrons to another compound.
11. A group of animals that have no backbone, unlike animals such as reptiles, amphibians, fish, birds and mammals who all have a backbone.
12. A process in which one substance permeates another; a fluid permeates or is dissolved by a liquid or solid.
13. The branch of biology that deals with classification and nomenclature; taxonomy.
14. Usually characterized by a chemical change, and they yield one or more products, which usually have properties different from the reactants
15. A fluid or air-filled cavity or sac.

A. Vesicle
E. Blastocyst
I. Barr body
M. Bile
B. Bioengineering
F. Atom
J. Systematics
N. Absorption
C. Invertebrate
G. Chemical reaction
K. Epistasis
O. Sexual Reproduction
D. Electron Donor
H. Larva
L. Pharmacology

14. Find the hidden words. The words have been placed horizontally, vertically, or diagonally. When you locate a word, draw an ellipse around it.

| X | U | Z | D | P | B | L | T | Y | J | U | F | S | M | T | O | R | Y | K | Y | Q | G | Y |
|---|---|---|---|---|---|---|---|---|---|---|---|---|---|---|---|---|---|---|---|---|---|---|
| P | A | Q | E | X | S | I | M | N | S | D | M | S | L | T | E | F | T | S | S | B | B | F |
| B | I | O | L | O | G | Y | T | E | S | T | O | S | T | E | R | O | N | E | Y | F | E | G |
| D | E | H | Y | D | R | A | T | I | O | N | R | E | A | C | T | I | O | N | M | L | N | S |
| F | A | C | U | L | T | A | T | I | V | E | A | N | A | E | R | O | B | E | B | K | T | M |
| V | A | L | E | N | C | E | B | A | N | D | Z | R | O | R | M | R | V | C | I | K | H | C |
| Z | W | N | A | P | W | H | M | P | A | A | D | Y | T | F | F | X | F | H | O | S | I | J |
| U | E | M | M | F | I | U | Z | A | R | U | W | B | Q | F | M | I | F | O | G | R | C | L |
| I | N | T | E | G | R | A | T | I | V | E | B | I | O | L | O | G | Y | L | E | I | Z | Y |
| E | M | B | R | Y | O | L | O | G | Y | T | W | S | K | J | L | A | Y | E | N | I | O | L |
| O | L | D | B | I | V | K | B | U | H | C | I | L | X | F | E | D | B | S | E | I | N | N |
| W | A | F | U | K | K | A | H | T | C | W | H | V | Q | P | C | C | J | T | S | T | E | A |
| H | K | Y | D | P | O | L | L | I | N | A | T | I | O | N | U | W | E | E | I | G | Q | H |
| Y | N | G | I | S | L | M | L | I | U | T | E | R | U | S | L | R | T | R | S | Q | I | N |
| Q | Z | Y | Z | H | S | A | C | O | E | L | O | M | A | T | E | W | V | O | V | K | B | A |
| C | X | W | I | T | R | A | N | S | F | E | R | R | N | A | Q | D | T | L | S | I | G | V |

1. An evolutionary theory that explains the origin of eukaryotic cells from prokaryotes.
2. The ecological region at the lowest level of a body of water such as an ocean or a lake.
3. Study of living organisms.
4. Organism which can produce energy through aerobic respiration and then switching to anaerobic respiration depending on the amounts of oxygen.
5. The organ in the lower body of a woman or female mammal where offspring are conceived and in which they gestate before birth; the womb.
6. A steroid hormone from the androgen group and is found in humans and other vertebrates.
7. The highest range of electron energies in which electrons are normally present at absolute zero temperature.
8. RNA consisting of folded molecules that transport amino acids from the cytoplasm of a cell to a ribosome.
9. A label frequently used to describe various forms of cross-disciplinary and multitaxon research.
10. The act of transferring pollen grains from the male anther of a flower to the female stigma.
11. Usually defined as a chemical reaction that involves the loss of a water molecule from the reacting molecule.
12. An organic lipid molecule that is biosynthesized by all animal cells because it is an essential structural component of all animal cell membranes.
13. The smallest particle in a chemical element or compound that has the chemical properties of that element or compound.
14. Animals, like flatworms and jellyfish, that have no body cavity (coelom).
15. The branch of biology that studies the development of gametes (sex cells), fertilization, and development of embryos and fetuses.

A. Molecule
D. Symbiogenesis
G. Uterus
J. Valence band
M. Integrative Biology
B. Facultative Anaerobe
E. Cholesterol
H. Testosterone
K. Acoelomate
N. Pollination
C. Embryology
F. Benthic zone
I. Transfer RNA
L. Dehydration Reaction
O. Biology

15. Find the hidden words. The words have been placed horizontally, vertically, or diagonally. When you locate a word, draw an ellipse around it.

| Z | Z | O | S | I | N | X | L | X | Y | V | O | I | M | I | K | E | V | P | U | E | C | H |
|---|---|---|---|---|---|---|---|---|---|---|---|---|---|---|---|---|---|---|---|---|---|---|
| E | L | E | C | T | R | O | M | A | G | N | E | T | I | C | S | P | E | C | T | R | U | M |
| C | Z | F | I | K | S | R | T | G | E | M | C | E | L | L | M | E | M | B | R | A | N | E |
| E | I | V | I | C | F | F | B | I | O | L | O | G | Y | M | E | D | U | L | L | A | H | S |
| C | W | G | E | N | E | T | I | C | S | Q | C | W | K | A | D | I | R | B | A | W | S | L |
| P | L | A | S | M | O | L | Y | S | I | S | T | D | F | M | S | F | E | P | J | W | I | Z |
| O | W | T | J | O | W | K | F | G | J | D | M | Z | S | O | L | O | D | L | H | Q | J | O |
| E | L | E | C | T | R | O | N | M | I | C | R | O | S | C | O | P | E | D | Y | A | S | P |
| M | I | N | T | E | G | R | A | T | I | V | E | B | I | O | L | O | G | Y | X | G | G | F |
| N | L | L | G | O | H | M | D | M | N | F | J | A | S | M | A | R | S | N | B | F | K | B |
| J | F | H | U | I | W | H | Y | H | Z | C | T | E | S | T | O | S | T | E | R | O | N | E |
| X | Y | O | G | H | W | E | N | D | O | T | H | E | R | M | G | R | H | I | V | C | D | F |
| Y | I | F | G | E | N | E | T | I | C | C | O | D | E | O | V | E | F | N | B | U | M | C |
| G | Y | U | Z | P | W | N | F | G | H | C | U | Y | U | J | W | U | O | D | F | G | B | C |
| W | A | Q | T | D | D | T | B | D | L | M | A | J | C | H | B | L | H | W | X | X | V | O |
| G | U | L | I | I | N | T | E | R | N | A | T | I | O | N | A | L | S | Y | S | T | E | M |

1. A motor protein in cells which converts the chemical energy contained in ATP into the mechanical energy of movement
2. Contraction of the protoplast of a plant cell as a result of loss of water from the cell.
3. A label frequently used to describe various forms of cross-disciplinary and multitaxon research.
4. A type of microscope that uses a beam of electrons to create an image of the specimen. it is capable of much higher magnifications.
5. The nucleotide triplets of DNA and RNA molecules that carry genetic information in living cells.
6. The study of heredity
7. Study of living organisms.
8. The collective term for all possible frequencies of electromagnetic radiation.
9. A steroid hormone from the androgen group and is found in humans and other vertebrates.
10. The modern form of the metric system and is the most widely used system of measurement.
11. The semipermeable membrane surrounding the cytoplasm of a cell.
12. An animal that is dependent on or capable of the internal generation of heat; a warm
13. The continuation of the spinal cord within the skull, forming the lowest part of the brainstem and containing control centers for the heart and lungs.

A. Endotherm
D. Testosterone
G. Plasmolysis
J. Electromagnetic Spectrum
M. Genetics

B. Cell membrane
E. Electron Microscope
H. Integrative Biology
K. International System

C. Dynein
F. Biology
I. Genetic Code
L. Medulla

16. Find the hidden words. The words have been placed horizontally, vertically, or diagonally. When you locate a word, draw an ellipse around it.

| L | C | B | M | R | H | V | E | V | Y | Y | Z | E | C | K | C | M | F | Z | I | M | T | A |
|---|---|---|---|---|---|---|---|---|---|---|---|---|---|---|---|---|---|---|---|---|---|---|
| U | H | C | M | M | R | Y | K | E | E | A | M | P | J | Z | R | U | H | O | L | E | Q | W |
| N | E | E | D | J | P | S | Y | C | H | O | B | I | O | L | O | G | Y | C | I | X | T | L |
| S | M | L | W | F | U | A | L | O | L | Z | A | D | A | J | L | A | R | Y | L | P | D | S |
| I | I | L | E | Q | N | E | V | X | I | N | U | E | M | A | C | R | O | P | H | A | G | E |
| Q | C | D | I | K | I | A | Q | S | G | T | R | M | M | D | H | P | Z | G | G | I | O | L |
| V | A | F | N | W | V | F | X | T | A | N | A | I | F | F | L | G | B | I | B | Z | C | X |
| W | L | Y | S | W | P | R | I | E | M | U | C | O | G | F | U | E | Z | E | L | B | V | C |
| O | R | C | U | I | P | B | R | R | E | K | I | L | F | X | D | V | F | M | K | V | F | Q |
| O | E | W | L | J | I | M | Z | O | N | U | L | O | M | L | P | Q | L | T | N | A | T | J |
| D | A | K | I | Z | G | S | J | I | T | A | G | G | N | Q | S | N | M | P | U | U | Z | Z |
| J | C | H | N | C | T | I | D | D | H | V | E | Y | M | A | Y | L | J | D | B | V | C | L |
| O | T | M | G | V | D | U | V | G | G | Z | V | V | W | M | U | D | S | R | Q | B | W | Y |
| W | I | E | O | B | I | O | M | E | C | H | A | N | I | C | S | F | O | F | I | K | K | U |
| S | O | I | K | M | S | Y | S | T | E | M | A | T | I | C | S | C | L | Z | Y | M | W | B |
| W | N | I | D | E | O | X | Y | R | I | B | O | N | U | C | L | E | I | C | A | C | I | D |

1. Helps keep blood sugar level from getting too high (hyperglycemia) or too low (hypoglycemia).
2. The application of the principles of biology to the study of physiological, genetic, and developmental mechanisms of behavior in humans and other animals.
3. The chemical name for DNA.
4. An organic compound with four rings arranged in a specific configuration. examples include the dietary lipid cholesterol and the sex hormones.
5. The study and analysis of the patterns, causes, and effects of health and disease conditions in defined populations.
6. Type of lymphocyte in the humeral immunity of the adaptive immune system.
7. The study of the structure and function of biological systems by means of the methods of "mechanics."
8. A kind of swallowing cell, which means it functions by literally swallowing up other particles or smaller cells.
9. The inner layer of the stems of woody plants; composed of xylem.
10. The branch of biology that deals with classification and nomenclature; taxonomy.
11. One of the four nucleobases in the nucleic acid of RNA that are represented by the letters a, g, c and u.
12. The fibrous connective tissue that connects bones to other bones.
13. Usually characterized by a chemical change, and they yield one or more products, which usually have properties different from the reactants

A. Biomechanics
D. Systematics
G. B cell
J. Ligament
M. Steroid

B. Chemical reaction
E. Uracil
H. Epidemiology
K. Macrophage

C. Wood
F. Insulin
I. Psychobiology
L. Deoxyribonucleic Acid

17. Find the hidden words. The words have been placed horizontally, vertically, or diagonally. When you locate a word, draw an ellipse around it.

| | | | | | | | | | | | | | | | | | | | | | | |
|---|---|---|---|---|---|---|---|---|---|---|---|---|---|---|---|---|---|---|---|---|---|---|
| R | E | M | R | F | K | K | E | A | P | Q | P | C | H | X | F | Q | Y | V | O | B | D | O |
| C | O | N | S | E | R | V | A | T | I | O | N | B | I | O | L | O | G | Y | B | H | B | G |
| R | S | O | H | Z | W | G | E | N | E | P | O | O | L | A | W | W | B | B | N | C | A | A |
| P | R | T | U | T | W | A | E | B | S | W | X | G | H | G | O | Q | L | J | E | D | S | M |
| L | P | T | M | O | F | K | W | D | P | L | A | N | T | N | U | T | R | I | T | I | O | N |
| D | V | U | A | O | M | L | V | H | L | A | C | Q | Z | S | B | Q | T | P | I | K | Q | D |
| Y | W | H | N | N | U | C | L | E | I | C | A | C | I | D | S | E | Q | U | E | N | C | E |
| C | G | A | N | D | A | H | B | U | T | E | O | S | C | L | S | U | D | V | D | Y | D | B |
| C | M | M | U | N | S | N | I | D | V | Q | C | L | N | Z | X | X | H | K | E | R | H | D |
| F | O | N | T | I | L | K | O | A | Z | E | B | V | F | P | N | F | U | V | E | P | O | P |
| W | L | I | R | M | E | R | M | S | B | T | E | N | K | J | Y | D | B | C | E | L | L | V |
| U | E | O | I | X | S | Q | A | C | S | O | Z | T | U | W | V | Z | U | D | C | C | V | Q |
| C | L | T | T | Q | B | R | S | S | J | G | V | Q | Q | L | G | M | R | K | W | C | N | M |
| V | B | E | I | X | S | K | S | U | X | B | Z | B | L | U | R | E | A | H | O | I | B | K |
| E | W | S | O | C | L | O | N | I | N | G | B | X | T | L | S | M | O | N | O | M | E | R |
| I | D | J | N | P | J | I | J | G | A | P | I | M | O | L | A | R | I | T | Y | U | A | N |

1. The si unit of measurement used to measure the number of things, usually atoms or molecules.
2. Refers to the provision of essential nutrients necessary to support human life and health.
3. Type of lymphocyte in the humeral immunity of the adaptive immune system.
4. The stock of different genes in an interbreeding population.
5. Serves an important role in the metabolism of nitrogen-containing compounds by animals and is the main nitrogen-containing substance in the urine of mammals.
6. A succession of letters that indicate the order of nucleotides within a DNA (using GACT or RNA (GACU) molecule.
7. The study of the chemical elements and compounds necessary for plant growth, plant metabolism and their external supply.
8. Propagate (an organism or cell) to make an identical copy of.
9. Organisms that produce an egg composed of shell and membranes that creates a protected environment in which the embryo can develop out of water
10. A unit of concentration measuring the number of moles of a solute per liter of solution.
11. Organic matter derived from living, or recently living organisms.
12. A molecule that can be bonded to other identical molecules to form a polymer.
13. The scientific study of nature and of earth's biodiversity with the aim of protecting species, their habitats, and ecosystems from excessive rates of extinction.

A. Human Nutrition
D. Biomass
G. Cloning
J. Nucleic Acid Sequence
M. B cell
B. Gene Pool
E. Monomer
H. Plant Nutrition
K. Molarity
C. Mole
F. Conservation Biology
I. Amniotes
L. Urea

18. Find the hidden words. The words have been placed horizontally, vertically, or diagonally. When you locate a word, draw an ellipse around it.

| X | R | W | V | H | H | T | F | I | W | Y | L | G | G | Z | A | Q | T | K | I | O | P | A |
|---|---|---|---|---|---|---|---|---|---|---|---|---|---|---|---|---|---|---|---|---|---|---|
| E | N | T | P | V | K | S | G | N | A | X | G | F | F | B | L | D | Z | D | U | M | R | X |
| B | D | G | Z | Y | P | K | R | Z | H | Q | R | I | O | S | Y | U | Q | Q | L | K | J | A |
| U | U | O | E | C | O | L | O | G | I | C | A | L | E | F | F | I | C | I | E | N | C | Y |
| H | E | L | E | C | T | R | O | N | T | R | A | N | S | P | O | R | T | C | H | A | I | N |
| G | J | L | V | O | N | Q | R | M | O | L | T | Q | D | I | X | Y | P | O | T | X | L | B |
| I | E | V | G | M | S | C | M | E | K | I | D | I | O | M | B | D | R | W | F | K | J | E |
| T | R | A | N | S | C | R | I | P | T | I | O | N | W | A | H | C | M | B | E | G | U | P |
| J | U | H | C | H | Y | D | R | O | C | A | R | B | O | N | R | T | H | M | O | L | E | I |
| D | Z | J | M | O | L | E | C | U | L | A | R | P | H | Y | S | I | C | S | B | G | J | S |
| I | Z | Z | J | M | N | K | B | A | B | A | C | T | E | R | I | O | P | H | A | G | E | T |
| C | H | E | M | I | C | A | L | E | Q | U | I | L | I | B | R | I | U | M | G | R | Z | A |
| H | V | Y | M | A | C | R | O | M | O | L | E | C | U | L | E | K | G | B | H | Y | P | S |
| Y | J | B | M | U | I | W | O | X | P | R | O | T | E | I | N | W | I | C | M | R | I | I |
| C | C | P | Q | V | T | J | O | E | N | D | O | C | Y | T | O | S | I | S | Q | C | J | S |
| X | I | T | H | Y | M | I | N | E | T | T | I | T | I | U | K | P | Y | W | R | F | O | N |

1. A form of active transport in which a cell transports molecules into the cell.
2. Describes the efficiency with which energy is transferred from one trophic level to the next.
3. The interaction of genes that are not alleles. The suppression of the effect of one such gene by another.
4. The site of oxidative phosphorylation in eukaryotes.
5. The study of the physical properties of molecules, the chemical bonds between atoms as well as the molecular dynamics.
6. The state in which both reactants and products are present in concentrations which have no further tendency to change with time.
7. In organic chemistry, a hydrocarbon is an organic compound consisting entirely of hydrogen and carbon.
8. The first step of gene expression, in which a segment of DNA is copied into RNA (mRNA) by the enzyme RNA polymerase.
9. Virus that infects and multiplies within bacteria.
10. A very large molecule, such as protein, commonly created by polymerization of smaller subunits (monomers).
11. One of the four nucleobases in the nucleic acid of DNA that are represented by the letters g–c–a–t.
12. The si unit of measurement used to measure the number of things, usually atoms or molecules.
13. Large biomolecules, or macromolecules, consisting of one or more long chains of amino acid residues.

A. Hydrocarbon
D. Electron Transport Chain
G. Thymine
J. Bacteriophage
M. Molecular physics

B. Epistasis
E. Protein
H. Macromolecule
K. Mole

C. Transcription
F. Chemical equilibrium
I. Endocytosis
L. Ecological Efficiency

19. Find the hidden words. The words have been placed horizontally, vertically, or diagonally. When you locate a word, draw an ellipse around it.

| V | C | M | H | I | S | T | O | L | O | G | Y | A | C | T | I | V | E | S | I | T | E | M |
|---|---|---|---|---|---|---|---|---|---|---|---|---|---|---|---|---|---|---|---|---|---|---|
| J | V | A | S | O | D | I | L | A | T | I | O | N | E | P | I | S | T | A | S | I | S | A |
| Q | I | L | W | L | V | F | Q | X | A | D | Q | Z | M | E | O | P | N | C | I | E | A | C |
| O | Z | V | W | D | M | A | C | R | O | M | O | L | E | C | U | L | E | B | T | Z | J | R |
| I | X | A | A | Z | A | M | Y | G | C | H | D | V | A | O | A | Y | P | P | D | T | H | O |
| A | D | F | A | C | U | L | T | A | T | I | V | E | A | N | A | E | R | O | B | E | E | E |
| Q | U | L | N | E | U | R | O | T | R | A | N | S | M | I | T | T | E | R | E | A | O | V |
| S | D | W | Y | R | V | S | Y | M | F | O | D | T | O | W | F | W | X | O | T | L | V | O |
| I | N | T | E | G | R | A | T | I | V | E | B | I | O | L | O | G | Y | X | H | N | M | L |
| Q | G | B | I | T | V | J | F | O | M | J | O | G | Z | L | E | J | S | I | O | Z | D | U |
| J | P | Q | S | D | Y | I | T | G | Z | E | R | I | E | Q | F | S | P | N | L | Y | D | T |
| B | I | O | C | H | E | M | I | S | T | R | Y | A | C | Z | Z | R | F | I | O | G | K | I |
| S | F | S | M | Y | K | C | B | P | I | E | V | L | M | P | Z | O | H | S | G | J | I | O |
| F | M | T | H | U | M | A | N | N | U | T | R | I | T | I | O | N | F | J | Y | W | A | N |
| J | P | Z | N | V | R | X | B | A | G | R | T | T | N | E | C | H | I | D | Q | M | A |
| K | C | E | L | L | N | U | C | L | E | U | S | Y | J | M | Y | Y | F | G | M | N | D | B |

1. The interaction of genes that are not alleles. The suppression of the effect of one such gene by another.
2. The dilatation of blood vessels, which decreases blood pressure.
3. The scientific and objective study of non-human animal behavior rather than human behavior and usually with a focus on behavior under natural conditions.
4. Refers to genetically determined structures or attributes that have apparently lost most or all their ancestral function in a given species.
5. The study of the microscopic anatomy of cells and tissues of plants and animals.
6. The "control room" for the cell. the nucleus gives out all the orders.
7. Organism which can produce energy through aerobic respiration and then switching to anaerobic respiration depending on the amounts of oxygen.
8. Refers to the provision of essential nutrients necessary to support human life and health.
9. The part of an enzyme or antibody where the chemical reaction occurs
10. The branch of science that explores the chemical processes within and related to living organisms.
11. A very large molecule, such as protein, commonly created by polymerization of smaller subunits (monomers).
12. Known as chemical messengers, are endogenous chemicals that enable neurotransmission.
13. A label frequently used to describe various forms of cross-disciplinary and multitaxon research.
14. Evolution on a scale of separated gene pools. studies focus on change that occurs at or above the level of species, in contrast with microevolution.

A. Vestigiality
B. Facultative Anaerobe
C. Vasodilation
D. Macroevolution
E. Macromolecule
F. Epistasis
G. Biochemistry
H. Histology
I. Active site
J. Integrative Biology
K. Human Nutrition
L. Ethology
M. Cell nucleus
N. Neurotransmitter

20. Find the hidden words. The words have been placed horizontally, vertically, or diagonally. When you locate a word, draw an ellipse around it.

| A | D | E | N | O | S | I | N | E | T | R | I | P | H | O | S | P | H | A | T | E | K | T |
|---|---|---|---|---|---|---|---|---|---|---|---|---|---|---|---|---|---|---|---|---|---|---|
| B | I | O | G | E | O | G | R | A | P | H | Y | L | Q | I | S | O | M | E | R | V | I | E |
| O | O | Y | I | P | Z | P | U | A | V | A | L | E | N | C | E | B | A | N | D | J | M | W |
| G | F | N | J | F | P | B | X | T | S | U | P | O | L | Y | P | L | O | I | D | Y | O | T |
| O | E | L | E | C | T | R | O | N | T | R | A | N | S | P | O | R | T | C | H | A | I | N |
| R | J | U | T | M | A | C | T | I | V | E | T | R | A | N | S | P | O | R | T | L | A | Y |
| W | H | O | L | E | G | E | N | O | M | E | S | E | Q | U | E | N | C | I | N | G | B | X |
| C | C | U | S | Y | M | B | I | O | G | E | N | E | S | I | S | B | M | I | E | E | W | Z |
| Q | W | P | L | A | C | E | B | O | W | W | K | G | B | U | G | O | L | L | W | T | J | O |
| A | I | G | Z | H | X | A | W | H | D | P | G | C | U | O | E | T | O | O | N | Y | O | D |
| R | U | E | T | H | O | L | O | G | Y | N | K | M | K | R | N | A | O | N | F | E | T | N |
| U | E | C | E | X | Z | Z | T | O | T | G | D | D | G | F | E | N | W | W | J | V | U | L |
| I | N | S | O | V | M | I | I | U | X | L | N | O | A | K | T | Y | L | K | Q | Z | P | J |
| C | P | H | Y | T | O | P | A | T | H | O | L | O | G | Y | I | B | H | H | J | D | M | R |
| R | W | I | Y | C | L | Q | K | Q | B | M | R | L | U | V | C | U | Q | O | G | V | L | M |
| S | W | F | B | G | M | L | H | L | J | W | Q | D | B | C | S | O | M | P | T | B | U | O |

1. A harmless pill, medicine, or procedure prescribed more for the psychological benefit to the patient than for any physiological effect.
2. The site of oxidative phosphorylation in eukaryotes.
3. The study of plants.
4. An evolutionary theory that explains the origin of eukaryotic cells from prokaryotes.
5. A molecule with the same chemical formula as another molecule, but with a different chemical structure.
6. The study of heredity
7. The study of the distribution of species and ecosystems in geographic space and through time.
8. The science of diagnosing and managing plant diseases.
9. A laboratory process that determines the complete DNA sequence of an organism's genome at a single time.
10. Containing more than two homologous sets of chromosomes.
11. The scientific and objective study of non-human animal behavior rather than human behavior and usually with a focus on behavior under natural conditions.
12. The highest range of electron energies in which electrons are normally present at absolute zero temperature.
13. A nucleotide derived from adenosine that occurs in muscle tissue; the major source of energy for cellular reactions.
14. Transport of a substance (as a protein or drug) across a cell membrane against the concentration gradient; requires an expenditure of energy

A. Biogeography
B. Isomer
C. Symbiogenesis
D. Placebo
E. Whole Genome Sequencing
F. Polyploidy
G. Phytopathology
H. Active Transport
I. Electron Transport Chain
J. Adenosine Triphosphate
K. Genetics
L. Botany
M. Ethology
N. Valence band

1. Find the hidden words. The words have been placed horizontally, vertically, or diagonally. When you locate a word, draw an ellipse around it.

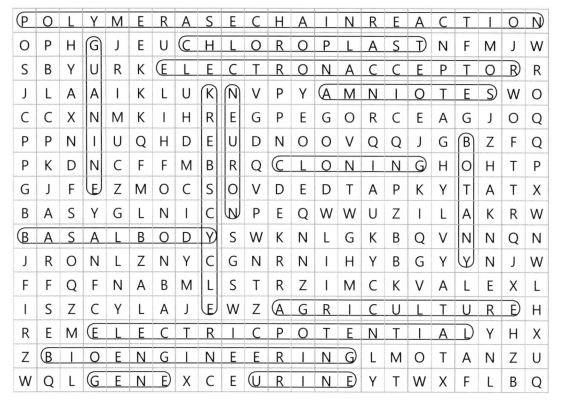

1. An electrically excitable cell that processes and transmits information through electrical and chemical signals.
2. One of the four main nucleobases found in the nucleic acids DNA and RNA, the others being adenine, cytosine, and thymine.
3. The practice of cultivating land, growing food, and raising stock.
4. A liquid by-product of the body secreted by the kidneys through a process called urination (or micturition) and excreted through the urethra.
5. The study of plants.
6. A chemical entity that accepts electrons transferred to it from another compound.
7. A gene is a locus (or region) of DNA that encodes a functional RNA or protein product and is the molecular unit of heredity.
8. The amount of work needed to move a unit charge from a reference point to a specific point against an electric field.
9. The application of concepts and methods of biology to solve real world problems.
10. Organisms that produce an egg composed of shell and membranes that creates a protected environment in which the embryo can develop out of water
11. A technique used in molecular biology to amplify a single copy or a few copies of a piece of DNA across several orders of magnitude.
12. Propagate (an organism or cell) to make an identical copy of.
13. the sequence of reactions by which most living cells generate energy during the process of aerobic respiration.
14. An organelle formed from a centriole, and a short cylindrical array of microtubules.
15. Work to convert light energy of the sun into sugars that can be used by cells.

A. Botany
D. Amniotes
G. Guanine
J. Neuron
M. Agriculture

B. Polymerase Chain Reaction
E. Basal body
H. Urine
K. Electric Potential
N. Krebs Cycle

C. Gene
F. Electron Acceptor
I. Bioengineering
L. Chloroplast
O. Cloning

2. Find the hidden words. The words have been placed horizontally, vertically, or diagonally. When you locate a word, draw an ellipse around it.

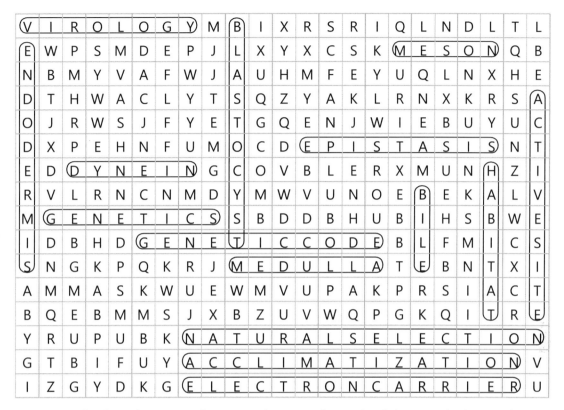

1. An inner layer of cells in the cortex of a root and of some stems, surrounding a vascular bundle.
2. A dark green to yellowish brown fluid, produced by the liver of most vertebrates, that aids the digestion of lipids in the small intestine.
3. The continuation of the spinal cord within the skull, forming the lowest part of the brainstem and containing control centers for the heart and lungs.
4. A mammalian blastula in which some differentiation of cells has occurred.
5. Adaptation to a new climate (a new temperature or altitude or environment).
6. A place for animals, people and plants and non-living things
7. The nucleotide triplets of DNA and RNA molecules that carry genetic information in living cells.
8. The interaction of genes that are not alleles. The suppression of the effect of one such gene by another.

9. The study of viruses-submicroscopic, parasitic particles of genetic material contained in a protein coat and virus-like agents.
10. A process in nature in which organisms possessing certain genotypic characteristics that make them better adjusted to an environment tend to survive.
11. The study of heredity
12. Hadronic subatomic particles composed of one quark and one antiquark, bound together by the strong interaction.
13. A motor protein in cells which converts the chemical energy contained in ATP into the mechanical energy of movement
14. Any of various molecules that can accept one or two electrons from one molecule and donating them to another in the process of electron transport.
15. The part of an enzyme or antibody where the chemical reaction occurs

| | | | |
|---|---|---|---|
| A. Medulla | B. Virology | C. Meson | D. Endodermis |
| E. Bile | F. Genetics | G. Dynein | H. Blastocyst |
| I. Active site | J. Electron Carrier | K. Epistasis | L. Genetic Code |
| M. Habitat | N. Natural Selection | O. Acclimatization | |

3. Find the hidden words. The words have been placed horizontally, vertically, or diagonally. When you locate a word, draw an ellipse around it.

| M | A | Z | T | J | V | E | P | I | N | E | P | H | R | I | N | E | I | H | B | Z | K | D |
|---|---|---|---|---|---|---|---|---|---|---|---|---|---|---|---|---|---|---|---|---|---|---|
| Z | J | M | R | K | I | D | E | A | R | P | A | X | V | G | H | D | S | F | H | S | W | H |
| O | V | D | A | R | W | I | N | I | A | N | F | I | T | N | E | S | S | H | A | K | L | T |
| G | F | K | V | W | Y | N | P | N | E | N | D | O | C | R | I | N | E | G | L | A | N | D |
| U | G | C | U | V | L | Y | W | E | C | T | O | T | H | E | R | M | N | O | B | D | J | T |
| D | K | C | C | M | X | W | D | H | T | M | Y | O | S | I | N | S | G | K | J | Q | B | Z |
| I | U | O | E | A | L | V | E | S | T | I | G | I | A | L | I | T | Y | A | Q | C | L | C |
| W | L | M | V | S | K | P | W | L | H | H | E | T | E | R | O | S | I | S | K | T | V | P |
| T | K | M | N | S | J | N | K | C | I | U | O | F | G | P | F | I | C | U | A | Q | V | Z |
| S | U | X | I | D | B | I | O | D | I | V | E | R | S | I | T | Y | Q | N | Y | J | Q | F |
| N | E | V | T | E | Y | M | H | P | A | A | O | Q | Y | P | D | A | R | C | E | Q | T | E |
| U | T | S | R | N | Q | A | W | G | E | N | E | P | O | O | L | X | E | Z | D | J | S | B |
| T | L | K | P | S | N | K | P | A | B | S | O | L | U | T | E | Z | E | R | O | V | K | B |
| W | H | F | Q | I | W | S | Y | N | T | H | E | T | I | C | B | I | O | L | O | G | Y | V |
| E | A | L | I | T | K | B | B | A | R | R | B | O | D | Y | A | N | A | T | O | M | Y | B |
| G | W | G | S | Y | D | W | P | N | O | X | A | B | S | O | R | P | T | I | O | N | B | G |

1. Large superfamily of motor proteins that move along actin filaments, while hydrolyzing ATP.
2. An interdisciplinary branch of biology and engineering.
3. The stock of different genes in an interbreeding population.
4. Density is mass per volume.
5. Refers to genetically determined structures or attributes that have apparently lost most or all their ancestral function in a given species.
6. The inactive x chromosome in a female somatic cell, rendered inactive in a process called lyonization
7. A process in which one substance permeates another; a fluid permeates or is dissolved by a liquid or solid.
8. The tendency of a crossbred individual to show qualities superior to those of both parents.
9. A organism in which internal physiological sources of heat are of relatively small or quite negligible importance in controlling body temperature. "cold blooded".
10. The lowest theoretically attainable temperature (at which the kinetic energy of atoms and molecules is minimal)
11. Another term for adrenaline.
12. The variety of life in the world or in a habitat or ecosystem.
13. The genetic contribution of an individual to the next generation's gene pool relative to the average for the population.
14. Glands that secrete their products, hormones, directly into the blood rather than through a duct.
15. The branch of morphology that deals with the structure of animals

A. Barr body
E. Vestigiality
I. Absolute Zero
M. Mass Density

B. Myosin
F. Biodiversity
J. Endocrine Gland
N. Synthetic Biology

C. Anatomy
G. Gene Pool
K. Absorption
O. Ectotherm

D. Heterosis
H. Epinephrine
L. Darwinian Fitness

4. Find the hidden words. The words have been placed horizontally, vertically, or diagonally. When you locate a word, draw an ellipse around it.

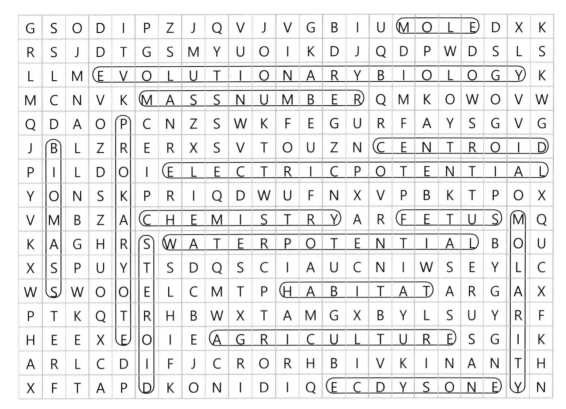

1. A branch of physical science that studies the composition, structure, properties and change of matter.
2. A human embryo after eight weeks of development.
3. A microscopic single celled organism that has no distinct nucleus
4. The amount of work needed to move a unit charge from a reference point to a specific point against an electric field.
5. The total number of protons and neutrons (together known as nucleons) in an atomic nucleus
6. A place for animals, people and plants and non-living things
7. A measure of the potential energy in water as well as the difference between the potential in a water sample and pure water.
8. The intersection of the three medians of the triangle (each median connecting a vertex with the midpoint of the opposite side).

9. An organic compound with four rings arranged in a specific configuration. examples include the dietary lipid cholesterol and the sex hormones.
10. Organic matter derived from living, or recently living organisms.
11. The practice of cultivating land, growing food, and raising stock.
12. The si unit of measurement used to measure the number of things, usually atoms or molecules.
13. A steroidal prohormone of the major insect molting hormone is secreted from the prothoracic glands.
14. A unit of concentration measuring the number of moles of a solute per liter of solution.
15. The subfield of biology that studies the evolutionary processes that produced the diversity of life on earth starting from a single origin of life.

A. Molarity
E. Mass Number
I. Centroid
M. Habitat

B. Steroid
F. Mole
J. Electric Potential
N. Prokaryote

C. Fetus
G. Evolutionary Biology
K. Agriculture
O. Ecdysone

D. Biomass
H. Chemistry
L. Water Potential

5. Find the hidden words. The words have been placed horizontally, vertically, or diagonally. When you locate a word, draw an ellipse around it.

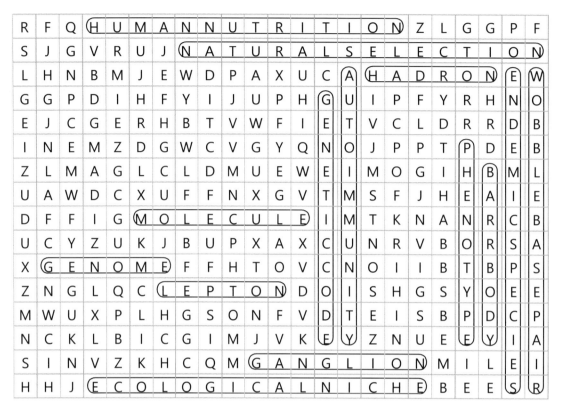

1. A process in nature in which organisms possessing certain genotypic characteristics that make them better adjusted to an environment tend to survive.
2. The inactive x chromosome in a female somatic cell, rendered inactive in a process called lyonization
3. The haploid set of chromosomes in a gamete or microorganism, or in each cell of a multicellular organism.
4. The system of immune responses of an organism against its own healthy cells and tissues.
5. The nucleotide triplets of DNA and RNA molecules that carry genetic information in living cells.
6. A pairing between two nucleotides in RNA molecules that does not follow Watson crick base pair rules
7. Refers to the provision of essential nutrients necessary to support human life and health.

8. A cluster (functional group) of nerve cell bodies in a centralized nervous system.
9. The ecological state of a species being unique to a defined geographic location, such as an island, nation, country or other defined zone, or habitat type.
10. An elementary, half-integer spin particle that does not undergo strong interactions.
11. The role and position a species has in its environment; how it meets its needs for food and shelter, how it survives, and how it reproduces.
12. The smallest particle in a chemical element or compound that has the chemical properties of that element or compound.
13. Any particle that is made from quarks, antiquarks and gluons.
14. The set of observable characteristics of an individual resulting from the interaction of its genotype with the environment.

A. Genetic Code
B. Lepton
C. Genome
D. Ganglion
E. Ecological Niche
F. Natural Selection
G. Wobble Base Pair
H. Molecule
I. Hadron
J. Phenotype
K. Autoimmunity
L. Endemic Species
M. Barr body
N. Human Nutrition

6. Find the hidden words. The words have been placed horizontally, vertically, or diagonally. When you locate a word, draw an ellipse around it.

| W | H | K | O | S | Q | H | Z | X | K | H | O | Z | K | Q | L | Z | F | F | O | S | C | J |
|---|---|---|---|---|---|---|---|---|---|---|---|---|---|---|---|---|---|---|---|---|---|---|
| L | V | P | O | R | G | A | N | I | S | M | H | Y | X | E | C | M | I | V | J | Y | X | H |
| P | L | A | S | M | O | L | Y | S | I | S | A | T | V | F | S | L | J | R | J | X | N | X |
| V | V | H | D | W | E | P | L | T | X | Z | B | T | C | R | J | U | V | Y | Y | T | P | L |
| S | D | G | K | A | P | W | H | T | R | C | I | X | C | B | B | I | U | I | M | F | Y | F |
| A | I | A | S | N | I | I | Q | O | T | K | T | J | E | J | U | N | U | M | E | X | L | F |
| C | S | B | T | W | N | S | D | Z | F | W | A | V | A | Q | H | L | B | Q | M | N | R | O |
| G | S | U | F | R | E | N | O | R | F | Y | T | H | E | T | E | R | O | S | I | S | R | O |
| T | E | P | Z | Q | P | M | O | L | E | C | U | L | A | R | P | H | Y | S | I | C | S | D |
| S | P | P | N | U | H | F | U | L | E | C | H | E | M | I | C | A | L | B | O | N | D | C |
| S | W | E | S | T | R | O | G | E | N | A | F | M | D | Y | Q | G | F | K | X | W | B | H |
| J | E | M | U | H | I | C | H | E | M | I | C | A | L | C | O | M | P | O | U | N | D | A |
| E | C | V | B | I | N | U | I | A | W | H | E | R | P | E | T | O | L | O | G | Y | A | I |
| W | A | X | I | A | E | Y | Q | O | M | C | H | E | M | I | S | T | R | Y | S | V | T | N |
| C | B | I | O | M | E | D | I | C | A | L | E | N | G | I | N | E | E | R | I | N | G | Y |
| K | O | T | W | N | G | J | I | K | N | H | C | X | V | R | K | D | C | B | P | K | E | M |

1. A place for animals, people and plants and non-living things
2. A branch of physical science that studies the composition, structure, properties and change of matter.
3. An individual animal, plant, or single-celled life form.
4. A hierarchical series of organisms each dependent on the next as a source of food.
5. The primary female sex hormone. it is responsible for the development and regulation of the female reproductive system and secondary sex characteristics.
6. Another term for adrenaline.
7. The study of the physical properties of molecules, the chemical bonds between atoms as well as the molecular dynamics.
8. A chemical substance consisting of two or more different chemically bonded chemical elements, with a fixed ratio determining the composition.
9. The midsection of the small intestine of many higher vertebrates like mammals, birds, reptiles. it is present between the duodenum and the ileum.
10. Contraction of the protoplast of a plant cell as a result of loss of water from the cell.
11. The application of engineering principles and design concepts to medicine and biology for healthcare purposes (e.g. diagnostic or therapeutic).
12. The branch of zoology concerned with reptiles and amphibians.
13. A lasting attraction between atoms that enables the formation of chemical compounds.
14. The tendency of a crossbred individual to show qualities superior to those of both parents.

A. Plasmolysis
B. Chemical compound
C. Food Chain
D. Chemistry
E. Habitat
F. Heterosis
G. Estrogen
H. Epinephrine
I. Molecular physics
J. Organism
K. Biomedical engineering
L. Chemical bond
M. Herpetology
N. Jejunum

7.  Find the hidden words. The words have been placed horizontally, vertically, or diagonally. When you locate a word, draw an ellipse around it.

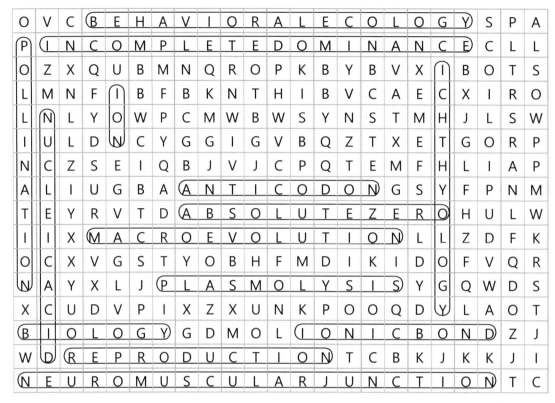

1.  The study of the evolutionary basis for animal behavior due to ecological pressures.
2.  The lowest theoretically attainable temperature (at which the kinetic energy of atoms and molecules is minimal)
3.  Known as fish science, is the branch of biology devoted to the study of fish.
4.  A complex organic substance present in living cells, especially DNA or RNA, whose molecules consist of many nucleotides linked in a long chain.
5.  Study of living organisms.
6.  Evolution on a scale of separated gene pools. studies focus on change that occurs at or above the level of species, in contrast with microevolution.
7.  A sequence of three nucleotides forming a unit of genetic code in a transfer RNA molecule, corresponding to a complementary codon in messenger RNA.
8.  An atom or molecule with a net electric charge due to the loss or gain of one or more electrons.
9.  Contraction of the protoplast of a plant cell as a result of loss of water from the cell.
10. The act of transferring pollen grains from the male anther of a flower to the female stigma.
11. The complete transfer of valence electron(s) between atoms. it is a type of chemical bond that generates two oppositely charged ions.
12. Giving birth to one of its kind, sexually or asexually.
13. A form of intermediate inheritance in which one allele for a specific trait is not completely expressed over its paired allele.
14. A chemical synapse formed by the contact between a motor neuron and a muscle fiber.

A.  Ionic Bond
B.  Plasmolysis
C.  Absolute Zero
D.  Nucleic Acid
E.  Behavioral ecology
F.  Ion
G.  Ichthyology
H.  Pollination
I.  Neuromuscular Junction
J.  Incomplete Dominance
K.  Biology
L.  Anticodon
M.  Macroevolution
N.  Reproduction

8. Find the hidden words. The words have been placed horizontally, vertically, or diagonally. When you locate a word, draw an ellipse around it.

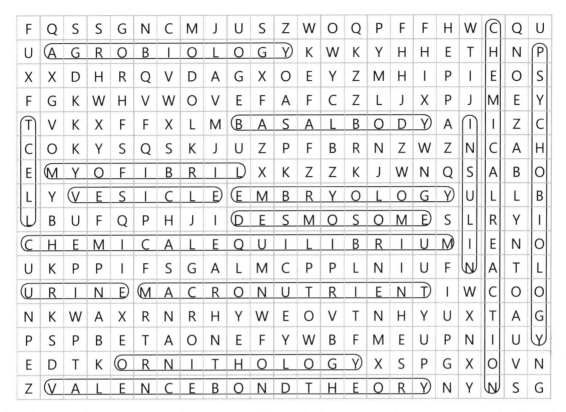

1. A lymphocyte of a type produced or processed by the thymus gland and actively participating in the immune response.
2. A branch of zoology that concerns the study of birds.
3. Usually characterized by a chemical change, and they yield one or more products, which usually have properties different from the reactants
4. Nutrients that provide calories or energy. nutrients are substances needed for growth, metabolism, and for other body functions.
5. The application of the principles of biology to the study of physiological, genetic, and developmental mechanisms of behavior in humans and other animals.
6. A liquid by-product of the body secreted by the kidneys through a process called urination (or micturition) and excreted through the urethra.
7. Any of the elongated contractile threads found in striated muscle cells.
8. An organelle formed from a centriole, and a short cylindrical array of microtubules.
9. The study of plant nutrition and growth especially to increase crop yield
10. A fluid or air-filled cavity or sac.
11. The state in which both reactants and products are present in concentrations which have no further tendency to change with time.
12. Helps keep blood sugar level from getting too high (hyperglycemia) or too low (hypoglycemia).
13. Also known as a macula adhaerens, is a cell structure specialized for cell to cell adhesion.
14. The branch of biology that studies the development of gametes (sex cells), fertilization, and development of embryos and fetuses.
15. A straightforward extension of Lewis structures. states that electrons in a covalent bond reside in a region that is the overlap of individual atomic orbitals.

A. Urine
B. Ornithology
C. Chemical reaction
D. Agrobiology
E. Macronutrient
F. Chemical equilibrium
G. Psychobiology
H. Embryology
I. Basal body
J. Desmosome
K. Vesicle
L. T Cell
M. Myofibril
N. Insulin
O. Valence bond theory

9. Find the hidden words. The words have been placed horizontally, vertically, or diagonally. When you locate a word, draw an ellipse around it.

| T | W | U | N | C | T | J | R | F | U | S | P | F | B | B | I | T | J | S | J | P | V | O |
|---|---|---|---|---|---|---|---|---|---|---|---|---|---|---|---|---|---|---|---|---|---|---|
| A | K | G | M | Y | Y | I | U | A | X | M | O | I | E | I | B | T | F | F | F | H | V | U |
| Z | Y | G | O | T | E | O | F | G | P | P | N | Z | V | P | T | O | U | O | F | O | V | J |
| H | P | U | K | J | L | U | U | D | R | T | D | S | Q | E | M | E | J | A | T | R | L | F |
| A | X | I | L | I | Y | G | J | R | Z | D | I | R | L | D | Q | K | V | M | J | M | U | K |
| C | C | Y | W | K | H | E | G | K | K | O | L | K | E | A | H | S | M | Z | A | O | M | N |
| R | L | L | R | Q | V | B | E | W | T | O | N | K | R | U | U | X | Y | L | A | N | B | T |
| Y | Z | Z | H | L | E | N | D | A | N | G | E | R | E | D | S | P | E | C | I | E | S | R |
| O | G | E | N | E | T | I | C | C | O | D | E | Y | M | E | U | R | I | C | A | C | I | D |
| B | X | A | S | E | X | U | A | L | R | E | P | R | O | D | U | C | T | I | O | N | X | W |
| I | L | W | G | Z | R | G | G | O | O | F | Z | J | Q | W | A | B | T | K | J | U | B | Y |
| O | Y | S | N | M | E | G | Y | N | D | N | A | S | E | Q | U | E | N | C | I | N | G | W |
| L | O | A | Z | V | S | B | N | I | K | V | F | S | E | M | W | T | Q | I | K | K | Q | F |
| O | C | U | D | W | X | N | E | N | V | A | L | E | N | C | E | B | A | N | D | T | N | M |
| G | A | H | R | Q | Z | K | U | G | D | E | P | O | L | A | R | I | Z | A | T | I | O | N |
| Y | E | I | N | T | E | R | N | A | L | F | E | R | T | I | L | I | Z | A | T | I | O | N |

1. A heterocyclic compound of carbon, nitrogen, oxygen, and hydrogen. it forms ions and salts known as urates and acid urates, such as ammonium acid urate.
2. The highest range of electron energies in which electrons are normally present at absolute zero temperature.
3. Threatened by factors such as habitat loss, hunting, disease and climate change, and usually have declining populations or a very limited range.
4. A form of terrestrial locomotion where an organism moves by means of its two rear limbs or legs.
5. The process of determining the precise order of nucleotides within a DNA molecule.
6. Propagate (an organism or cell) to make an identical copy of.
7. A diploid cell resulting from the fusion of two haploid gametes; a fertilized ovum.
8. Process of reproduction involving a single parent that results in offspring that are genetically identical to the parent.
9. A chemical substance produced in the body that controls and regulates the activity of certain cells or organs.
10. The branch of biology that studies the effects of low temperatures on living things within earth's cryosphere or in science.
11. Fertilization that takes place inside the egg-producing individual.
12. The nucleotide triplets of DNA and RNA molecules that carry genetic information in living cells.
13. The process of reversing the charge across a cell membrane (usually a neuron), so causing an action potential.

A. DNA Sequencing
B. Genetic Code
C. Cryobiology
D. Hormone
E. Endangered Species
F. Asexual Reproduction
G. Depolarization
H. Internal Fertilization
I. Uric acid
J. Valence band
K. Zygote
L. Cloning
M. Bipedal

10. Find the hidden words. The words have been placed horizontally, vertically, or diagonally. When you locate a word, draw an ellipse around it.

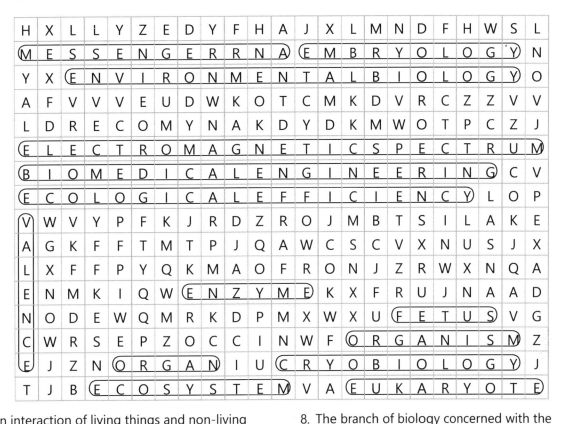

| H | X | L | L | Y | Z | E | D | Y | F | H | A | J | X | L | M | N | D | F | H | W | S | L |
|---|---|---|---|---|---|---|---|---|---|---|---|---|---|---|---|---|---|---|---|---|---|---|
| M | E | S | S | E | N | G | E | R | R | N | A | E | M | B | R | Y | O | L | O | G | Y | N |
| Y | X | E | N | V | I | R | O | N | M | E | N | T | A | L | B | I | O | L | O | G | Y | O |
| A | F | V | V | V | E | U | D | W | K | O | T | C | M | K | D | V | R | C | Z | Z | V | V |
| L | D | R | E | C | O | M | Y | N | A | K | D | Y | D | K | M | W | O | T | P | C | Z | J |
| E | L | E | C | T | R | O | M | A | G | N | E | T | I | C | S | P | E | C | T | R | U | M |
| B | I | O | M | E | D | I | C | A | L | E | N | G | I | N | E | E | R | I | N | G | C | V |
| E | C | O | L | O | G | I | C | A | L | E | F | F | I | C | I | E | N | C | Y | L | O | P |
| V | W | V | Y | P | F | K | J | R | D | Z | R | O | J | M | B | T | S | I | L | A | K | E |
| A | G | K | F | F | T | M | T | P | J | Q | A | W | C | S | C | V | X | N | U | S | J | X |
| L | X | F | F | P | Y | Q | K | M | A | O | F | R | O | N | J | Z | R | W | X | N | Q | A |
| E | N | M | K | I | Q | W | E | N | Z | Y | M | E | K | X | F | R | U | J | N | A | A | D |
| N | O | D | E | W | Q | M | R | K | D | P | M | X | W | X | U | F | E | T | U | S | V | G |
| C | W | R | S | E | P | Z | O | C | C | I | N | W | F | O | R | G | A | N | I | S | M | Z |
| E | J | Z | N | O | R | G | A | N | I | U | C | R | Y | O | B | I | O | L | O | G | Y | J |
| T | J | B | E | C | O | S | Y | S | T | E | M | V | A | E | U | K | A | R | Y | O | T | E |

1. An interaction of living things and non-living things in a physical environment.
2. Biological molecules (proteins) that act as catalysts and help complex reactions occur everywhere in life.
3. The branch of biology that studies the development of gametes (sex cells), fertilization, and development of embryos and fetuses.
4. Describes the efficiency with which energy is transferred from one trophic level to the next.
5. Refers to the number of elements to which it can connect.
6. The collective term for all possible frequencies of electromagnetic radiation.
7. The application of engineering principles and design concepts to medicine and biology for healthcare purposes (e.g. diagnostic or therapeutic).

8. The branch of biology concerned with the relations between organisms and their environment.
9. The form of rna in which genetic information transcribed from dna as a sequence of bases is transferred to a ribosome.
10. Any organism whose cells contain a nucleus and other organelles enclosed within membranes.
11. An individual animal, plant, or single-celled life form.
12. A human embryo after eight weeks of development.
13. The branch of biology that studies the effects of low temperatures on living things within earth's cryosphere or in science.
14. A part of an organism that is typically self-contained and has a specific vital function, such as the heart or liver in humans.

A. Ecosystem
D. Valence
G. Electromagnetic Spectrum
J. Fetus
M. Organism

B. Biomedical engineering
E. Cryobiology
H. Embryology
K. Enzyme
N. Eukaryote

C. Ecological Efficiency
F. Messenger RNA
I. Environmental Biology
L. Organ

11. Find the hidden words. The words have been placed horizontally, vertically, or diagonally. When you locate a word, draw an ellipse around it.

```
F  S  M  E  I  O  S  I  S  B  K  M  A  H  W  Z  C  Q  I  H  Y  Z  D
Q  I  U  E  V  O  L  U  T  I  O  N  A  R  Y  B  I  O  L  O  G  Y  T
O  U  E  N  D  O  P  L  A  S  M  I  C  R  E  T  I  C  U  L  U  M  R
D  N  G  D  N  X  P  C  Y  J  P  A  M  N  N  P  X  R  E  J  X  D  A
P  I  E  B  A  Q  X  C  J  B  S  O  J  L  Q  T  Y  E  V  X  R  M  N
H  T  N  M  I  O  R  S  W  M  P  D  S  I  K  T  P  P  G  M  F  N  S
C  S  E  M  P  U  G  B  F  U  G  J  T  P  O  R  R  R  F  S  B  L  L
V  E  L  E  M  E  N  T  A  J  I  U  K  O  N  D  F  O  I  I  U  T  A
L  E  P  T  O  N  K  E  G  T  I  U  F  P  W  E  M  D  G  G  I  W  T
M  M  T  A  L  A  E  C  B  N  U  Q  E  R  D  S  U  U  S  F  H  A  I
S  H  I  S  T  O  L  O  G  Y  X  A  M  O  Z  M  M  C  U  J  W  A  O
V  A  L  E  N  C  E  T  V  O  F  O  S  T  N  O  V  T  I  R  N  U  N
H  D  T  G  Q  P  P  Y  F  A  M  R  F  E  F  S  N  I  K  W  A  N  G
F  C  E  E  G  Z  O  P  B  M  Q  Y  K  I  N  O  T  O  F  L  U  H  G
J  X  F  E  W  N  E  E  I  Z  B  H  Q  N  V  M  U  N  K  H  S  D  Z
N  G  B  N  D  O  B  C  D  L  A  C  Q  P  U  E  E  J  A  X  H  Q  B
```

1. A biochemical assembly that contains both proteins and lipids, bound to the proteins, which allow fats to move through the water inside and outside cells.
2. A species of atoms having the same number of protons in their atomic nuclei.
3. Describes a genetically distinct geographic variety, population or race within a species, which is adapted to specific environmental conditions.
4. A system of physical units-based on the meter, kilogram, second, ampere, kelvin, candela, and mole, together with a set of prefixes.
5. The decoding of genetic instructions for making proteins.
6. Also known as a macula adhaerens, is a cell structure specialized for cell to cell adhesion.
7. A network of membranous tubules within the cytoplasm of a eukaryotic cell, continuous with the nuclear membrane.
8. Giving birth to one of its kind, sexually or asexually.
9. A type of cell division that reduces the number of chromosomes in the parent cell by half and produces four gamete cells.
10. The study of the microscopic anatomy of cells and tissues of plants and animals.
11. Refers to the number of elements to which it can connect.
12. The subfield of biology that studies the evolutionary processes that produced the diversity of life on earth starting from a single origin of life.
13. A gene is a locus (or region) of DNA that encodes a functional RNA or protein product and is the molecular unit of heredity.
14. An elementary, half-integer spin particle that does not undergo strong interactions.

A. Element
D. Evolutionary Biology
G. Gene
J. Valence
M. Lepton

B. Histology
E. Meiosis
H. Translation
K. Reproduction
N. Endoplasmic Reticulum

C. Ecotype
F. Desmosome
I. SI units
L. Lipoprotein

# 12. Find the hidden words. The words have been placed horizontally, vertically, or diagonally. When you locate a word, draw an ellipse around it.

```
Q I N D E P E N D E N T A S S O R T M E N T D
P A F Z D P D M N I V T Z H J C P V K A X Z E
P H U M A N N U T R I T I O N Y Q A A B Q A N
S H U W I L Q M N X P X N Z Z M U G V V U W I
Y A Y H L G A T Q C O Z C P Y D F R S M M I T
C I V W E A X W B X M E U H F G U O Z J M K R
H B K X W K J P V P W U U L I J M B M B E T I
O H O J O R G A N I S M Z O V D X I U T V E F
B D W F B L Y K Z L V K C E H E D O R W L S I
I T T V P F W S K C S N O M W Z K L S X O G C
O X B A C T E R I A O B B T Y W L O B V R L A
L A D E N Y L A T E C Y C L A S E G B J B B T
O D E P O L A R I Z A T I O N L I Y G Z F S I
G N I G X E L E C T R O N S H E L D G O C W O
Y M F B I O G E O G R A P H Y C P N D S R B N
R J C H L O R O P L A S T D E C I D U O U S K
```

1. The study of plant nutrition and growth especially to increase crop yield
2. The vascular tissue in plants that conducts sugars and other metabolic products downward from the leaves.
3. An electron shell is the outside part of an atom around the atomic nucleus. it is a group of atomic orbitals with the same value of the principal quantum number n.
4. Means "falling off at maturity" or "tending to fall off", and it is typically used in order to refer to trees or shrubs that lose their leaves seasonally.
5. The study of the distribution of species and ecosystems in geographic space and through time.
6. Refers to the provision of essential nutrients necessary to support human life and health.
7. A microbially facilitated process of nitrate reduction that may ultimately produce molecular nitrogen.
8. The principle, originated by Gregor Mendel, stating that when two or more characteristics are inherited, individual hereditary factors assort independently.
9. Single-cell microscopic organisms which lack a true nucleus. they represent one of the three domains.
10. An individual animal, plant, or single-celled life form.
11. The application of the principles of biology to the study of physiological, genetic, and developmental mechanisms of behavior in humans and other animals.
12. An enzyme that catalyzes the formation of cyclic amp from ATP.
13. Work to convert light energy of the sun into sugars that can be used by cells.
14. The process of reversing the charge across a cell membrane (usually a neuron), so causing an action potential.

A. Deciduous
B. Human Nutrition
C. Biogeography
D. Organism
E. Agrobiology
F. Electron Shell
G. Chloroplast
H. Bacteria
I. Adenylate cyclase
J. Depolarization
K. Independent Assortment
L. Denitrification
M. Phloem
N. Psychobiology

13. Find the hidden words. The words have been placed horizontally, vertically, or diagonally. When you locate a word, draw an ellipse around it.

| E | U | X | S | Y | S | T | E | M | A | T | I | C | S | B | G | I | H | L | V | T | Z | F |
|---|---|---|---|---|---|---|---|---|---|---|---|---|---|---|---|---|---|---|---|---|---|---|
| Z | P | H | A | R | M | A | C | O | L | O | G | Y | G | L | B | Q | R | O | P | I | L | Y |
| A | Z | J | O | L | B | E | X | C | P | M | A | B | N | A | Y | Q | H | Y | F | J | I | E |
| S | X | N | P | A | I | V | U | I | P | N | Q | W | K | S | H | A | P | D | U | N | R | D |
| B | J | J | F | R | O | E | H | Z | E | E | L | E | C | T | R | O | N | D | O | N | O | R |
| A | L | I | L | V | E | S | I | B | I | L | E | A | S | O | I | G | A | H | G | C | M | U |
| R | U | V | I | A | N | I | O | Y | Q | P | U | T | M | C | I | M | M | K | O | G | Y | U |
| R | M | Q | N | K | G | C | I | A | E | E | X | O | N | Y | E | G | T | I | B | I | T | X |
| B | H | B | V | G | I | L | Q | J | K | Z | Z | W | Z | S | W | I | U | A | C | M | U | L |
| O | Y | J | L | V | N | E | E | K | B | C | K | N | T | T | Z | L | E | Q | Q | Y | W | Z |
| D | F | Z | D | S | E | X | U | A | L | R | E | P | R | O | D | U | C | T | I | O | N | A |
| Y | J | B | E | I | E | P | T | E | D | G | O | P | J | K | M | M | X | L | F | O | Z | W |
| F | Z | N | S | R | R | D | B | F | M | P | M | U | E | P | I | S | T | A | S | I | S | J |
| B | T | Z | C | L | I | I | G | J | M | L | W | A | B | S | O | R | P | T | I | O | N | U |
| G | E | L | Z | O | N | I | N | V | E | R | T | E | B | R | A | T | E | Z | L | E | E | E |
| B | R | P | Y | Q | G | C | C | H | E | M | I | C | A | L | R | E | A | C | T | I | O | N |

1. The smallest component of an element having the chemical properties of the element
2. The interaction of genes that are not alleles. The suppression of the effect of one such gene by another.
3. The application of concepts and methods of biology to solve real world problems.
4. A mammalian blastula in which some differentiation of cells has occurred.
5. The science of drug action on biological systems.
6. Type of reproduction in which cells from two parents unite to form the first cell of a new organism.
7. A dark green to yellowish brown fluid, produced by the liver of most vertebrates, that aids the digestion of lipids in the small intestine.
8. The inactive x chromosome in a female somatic cell, rendered inactive in a process called lyonization

9. A distinct juvenile form many animals undergo before metamorphosis into adults. animals with indirect development such as insects, amphibians, or cnidarians.
10. A chemical entity that donates electrons to another compound.
11. A group of animals that have no backbone, unlike animals such as reptiles, amphibians, fish, birds and mammals who all have a backbone.
12. A process in which one substance permeates another; a fluid permeates or is dissolved by a liquid or solid.
13. The branch of biology that deals with classification and nomenclature; taxonomy.
14. Usually characterized by a chemical change, and they yield one or more products, which usually have properties different from the reactants
15. A fluid or air-filled cavity or sac.

A. Vesicle
E. Blastocyst
I. Barr body
M. Bile

B. Bioengineering
F. Atom
J. Systematics
N. Absorption

C. Invertebrate
G. Chemical reaction
K. Epistasis
O. Sexual Reproduction

D. Electron Donor
H. Larva
L. Pharmacology

14. Find the hidden words. The words have been placed horizontally, vertically, or diagonally. When you locate a word, draw an ellipse around it.

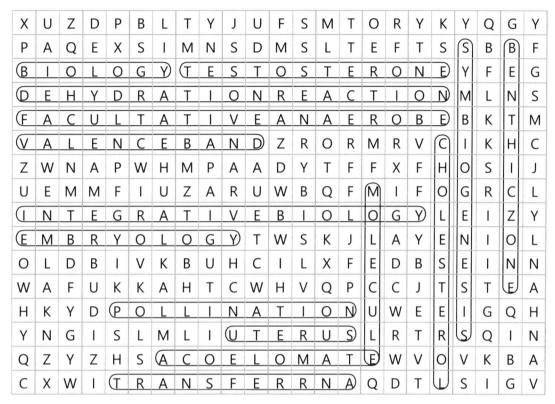

1. An evolutionary theory that explains the origin of eukaryotic cells from prokaryotes.
2. The ecological region at the lowest level of a body of water such as an ocean or a lake.
3. Study of living organisms.
4. Organism which can produce energy through aerobic respiration and then switching to anaerobic respiration depending on the amounts of oxygen.
5. The organ in the lower body of a woman or female mammal where offspring are conceived and in which they gestate before birth; the womb.
6. A steroid hormone from the androgen group and is found in humans and other vertebrates.
7. The highest range of electron energies in which electrons are normally present at absolute zero temperature.
8. RNA consisting of folded molecules that transport amino acids from the cytoplasm of a cell to a ribosome.
9. A label frequently used to describe various forms of cross-disciplinary and multitaxon research.
10. The act of transferring pollen grains from the male anther of a flower to the female stigma.
11. Usually defined as a chemical reaction that involves the loss of a water molecule from the reacting molecule.
12. An organic lipid molecule that is biosynthesized by all animal cells because it is an essential structural component of all animal cell membranes.
13. The smallest particle in a chemical element or compound that has the chemical properties of that element or compound.
14. Animals, like flatworms and jellyfish, that have no body cavity (coelom).
15. The branch of biology that studies the development of gametes (sex cells), fertilization, and development of embryos and fetuses.

A. Molecule
B. Facultative Anaerobe
C. Embryology
D. Symbiogenesis
E. Cholesterol
F. Benthic zone
G. Uterus
H. Testosterone
I. Transfer RNA
J. Valence band
K. Acoelomate
L. Dehydration Reaction
M. Integrative Biology
N. Pollination
O. Biology

15. Find the hidden words. The words have been placed horizontally, vertically, or diagonally. When you locate a word, draw an ellipse around it.

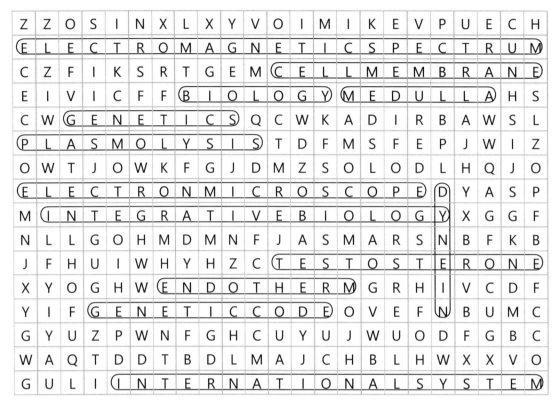

1. A motor protein in cells which converts the chemical energy contained in ATP into the mechanical energy of movement
2. Contraction of the protoplast of a plant cell as a result of loss of water from the cell.
3. A label frequently used to describe various forms of cross-disciplinary and multitaxon research.
4. A type of microscope that uses a beam of electrons to create an image of the specimen. it is capable of much higher magnifications.
5. The nucleotide triplets of DNA and RNA molecules that carry genetic information in living cells.
6. The study of heredity
7. Study of living organisms.

8. The collective term for all possible frequencies of electromagnetic radiation.
9. A steroid hormone from the androgen group and is found in humans and other vertebrates.
10. The modern form of the metric system and is the most widely used system of measurement.
11. The semipermeable membrane surrounding the cytoplasm of a cell.
12. An animal that is dependent on or capable of the internal generation of heat; a warm
13. The continuation of the spinal cord within the skull, forming the lowest part of the brainstem and containing control centers for the heart and lungs.

A. Endotherm
D. Testosterone
G. Plasmolysis
J. Electromagnetic Spectrum
M. Genetics

B. Cell membrane
E. Electron Microscope
H. Integrative Biology
K. International System

C. Dynein
F. Biology
I. Genetic Code
L. Medulla

16. Find the hidden words. The words have been placed horizontally, vertically, or diagonally. When you locate a word, draw an ellipse around it.

| L | C | B | M | R | H | V | E | V | Y | Y | Z | E | C | K | C | M | F | Z | I | M | T | A |
|---|---|---|---|---|---|---|---|---|---|---|---|---|---|---|---|---|---|---|---|---|---|---|
| U | H | C | M | M | R | Y | K | E | E | A | M | P | J | Z | R | U | H | O | L | E | Q | W |
| N | E | E | D | J | P | S | Y | C | H | O | B | I | O | L | O | G | Y | C | I | X | T | L |
| S | M | L | W | F | U | A | L | O | L | Z | A | D | A | J | L | A | R | Y | L | P | D | S |
| I | I | U | E | Q | N | E | V | X | I | N | U | E | M | A | C | R | O | P | H | A | G | E |
| Q | C | D | I | K | I | A | Q | S | G | T | R | M | M | D | H | P | Z | G | G | I | O | L |
| V | A | F | N | W | V | F | X | T | A | N | A | I | F | F | L | G | B | I | B | Z | C | X |
| W | L | Y | S | W | P | R | I | E | M | U | C | O | G | F | U | E | Z | E | L | B | V | C |
| O | R | C | U | I | P | B | R | R | E | K | I | L | F | X | D | V | F | M | K | V | F | Q |
| O | E | W | L | J | I | M | Z | O | N | U | U | O | M | L | P | Q | L | T | N | A | T | J |
| D | A | K | I | Z | G | S | J | I | T | A | G | G | N | Q | S | N | M | P | U | U | Z | Z |
| J | C | H | N | C | T | I | D | D | H | V | E | Y | M | A | Y | L | J | D | B | V | C | L |
| O | T | M | G | V | D | U | V | G | G | Z | V | V | W | M | U | D | S | R | Q | B | W | Y |
| W | I | E | O | B | I | O | M | E | C | H | A | N | I | C | S | F | O | F | I | K | K | U |
| S | O | I | K | M | S | Y | S | T | E | M | A | T | I | C | S | C | L | Z | Y | M | W | B |
| W | N | I | D | E | O | X | Y | R | I | B | O | N | U | C | L | E | I | C | A | C | I | D |

1. Helps keep blood sugar level from getting too high (hyperglycemia) or too low (hypoglycemia).
2. The application of the principles of biology to the study of physiological, genetic, and developmental mechanisms of behavior in humans and other animals.
3. The chemical name for DNA.
4. An organic compound with four rings arranged in a specific configuration. examples include the dietary lipid cholesterol and the sex hormones.
5. The study and analysis of the patterns, causes, and effects of health and disease conditions in defined populations.
6. Type of lymphocyte in the humeral immunity of the adaptive immune system.
7. The study of the structure and function of biological systems by means of the methods of "mechanics."
8. A kind of swallowing cell, which means it functions by literally swallowing up other particles or smaller cells.
9. The inner layer of the stems of woody plants; composed of xylem.
10. The branch of biology that deals with classification and nomenclature; taxonomy.
11. One of the four nucleobases in the nucleic acid of RNA that are represented by the letters a, g, c and u.
12. The fibrous connective tissue that connects bones to other bones.
13. Usually characterized by a chemical change, and they yield one or more products, which usually have properties different from the reactants

A. Biomechanics
D. Systematics
G. B cell
J. Ligament
M. Steroid

B. Chemical reaction
E. Uracil
H. Epidemiology
K. Macrophage

C. Wood
F. Insulin
I. Psychobiology
L. Deoxyribonucleic Acid

17. Find the hidden words. The words have been placed horizontally, vertically, or diagonally. When you locate a word, draw an ellipse around it.

| R | E | M | R | F | K | K | E | A | P | Q | P | C | H | X | F | Q | Y | V | O | B | D | O |
|---|---|---|---|---|---|---|---|---|---|---|---|---|---|---|---|---|---|---|---|---|---|---|
| C | O | N | S | E | R | V | A | T | I | O | N | B | I | O | L | O | G | Y | B | H | B | G |
| R | S | O | H | Z | W | G | E | N | E | P | O | O | L | A | W | W | B | B | N | C | A | A |
| P | R | T | U | T | W | A | E | B | S | W | X | G | H | G | O | Q | L | J | E | D | S | M |
| L | P | T | M | O | F | K | W | D | P | L | A | N | T | N | U | T | R | I | T | I | O | N |
| D | V | U | A | O | M | L | V | H | L | A | C | Q | Z | S | B | Q | T | P | I | K | Q | D |
| Y | W | H | N | N | U | C | L | E | I | C | A | C | I | D | S | E | Q | U | E | N | C | E |
| C | G | A | N | D | A | H | B | U | T | E | O | S | C | L | S | U | D | V | D | Y | D | B |
| C | M | M | U | N | S | N | I | D | V | Q | C | L | N | Z | X | X | H | K | E | R | H | D |
| F | O | N | T | I | L | K | O | A | Z | E | B | V | F | P | N | F | U | V | E | P | O | P |
| W | L | I | R | M | E | R | M | S | B | T | E | N | K | J | Y | D | B | C | E | L | L | V |
| U | E | O | I | X | S | Q | A | C | S | O | Z | T | U | W | V | Z | U | D | C | C | V | Q |
| C | L | T | T | Q | B | R | S | S | J | G | V | Q | Q | L | G | M | R | K | W | C | N | M |
| V | B | E | I | X | S | K | S | U | X | B | Z | B | L | U | R | E | A | H | O | I | B | K |
| E | W | S | O | C | L | O | N | I | N | G | B | X | T | L | S | M | O | N | O | M | E | R |
| I | D | J | N | P | J | I | J | G | A | P | I | M | O | L | A | R | I | T | Y | U | A | N |

1. The si unit of measurement used to measure the number of things, usually atoms or molecules.
2. Refers to the provision of essential nutrients necessary to support human life and health.
3. Type of lymphocyte in the humeral immunity of the adaptive immune system.
4. The stock of different genes in an interbreeding population.
5. Serves an important role in the metabolism of nitrogen-containing compounds by animals and is the main nitrogen-containing substance in the urine of mammals.
6. A succession of letters that indicate the order of nucleotides within a DNA (using GACT or RNA (GACU) molecule.
7. The study of the chemical elements and compounds necessary for plant growth, plant metabolism and their external supply.
8. Propagate (an organism or cell) to make an identical copy of.
9. Organisms that produce an egg composed of shell and membranes that creates a protected environment in which the embryo can develop out of water
10. A unit of concentration measuring the number of moles of a solute per liter of solution.
11. Organic matter derived from living, or recently living organisms.
12. A molecule that can be bonded to other identical molecules to form a polymer.
13. The scientific study of nature and of earth's biodiversity with the aim of protecting species, their habitats, and ecosystems from excessive rates of extinction.

A. Human Nutrition
B. Gene Pool
C. Mole
D. Biomass
E. Monomer
F. Conservation Biology
G. Cloning
H. Plant Nutrition
I. Amniotes
J. Nucleic Acid Sequence
K. Molarity
L. Urea
M. B cell

18. Find the hidden words. The words have been placed horizontally, vertically, or diagonally. When you locate a word, draw an ellipse around it.

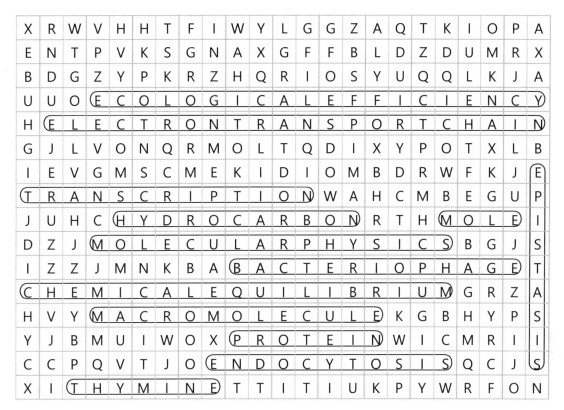

| X | R | W | V | H | H | T | F | I | W | Y | L | G | G | Z | A | Q | T | K | I | O | P | A |
|---|---|---|---|---|---|---|---|---|---|---|---|---|---|---|---|---|---|---|---|---|---|---|
| E | N | T | P | V | K | S | G | N | A | X | G | F | F | B | L | D | Z | D | U | M | R | X |
| B | D | G | Z | Y | P | K | R | Z | H | Q | R | I | O | S | Y | U | Q | Q | L | K | J | A |
| U | U | O | E | C | O | L | O | G | I | C | A | L | E | F | F | I | C | I | E | N | C | Y |
| H | E | L | E | C | T | R | O | N | T | R | A | N | S | P | O | R | T | C | H | A | I | N |
| G | J | L | V | O | N | Q | R | M | O | L | T | Q | D | I | X | Y | P | O | T | X | L | B |
| I | E | V | G | M | S | C | M | E | K | I | D | I | O | M | B | D | R | W | F | K | J | E |
| T | R | A | N | S | C | R | I | P | T | I | O | N | W | A | H | C | M | B | E | G | U | P |
| J | U | H | C | H | Y | D | R | O | C | A | R | B | O | N | R | T | H | M | O | L | E | I |
| D | Z | J | M | O | L | E | C | U | L | A | R | P | H | Y | S | I | C | S | B | G | J | S |
| I | Z | Z | J | M | N | K | B | A | B | A | C | T | E | R | I | O | P | H | A | G | E | T |
| C | H | E | M | I | C | A | L | E | Q | U | I | L | I | B | R | I | U | M | G | R | Z | A |
| H | V | Y | M | A | C | R | O | M | O | L | E | C | U | L | E | K | G | B | H | Y | P | S |
| Y | J | B | M | U | I | W | O | X | P | R | O | T | E | I | N | W | I | C | M | R | I | I |
| C | C | P | Q | V | T | J | O | E | N | D | O | C | Y | T | O | S | I | S | Q | C | J | S |
| X | I | T | H | Y | M | I | N | E | T | T | I | T | I | U | K | P | Y | W | R | F | O | N |

1. A form of active transport in which a cell transports molecules into the cell.
2. Describes the efficiency with which energy is transferred from one trophic level to the next.
3. The interaction of genes that are not alleles. The suppression of the effect of one such gene by another.
4. The site of oxidative phosphorylation in eukaryotes.
5. The study of the physical properties of molecules, the chemical bonds between atoms as well as the molecular dynamics.
6. The state in which both reactants and products are present in concentrations which have no further tendency to change with time.
7. In organic chemistry, a hydrocarbon is an organic compound consisting entirely of hydrogen and carbon.
8. The first step of gene expression, in which a segment of DNA is copied into RNA (mRNA) by the enzyme RNA polymerase.
9. Virus that infects and multiplies within bacteria.
10. A very large molecule, such as protein, commonly created by polymerization of smaller subunits (monomers).
11. One of the four nucleobases in the nucleic acid of DNA that are represented by the letters g–c–a–t.
12. The si unit of measurement used to measure the number of things, usually atoms or molecules.
13. Large biomolecules, or macromolecules, consisting of one or more long chains of amino acid residues.

A. Hydrocarbon
D. Electron Transport Chain
G. Thymine
J. Bacteriophage
M. Molecular physics

B. Epistasis
E. Protein
H. Macromolecule
K. Mole

C. Transcription
F. Chemical equilibrium
I. Endocytosis
L. Ecological Efficiency

19. Find the hidden words. The words have been placed horizontally, vertically, or diagonally. When you locate a word, draw an ellipse around it.

| V | C | M | H | I | S | T | O | L | O | G | Y | A | C | T | I | V | E | S | I | T | E | M |
|---|---|---|---|---|---|---|---|---|---|---|---|---|---|---|---|---|---|---|---|---|---|---|
| J | V | A | S | O | D | I | L | A | T | I | O | N | E | P | I | S | T | A | S | I | S | A |
| Q | I | L | W | L | V | F | Q | X | A | D | Q | Z | M | E | O | P | N | C | I | E | A | C |
| O | Z | V | W | D | M | A | C | R | O | M | O | L | E | C | U | L | E | B | T | Z | J | R |
| I | X | A | A | Z | A | M | Y | G | C | H | D | V | A | O | A | Y | P | P | D | T | H | O |
| A | D | F | A | C | U | L | T | A | T | I | V | E | A | N | A | E | R | O | B | E | E | E |
| Q | U | L | N | E | U | R | O | T | R | A | N | S | M | I | T | T | E | R | E | A | O | V |
| S | D | W | Y | R | V | S | Y | M | F | O | D | T | O | W | F | W | X | O | T | L | V | O |
| I | N | T | E | G | R | A | T | I | V | E | B | I | O | L | O | G | Y | X | H | N | M | L |
| Q | G | B | I | T | V | J | F | O | M | J | O | G | Z | L | E | J | S | I | O | Z | D | U |
| J | P | Q | S | D | Y | I | T | G | Z | R | I | E | Q | F | S | P | N | L | Y | D | T | |
| B | I | O | C | H | E | M | I | S | T | R | Y | A | C | Z | Z | R | F | I | O | G | K | I |
| S | F | S | M | Y | K | C | B | P | I | E | V | L | M | P | Z | O | H | S | G | J | I | O |
| F | M | T | H | U | M | A | N | N | U | T | R | I | T | I | O | N | F | J | Y | W | A | N |
| J | P | Z | N | V | R | X | B | A | G | R | T | T | N | E | C | H | I | D | Q | M | A | |
| K | C | E | L | L | N | U | C | L | E | U | S | Y | J | M | Y | Y | F | G | M | N | D | B |

1. The interaction of genes that are not alleles. The suppression of the effect of one such gene by another.
2. The dilatation of blood vessels, which decreases blood pressure.
3. The scientific and objective study of non-human animal behavior rather than human behavior and usually with a focus on behavior under natural conditions.
4. Refers to genetically determined structures or attributes that have apparently lost most or all their ancestral function in a given species.
5. The study of the microscopic anatomy of cells and tissues of plants and animals.
6. The "control room" for the cell. the nucleus gives out all the orders.
7. Organism which can produce energy through aerobic respiration and then switching to anaerobic respiration depending on the amounts of oxygen.
8. Refers to the provision of essential nutrients necessary to support human life and health.
9. The part of an enzyme or antibody where the chemical reaction occurs
10. The branch of science that explores the chemical processes within and related to living organisms.
11. A very large molecule, such as protein, commonly created by polymerization of smaller subunits (monomers).
12. Known as chemical messengers, are endogenous chemicals that enable neurotransmission.
13. A label frequently used to describe various forms of cross-disciplinary and multitaxon research.
14. Evolution on a scale of separated gene pools. studies focus on change that occurs at or above the level of species, in contrast with microevolution.

A. Vestigiality
E. Macromolecule
I. Active site
M. Cell nucleus
B. Facultative Anaerobe
F. Epistasis
J. Integrative Biology
N. Neurotransmitter
C. Vasodilation
G. Biochemistry
K. Human Nutrition
D. Macroevolution
H. Histology
L. Ethology

20. Find the hidden words. The words have been placed horizontally, vertically, or diagonally. When you locate a word, draw an ellipse around it.

| A | D | E | N | O | S | I | N | E | T | R | I | P | H | O | S | P | H | A | T | E | K | T |
|---|---|---|---|---|---|---|---|---|---|---|---|---|---|---|---|---|---|---|---|---|---|---|
| B | I | O | G | E | O | G | R | A | P | H | Y | L | Q | I | S | O | M | E | R | V | I | E |
| O | O | Y | I | P | Z | P | U | A | V | A | L | E | N | C | E | B | A | N | D | J | M | W |
| G | F | N | J | F | P | B | X | T | S | U | P | O | L | Y | P | L | O | I | D | Y | O | T |
| O | E | L | E | C | T | R | O | N | T | R | A | N | S | P | O | R | T | C | H | A | I | N |
| R | J | U | T | M | A | C | T | I | V | E | T | R | A | N | S | P | O | R | T | L | A | Y |
| W | H | O | L | E | G | E | N | O | M | E | S | E | Q | U | E | N | C | I | N | G | B | X |
| C | C | U | S | Y | M | B | I | O | G | E | N | E | S | I | S | B | M | I | E | E | W | Z |
| Q | W | P | L | A | C | E | B | O | W | W | K | G | B | U | G | O | L | L | W | T | J | O |
| A | I | G | Z | H | X | A | W | H | D | P | G | C | U | O | E | T | O | O | N | Y | O | D |
| R | U | E | T | H | O | L | O | G | Y | N | K | M | K | R | N | A | O | N | F | E | T | N |
| U | E | C | E | X | Z | Z | T | O | T | G | D | D | G | F | E | N | W | W | J | V | U | L |
| I | N | S | O | V | M | I | I | U | X | L | N | O | A | K | T | Y | L | K | Q | Z | P | J |
| C | P | H | Y | T | O | P | A | T | H | O | L | O | G | Y | I | B | H | H | J | D | M | R |
| R | W | I | Y | C | L | Q | K | Q | B | M | R | L | U | V | C | U | Q | O | G | V | L | M |
| S | W | F | B | G | M | L | H | L | J | W | Q | D | B | C | S | O | M | P | T | B | U | O |

1. A harmless pill, medicine, or procedure prescribed more for the psychological benefit to the patient than for any physiological effect.
2. The site of oxidative phosphorylation in eukaryotes.
3. The study of plants.
4. An evolutionary theory that explains the origin of eukaryotic cells from prokaryotes.
5. A molecule with the same chemical formula as another molecule, but with a different chemical structure.
6. The study of heredity
7. The study of the distribution of species and ecosystems in geographic space and through time.
8. The science of diagnosing and managing plant diseases.
9. A laboratory process that determines the complete DNA sequence of an organism's genome at a single time.
10. Containing more than two homologous sets of chromosomes.
11. The scientific and objective study of non-human animal behavior rather than human behavior and usually with a focus on behavior under natural conditions.
12. The highest range of electron energies in which electrons are normally present at absolute zero temperature.
13. A nucleotide derived from adenosine that occurs in muscle tissue; the major source of energy for cellular reactions.
14. Transport of a substance (as a protein or drug) across a cell membrane against the concentration gradient; requires an expenditure of energy

A. Biogeography
D. Placebo
G. Phytopathology
J. Adenosine Triphosphate
M. Ethology
B. Isomer
E. Whole Genome Sequencing
H. Active Transport
K. Genetics
N. Valence band
C. Symbiogenesis
F. Polyploidy
I. Electron Transport Chain
L. Botany

Made in the USA
Middletown, DE
01 December 2022

16529332R00115